Sheila Kitzinger is known worldwide for her books on childbirth, breast feeding and sexuality, including *The Experience of Childbirth*, *Pregnancy and Childbirth*, *Woman's Experience of Sex* and *The Crying Baby*. She lectures in many countries and, as an anthropologist, researches midwifery, birth and motherhood in diverse cultures. Celia is one of her five daughters.

Celia Kitzinger is a social psychologist and lecturer at the Polytechnic of East London. Her research into lesbian identity, human rights and children's experiences of unfairness in schools has been published in many journals. She lectures widely in North America and Europe. She is Assistant Editor of *The Psychologist*, and author of *The Social Construction of Lesbianism*.

GU00722739

TALKING WITH CHILDREN

ABOUT THINGS THAT MATTER

TALKING WITH CHILDREN

ABOUT THINGS THAT MATTER

Sheila Kitzinger and Celia Kitzinger

PANDORA

LONDON SYDNEY WELLINGTON

First published by Pandora Press, an imprint of the Trade Division
of Unwin Hyman, in 1989.
First published in paperback in 1990.
© Sheila Kitzinger and Celia Kitzinger, 1989.

PANDORA PRESS
Unwin Hyman Ltd
15–17 Broadwick Street,London W1V 1FP

Allen & Unwin Australia Pty Ltd
PO Box 764, 8 Napier Street, North Sydney, NSW 2060, Australia

Allen & Unwin NZ Ltd (in association with the Port Nicholson Press)
Compusales Building, 75 Ghuznee Street, Wellington, New Zealand

British Library Cataloguing in Publication Data
Kitzinger, Sheila, 1929–
    Talking with children: about things that matter.
    1. Children. Moral education
    I. Title   II. Kitzinger, Celia
    370.11'14

    ISBN 0-04-440733-5

Set in 11 on 13½ point Linotype Plantin
by Nene Phototypesetters Ltd, Northampton
and printed in Great Britain by Cox & Wyman Limited, Reading

To Sam
In the hope that he will help to make a better world

WHEN I WAS YOUR AGE

When I was your age, child –
When I was eight,
When I was ten,
When I was two
(How old are you?) –
When I was your age, child,
My father would have gone quite *wild*
Had I behaved the way you
Do.
What, food uneaten on my plate
When I was eight?
What, room in such a filthy state
When I was ten?
What, late
For school when I was two?
My father would have shouted, 'When
I was your age, child, my father would have *raved*
Had I behaved
The way you
Do.'

When I was your age, child, I
Should never have dreamed
Of sitting idly
Watching television half the night.
It would have seemed
Demented:
Television not then having been
Invented.
When I
Was your age, child, I did not lie
About
The house all day.
(I did not lie about anything at all – no liar I!)
I got out!

I ran away!

To sea!

(Though naturally I was back, with hair brushed and hands
    washed, in time for tea.)

When

I was your age, child, and the older generation

Offered now and then

A kindly explanation

Of what the world was like in their young day

I did not yawn in that rude way.

Why goodness me,

There being no television to see

(As I have, I think, already said)

We were dashed grateful

For any entertainment we could get instead,

However tedious and hateful.

So grow up, child! And be

Your age! (What *is* your age, then?

Eight? Or nine? Or two? Or ten?)

Remember, as you look at me –

When I was your age I was forty-three.

Michael Frayn, extract taken from *Allsorts* (a children's annual)

CONTENTS

ACKNOWLEDGEMENTS

We are grateful to the Rockefeller Foundation for awarding us both Writers' Fellowships that enabled us to spend a gorgeous September at Bellagio on Lake Como, wined, dined and cossetted, so that we could work together intensively on this book. It was an unforgettable experience!

Discussions with various people have proved very helpful, including Uwe Kitzinger, Jenny Kitzinger – on child sexual abuse, Polly Kitzinger, Tess McKenney and Martha Hatch. Sheila could not have managed without the invaluable secretarial help of Judith Schroeder. It is really lovely having somebody so skilled and so interested and involved in the work. Celia is grateful to the Leverhulme Trust who funded her research on children's experience of unfairness in school (pages 76; 83–4).

We want to thank all the women who answered the questionnaire in *Parents* magazine and those who talked to us about their beliefs and experiences.

We should also like to thank those who gave us permission to reproduce illustrations: Penny Simkin and Sandra VanDam Anderson for the children's drawings of birth on pages 112–13. These are taken from *Birth Through Children's Eyes* (1981) Seattle, Pennypress; Michael Heath for his generous permission to reproduce the cartoons on pages 4, 137 and 153; Jonathan Frost for Kurdish children's drawings of villages being raised, crops destroyed and their families killed on pages 240–1; Peters, Fraser & Dunlop

Group Ltd, for the Posy Simmons' cartoon on page 172. Finally, we should like to thank Michael Frayn for the verses on pages vi–viii, and Sheba Feminist Publishers for permission to reproduce on page 262 lines from Seni Seneviratne's 'Just Jealous' from *Charting the Journey: Writings by Black and Third World Women*, edited by Shabnam Grewal, *et al*.

PREFACE

There is a spate of books on the market about how to control children's behaviour – about avoiding sibling rivalry, solving sleep problems, exerting discipline, about how to get children to co-operate, toilet training, overcoming shyness, about coping with tantrums and hyperactivity, stealing, lying and bullying, about maintaining meaningful relationships and dealing with children's fears. There are books with aggressive titles like *Toddler Taming, Dare to Discipline, Spanking: Why. When. How?*; achievement-oriented books like *Raising Children for Success, How to Have a Smarter Baby*, and *How to Raise a Brighter Child*; sad books like *How to Really Love Your Child* and *When Your Child Drives You Crazy*; hopeful books with titles like *401 Ways to Get Your Kids to Work at Home* and *No-Fault Parenting*. After all this you might feel the need to read a book called *Battle Fatigue*. But there is very little about what you *believe* and the kind of person you hope your child will become.

For in spite of the theories and all our intentions to make a success of parenting, when it comes down to practical action we know that 'raising children is a kind of *desperate improvisation*'.[1] Much of what we do as parents is 'off the cuff'. We may aim at consistency, but that is just talk.

So what we believe, the values we hold in our own lives, the things that really matter to us, are bound to be revealed in everything that we do with our children. This is fundamental to the way in which we try to discipline, how we answer questions and talk with our children, and the whole quality of family life.

In this book we explore the values that mothers hold to be most important in their lives, those they want to communicate most urgently to their children, how they do this in practice, and where they think they succeed and fail.

There are many statistical studies of children and values done by psychologists, and we have incorporated material from these studies throughout the text. We deliberately chose not to do a statistical study, but to approach the subject in another way, believing that to discuss these matters in quantitative terms could not be of much help to parents wrestling with the day-to-day challenges of family life. We should like the book to provide a stimulus for parents to explore what they think and believe, and how they behave with their children. So instead of offering advice, we hope to raise questions which only readers themselves can answer.

The women who answered our questionnaire are not representative of all mothers, or even of all mothers in Britain. They were readers of a national parenting magazine and had to be motivated to want to take time off to fill in the questionnaire and to pay for a stamp to post it back. But the subjects they talk about are those that concern parents in all industrial societies – and to a large extent the world over. In exploring these issues we hope that parents can learn a little more about themselves and their own children, and appreciate that mothers of young children, who are often isolated in industrial cultures, can discover what some other mothers think, and so feel less alone.

The material from interviews is drawn mainly from discussions with mothers in Britain, together with others in Japan, France, Italy, Poland, Colombia, Mexico, Thailand and the USA.

Many practical books about children have been written, discussing subjects like nutrition and baby care, and dealing with problem behaviour, but few books which have focused mainly on moral and spiritual matters. Searching through titles of books published in North America and Britain we found, too, that the mass of them concern either infants and toddlers or adolescents.

There is much less material available concerning the ages between three and twelve. We decided that our main focus would be on this age span.

A great deal of this writing for parents is prescriptive, too. There are books which tell you what you *ought* to do, and each of them may have a different recipe for success. Consulting books like these turns out to be rather like using half a dozen recipe books to make a soufflé. We suspect that making a lot of rules is not very useful. This is because children are different, and families are part of cultures which vary enormously and are exposed to different stresses.

Men have asked us why there is little about fathers in this book. It is simply because no men answered the original questionnaire in the magazine, though we did not restrict the responses to mothers. Some of the interviews were conducted with fathers, especially where we hoped that their thinking on the subject of moral education would contribute to the cross-cultural dimension. So some quotations from interviews with fathers in Britain, the USA, Poland, Japan, Israel and Africa are included. But the main emphasis in these pages is on women's and children's lives and thinking.

We found it helpful to talk to adults about their own childhood memories, too, and here again cross-cultural aspects sharpened the issues raised. All accounts which draw on memory are in some way legendary, but these legends are themselves revealing. Why do we recollect some incidents in our childhood so keenly and why do they hold such deep meaning for us? Many adults are still angry, hurt and guilty about events that occurred forty years or more earlier in their lives. We have included some of this retrospective material, together with material from historical sources, where it is relevant, in order to provide a perspective in time.

We have also used freely anthropological, sociological, psychological and autobiographical material which can add to our understanding of the problems parents and children face. Sometimes, where an author has presented a childhood scene in especially sharp focus and in a way that stimulates thinking around the subject, we have drawn on sources in literature, too.

This is not a book that tells you how you ought to bring up your children. Instead, it is an exploration of the values parents – mostly mothers – think are important, the questions children ask, the discussions we have with children, and how we deal with all the conflicts and challenges connected with behaviour and relationships in a fast-changing world.

TALKING WITH CHILDREN

ABOUT THINGS THAT MATTER

CHAPTER
1

EXPECTATIONS

In raising children parents usually want to promote their own hard-won set of values. Sometimes that is a value system similar to the one they took from their own families two decades earlier. Sometimes it is a radical transformation, struck from intense childhood pain and carried to adulthood with a vow not to visit upon the next generation the destructive practices and philosophies that scarred their lives. Often it is some kind of compromise – aspects of our parents' values are incorporated into our own beliefs, and others rejected.

Encased in adult images of childhood are our own memories and dreams, our feelings about the childhood we have left behind – the one we had and that other one we feel we *should* have had. Many people have some unhappy memories of childhood, and for some such negative feelings flood in that they decide never to have children themselves. A woman who describes herself as a 'voluntary non-parent' says:

Every parent has been through the childhood experience – that unrewarding, tedious and frustrating period with little control over one's lifestyle, attitudes or behaviour, in which one's opinions are dismissed, dreams ridiculed and slightest sign of independence treated as a threat.

No adult I know has ever expressed the wish to repeat their own childhood. Yet they happily inflict it on others.[1]

Most mothers hope to avoid the mistakes their own mothers made – and to give their children things they missed out on themselves. They invest their personal hopes and fantasies in their children, their own unfulfilled dreams and ambitions. A mother of two children aged 6 and 3 says:

> I do cuddle my children an awful lot. I think this is why I tend to cuddle them, because I missed it. And I don't want them to miss it. I know what it's like to go without. Even when they're naughty you can be firm without being unkind. You've got to give them a cuddle. You can't just say, 'Oh, no. You've been naughty,' which is cruel. Which is what my mother done to me. It's cruel. I learned. And I always vowed I wouldn't do that to my children.[2]

The mother of a 22 month old son told us that she remembered as a child 'having a bad body odour and scruffy clothes because my mother could not be bothered to wash and clothe me adequately or to teach me to wash and clothe myself'. She is determined that her son will 'pride himself on his good appearance'. Another woman tries to compensate for her own deprived childhood by giving her daughter more than is necessary:

> She has a lot more clothes than she'll ever wear. I didn't have that. We had a lot of clothes to wear indoors but there was just one best. And everywhere you went you wore the same thing. It was really embarrassing with all my friends having new clothes. I don't want my children to feel that way. She'll always have more than she needs.[3]

Believing that children will have a better life than their parents gives a sense of meaning and purpose to child rearing. One woman describes her own life, saying that 'if you're normal working class, you've just got to carry on. All the frustration, the money troubles, you've got to manage from week to week.' She wants something better for her children. 'That's why we've only got two children – so we can give them as much as we can. To make life nice for them as it hasn't been for us'.[4] Another mother describes her own childhood: 'From the age of 8 I was a refugee Jew in a foreign land, despised and taunted at school, my father in a refugee camp for years.' She felt 'lonely, hopeless and sad a lot of the time' and with her own children has wanted, more than anything, to give them 'security, a solid home life, self-confidence, and a sense that they are as good as anyone'.

Yet women often find themselves repeating their own mother's behaviour with their children and are distressed by this: 'I told her to shut up and sit down and behave, and as I said it I heard my mother saying it to me – the same intonation, the same words, everything. And I was horrified.'

> There have been times . . . when I have become acutely aware of things coming out of my mouth or even entering my mind that were so my mother, and I think 'My God, where did that come from?' It came from her . . . When I react to my children I know I can feel a lot of my mother in me.[5]

The values we want to impart to children depend a great deal not just on our experience of our own childhood, but also on the value we attach to having children, and the reasons why we wanted them in the first place. Women who say they have children to make their marriage more secure are most likely to stress independence as an important quality for their children to develop.[6] 'My husband and I have enjoyed rearing our children, and it's brought us closer together,' one woman whose children are 8 and 9 told us, 'but we're looking forward to the time when they leave home and we can have more time together.' Another woman who says sadly that she found her baby son 'horrendously obnoxious' says: 'I had a love child, and I thought life would be romantic. But he was either grisly or a tornado.'

Childrearing is fascinating, exhausting, exciting, frustrating – and deeply rewarding. It is full of comedy, drama, sheer poetry – and sometimes tragedy, and you can never know in advance how it is going to be. When a woman enters on motherhood with romantic ideas about a baby who is always smiling and cooing, and who when

put down settles straight into blissful sleep, the reality of having a child in the home comes with the shock of cold reality. She may feel drained, sucked dry, worn out, her time and attention completely monopolised by a thriving creature whom she often invests with far more power than a baby can possess. She may even feel that she is being destroyed by her child.[7]

Media and fictional images of malign children, possessed by the devil, or from another planet, invading the homes of ordinary families, come close to reflecting the intense hostility even the most loving mothers sometimes feel towards the children who seem like aliens in their homes. Couples in the United States can avoid this risk entirely by buying a 'videobaby' to watch, advertised as 'clean, neat and tidy . . . a baby that never throws up on your shoulder or needs its diapers changed'.

In many cultures children are wanted because they work in the home or business or on the farm, and provide support for their parents in old age. In countries like this – Indonesia and Turkey, for example – obedience is a highly valued characteristic in children and they are trained to respect their elders and be loyal to their parents.

4

Some Western parents talk about children like this too. They say they want a child to 'look after me when I am old' or 'to enter the family business and run it when I am gone'.

In the past children were needed to help with agricultural work or the care of infants in Western countries too. The notion of childhood as a special period of life, a kind of quarantine before being allowed to join adults, a time when the child's behaviour and moral welfare has to be carefully monitored, is a modern idea. In the 1500s, 10 year olds participated fully in the affairs of adults. There was no thought that a person of that age was either intellectually or physically incapable of performing adult tasks. For working-class parents, the child's work was essential for economic survival. For middle-class parents, the brevity of life (with life expectancy about thirty-five or forty) meant that the child had to be able to manage adult affairs to ensure the transmission and continued ownership of property among family members.

People's lives comprised two broad periods, an extended 'infancy', which lasted until 7 or 8 years of age, during which time they were usually cared for by parents, and 'adulthood', when they were expected to share equally in the activities and responsibilities of the older adults, work more or less as they did, go to the same places of entertainment, play the same games, and read the same books. (There were no special books for children before the seventeenth century – fairy tales, now considered suitable only for children, were read aloud by ladies and gentlemen in the Paris salons.)

Working-class children were employed to weed, pick stones, scare birds, mind babies, guard sheep, cast the seed in the furrow and help with harvest work. In certain industries children began to work even earlier than in agriculture. In textile manufacture this was partly because the work could be performed under parental supervision and did not demand much physical strength. In the early 1720s, Daniel Defoe said that children aged about five were generally employed in the textile mills around Taunton and Colchester.[8] Children even younger than this were used to pick up cotton waste, creeping under unguarded machines where bigger people could not go.[9]

Childhood ended early in the upper classes too. In 1741 Lord Chesterfield wrote to his son:

> This is the last letter I shall write to you as a little boy, for tomorrow you will attain your nineth year, so that for the future I shall treat you as a youth. You must now commence a different course of life, a different course of studies. No more levity. Childish toys and playthings must be thrown aside, and your mind directed to serious objects. What was not unbecoming to a child would be disgraceful to a youth.[10]

In many other cultures today children are expected to take on a great deal of responsibility from an early age. Girls in the Nyansongo tribe in Western Kenya become nurses for babies when aged 5 to 8 years old, starting the job when the infant is about 2 months old and continuing until the child can walk securely. Since few of these girls go to school, they are available as nurses all day long, and feed, bathe and care for the infants while their mothers work in the field or go to market. Children are also expected to carry wood and water, prepare and cook food, garden and care for animals.[11] Poor children in India work from the age of about 7 or 8 to support their families. The brickmaking kiln at Shiliguri near Darjeeling employs fifty boys who labour from dawn to dark with no respite except the three-hour break in the middle of the day, when the gasping heat makes work impossible for all. Eight-year-old Ganesh has worked there for six months, carrying loads of bricks on his head, balanced on a board and cushioned by a turban. Each day he carries more than three tons of bricks to the kiln, for which he earns about £1.20.[12]

The self-conscious provision of a 'happy childhood' for children in the West is a luxury born of relative affluence. Yet in the West, children – even those with wealthy parents – take more responsibility than is generally acknowledged. Nearly a quarter of North American children over 6 cook their own and their siblings' dinner occasionally and more than one in every twenty do it most of the time. One 10-year-old says she has already heated up hundreds of microwave dinners in her short life, and if she has to do the cooking, when her parents come home from work they jolly well have to finish what she puts in front of them.[13] More than 10,000 children in Britain are the sole carers of a severely disabled parent. They may take their mother to the toilet, change sanitary towels, get up regularly during the night to turn her to prevent pressure sores, do all the cooking, cleaning, housework and control the family finances, and often have to take care of younger brothers and sisters.[14]

After the Industrial Revolution, as the urban middle class grew in size, middle-class families began to regard their children less as objects of utility and more as emerging people who enhance their parents' sense of self. Most North American mothers today give as their primary reason for wanting children their own need for love and companionship. The values they want in their children are personality characteristics such as warmth, cheerfulness and a loving, outgoing, responsive, caring nature – the sort of qualities you might hope for in a friend.[15] The child in a fifteenth-century farming village had an opportunity, each day, to realise that he was valuable to his parents – he could point to a ploughed field or a full woodpile as evidence. Children in the West today, valued not for what they achieve in contributing to the family's economic status, but for their psychological qualities, find it more difficult to get assurance from adults that they matter. And parental expectations of the personal satisfactions their children will bring are sometimes excessive, like the 15-year-old who feels rejected by her own parents and greets her baby with the words 'at least now someone will love me'. Or the woman in her thirties who battered her 6-month-old child, and justified this with, 'I waited seven years to have this baby and now she's here she doesn't *do* anything for me.'

Children can also be seen as a source of power and influence. In India a young bride enters her mother-in-law's house almost as a servant, and it is only through the bearing of a son that she gains power in that household over sisters-in-law who do not have sons, and eventually rises to the position of mother-in-law herself with power over her son's wives. In Western cultures, parenthood represents the achievement of adulthood – proof that you are at last grown up. Women who have so little power in the world outside the home are attributed huge powers within it, reflected in old sayings like 'the hand that rocks the cradle rules the world'. What happens in infancy is supposed to determine the course of the child's entire life: 'as the twig is bent, so is the tree inclined' or 'the fruit does not fall far from the tree'. This attributes to woman the power to mar her child's entire life. With that power comes tremendous responsibility.

Bad mothering is believed to cause irreparable damage and childhood traumas are used as alibis by adults to 'explain away' their questionable behaviour. Blaming mothers is common in psychology: in 125 articles analysed in one study, mothers were blamed for seventy-two different kinds of psychological disorder in their children, ranging from agoraphobia to arson, hyperactivity to schizophrenia, 'premature mourning' to 'homicidal trans-sexualism'. The reviewer says: 'In the articles we reviewed, not a single mother was ever described as emotionally healthy, although some fathers were, and no mother-child relationship was said to be healthy, although some father-child ones were described as ideal.' She is concerned about mother-blaming not just because it hurts mothers, but also because it 'prevents us from looking with fully open eyes at the total range of causes for children's unhappiness and psychological problems', which might include disturbing encounters with other adults or children, or familial stresses and tensions stemming from difficult social or economic circumstances.[16]

Psychological experts have always believed that they know what is wrong with mothers, and how they should do the job better. As long ago as 1928 one psychologist asserted that 'no one today knows enough to raise a child'. He argued that:

The world would be considerably better off if we were to stop having children for twenty years (except for those reared for experimental purposes) and were then to start again with enough facts to do the job with some degree of accuracy. Parenthood, instead of being an instinctive art, is a science, the details of which must be worked out by patient laboratory methods.[17]

Today, along with a plethora of childcare books and magazines packed with medical, psychological and psychiatric advice, parents may choose to take their children to be analysed by a computer program. One father whose son went through this describes it as a mixture of horoscope-style generalities, bland truisms, and eerily accurate diagnoses – although accuracy in this context just means that he and the computer shared some of the same ideas.[18]

The properly brought up child is supposed to grow into a well-adjusted and mature adult, testimony to the parents' – and particularly the mother's – childrearing techniques. A child is her handiwork, her creation, and the way the child turns out is a reflection on her. One woman, whose children were reading at two, playing the violin by four, and had personal computers with educational software from babyhood told us: 'I'm building quality children who will become quality adults.' Another uses a manufacturing analogy in which children are *products*, the output of the parental 'firm':

As parents we are responsible for setting up and monitoring a short 'production run' of a high quality complex 'article' in which prototypes are excluded, mistakes are costly and sometimes irreversible. For many years it has been my contention ... that parental 'firms' can reduce their risks by acquiring information and understanding about the principles of the 'production process' – both before the 'production line' is set up, and during the production process itself.[19]

In all the emphasis on the importance of careful childrearing, the needs, rights and personalities of the women who mother are frequently forgotten. According to the psychoanalyst Bruno Bettelheim:

We have grown to think that with the right formula, the right programme, we can create a perfect product. Factory assembly lines, industries where people slot together inanimate components, all the areas of life where we know we can create things that are 100 per cent as they are designed, have led people to assume that the same must be possible with children. It may not be conscious but it is an attitude of mind. People have turned to books, not for guidance, but for a blueprint which will allow them to construct to satisfaction, and the fear of failure is great. Of course, all this puts an enormous pressure on children and also on their parents – we should not expect to achieve a perfect child any more than we should expect to be perfect parents. Perfection is not within the grasp of ordinary human beings.[20]

Children's moral development cannot be the exclusive responsibility of mothers. Children are active participants in their own socialisation, and both mother and child live in a society which systematically encourages certain forms of development and not others.

The mother–child relationship, one of the essential factors of social change, is also one of the most difficult to modify. Its transformation cannot be achieved solely by educating the mothers. Women's living conditions and the discrimination they have to suffer prevent them from meeting their children's needs in order to prepare them effectively for life in a modern world.[21]

One vital element in this preparation for life in the modern world must be education for social and political change. Without that, there will be no future, for us, or for our children.

CHAPTER
2

LEARNING TO BE 'GOOD'

'Be a good girl now!' 'You can't come to the park unless you behave like a good boy.' 'Have you been really good?'

In one North American study more than half of all mothers chose 'being good' as the single most important quality they wanted in their children – more important than obedience, independence or academic success.[1] But what are we expecting of children when we want them to be 'good'?

In fact, there are at least two different meanings of being 'good', and even very young children know the difference between these two senses of the word. In his autobiography Geoffrey Dennis[2] distinguishes these meanings as they were applied in his own childhood:

> 'Be good' – meaning 'Do as you're told: Don't untidy that room: Clear up all the mess: Get ready for bed instead of finding excuses: Don't dawdle: Be sensible: Behave!', and the second meaning of 'good', the Sunday School meaning that children are good 'if you have pure hearts and kind natures: When you are gentle, unselfish, thoughtful for others. When you try to be like Jesus!'

While we do not all define goodness in Christian terms, most of us recognise this distinction between 'good' meaning conforming with social rules and customs, and 'good' meaning adherence to fundamental moral principles.

Gwen Raverat[3] remembers being taught very carefully and with great insistence how gentlepersons behaved:

Gentlemen don't tell lies; Ladies don't pick their noses; Gentlemen never avoid paying their bus fares; Ladies are always polite to servants; Gentlemen never show they are afraid; No Lady would wear a hat like that; Gentlemen are always generous with money, don't hit smaller boys; never read other people's letters ... This was quite different from the other set of values which emphasised honesty, kindness and moral courage.

POLITENESS

Adults spend a lot of time and energy trying to teach children to be polite. Many mothers who talked to us said this was like 'taming wild animals' or 'civilising savages'. Starting with a totally egocentric, utterly demanding newborn, or a toddler whose most important words appear to be 'No', 'It's mine', and 'Give me!', they struggled to create a polite, courteous, well-mannered person. The raw materials sometimes seem unpromising!

A few women who spoke to us chose 'politeness' as the most important virtue they wanted their child to learn – more important than religion, for example, self-confidence, independence or kindness. Politeness, they say, 'can get you a long way in life', 'enables you to get on well in any situation', 'earns respect from others', and 'means that the world is your oyster'. Lorraine, who thinks that 'being polite to people brings much better results in communication' went into some detail about how she teaches politeness to her 18-month-old son:

I think it very important that children learn 'please' and 'thank you' – to speak nicely to people who speak to them, and ask nicely for the things that they want. I was brought up this way and I know people do appreciate my manners. Being a polite child also means to me that they will respect their elders – hold doors open for women or elderly men etc. and I know that I won't have to worry when he goes to tea with his friends later on. I insist that he says 'ta' for everything given to him, as I do when he gives me anything. And 'pease', for when he wants something (he can't say please properly yet) again as I do when I want him to give me anything. I set the example and hope that he follows. Even when he's thrown something or done something objectionable I will ask him politely not to do it (obviously followed with appropriate telling off if three times asking doesn't work). I know he is beginning to understand.

Judy is teaching her 3-year-old son to be polite by allowing him to have his own way with most things when he asks for them nicely. Many women stress the importance of being polite themselves, to their children as well as to adults, so setting a good example. It is amazing how rudely adults can themselves behave in front of children, and yet expect them to grow up polite. They are often especially rude to children, adopting an insulting tone of voice, interrupting what they are doing or saying, and treating them as social inferiors.

We are often told that children today don't have any manners and that they are far less well-behaved than children of earlier generations. In fact, every generation seems to believe this! Aristotle, who was born in 322BC, complained about children who 'have bad manners and contempt for authority. They show disrespect for their elders.' He warned that children were becoming 'tyrants' and was disgusted to find that unlike the manners he was taught when he was a child, 'they no longer rise when elders enter the room. They contradict their parents, chatter before company, gobble up their food and tyrannize their teachers.'[4]

The word 'courtesy', like most other terms associated with good manners (politeness, etiquette, kindness, deportment, dignity, graciousness) comes from the French. The only related Anglo-Saxon word still in use is 'churlish', which means just the opposite. After the Norman invasion, French was widely spoken among the upper classes in Britain and 'courtesy books' were written for the children of royalty and nobles describing how to behave properly. They were often in verse so that children could easily memorise them, and were an important part of medieval education.

The most popular was *The Babees Book*,[5] composed in 1475, which begins with the injunction:

> Swete children have al-wy
> Your delyte in curtesye.

The image of the medieval feast as an orgy of gluttony with noblemen grabbing food in their fists and hurling discarded bones onto the floor for the dogs tells only one side of the story. There were also strict rules of deportment which dictated how napkins should be folded, the order of precedence in which distinguished guests should be seated at meals, and how knives must be used. Much of the advice given to children in the Middle Ages is similar to that they are offered today – not to put their elbows on the table or dirty the cloth, not to speak with their mouths full or pick their noses or put their knives in their mouths, not to whisper, to be alert to hand dishes to others who might want them and so on. Other instructions seem odd to today's ears: how to get water and pour it over the lord's hands at the end of a meal, to make the sign of the cross over their mouths before eating, to hold their hands over their mouths while spitting, and after carefully blowing their noses in thumb and forefinger, to step on whatever fell to the ground so that others did not have to look at it. Some people will always argue that children today are less polite than they used to be: certainly they no longer address their parents as 'Sir' and 'Madam', but, on the other hand, they do occasionally use their handkerchiefs and are likely to have a bath more than once a month.

Codes of manners and ideals of politeness vary in different cultures, too. In some societies it is polite to belch loudly at the end of a meal as a way of expressing appreciation of good food, and in Japan green tea must be drunk with a particular hissing slurp to show your enjoyment while holding the bowl in both hands with its pattern facing outwards so that others can admire it. In many Arab cultures it is considered the height of rudeness to reject offers of food, and the squeamish Westerner who turns down the offer of a sheep's eye, a special delicacy, may deeply offend a host. Whereas in England a polite child is expected to stand up for an adult in a crowded bus, in Italy adults offer their seats to children. When teaching in West Africa, an English man discovered that despite the British reputation for formality, English manners of greeting and making social contact seem almost slap-happy to Africans and offensively casual; African greetings are far more elaborate and ceremonial.[6]

Even within Britain codes of behaviour vary with social class. A middle-class teacher describes how she taught children at her kindergarten to say 'lavatory' because she considered the word 'toilet' vulgar. The working-class parents protested that 'lavatory' was the vulgar term and 'toilet' correct. Many educationalists have suggested that some of the alleged 'behaviour problems' attributed to working-class children in British schools are due to the different expectations and definitions of 'good behaviour' of their working-class parents and their (largely) middle-class teachers. In the nineteenth century, good manners was often described as 'good breeding': the way you behaved showed what kind of family and social class you came from. In many ways this is still true today. In the film 'A Fish Called Wanda' John Cleese says: 'I'm middle class and my aim in life is to get through life without being socially embarrassed!'

When people with different codes of manners interact, they often inadvertently offend one another. A young child is rather like an adult in a foreign culture. Polite behaviour seems so natural to us as adults that we forget that we once had to acquire it. Children have to learn not only that they should be 'well-mannered' but also what that means – all the intricate and elaborate behaviours involved that are as complicated for them as learning Japanese etiquette, and the exact depth of bow appropriate for each person to whom they are introduced, is for Westerners.

Children also encounter different codes of behaviour within their own culture – rules of politeness may be different with parents and with grandparents, at home and at school, in their own family and in that of their best friends. This is often a problem for parents who want to present children with a single coherent code of manners. But codes of conduct *are* different – in different cultures and sub-cultures, and in different generations – and it is no bad thing for children to become sensitive to these differences in habit and custom. Katherine Whitehorn adopted this approach with her children:

> I do not believe it is damaging to children to be asked to behave differently in different surroundings. They are more adaptable than that. Even ours, lined up and told that *chez* their grandparents they didn't get down from the table without asking and were not to swear, simply accepted such things as the custom of another country. You could even argue that if we want them to grow up as the sort of people who can respect other people's customs, be they Finns or Fijians, they should not be allowed to assume that what happens at home is the only way for things to be.[7]

Children can learn to be flexible and to slip into the conventions and decode the customs of different groups.

Children develop their own codes of manners when they understand the basic principle of consideration for others. A group of children was asked recently to give some examples of good manners. Answers were: 'Burying things when they're dead'; 'Winding back the video for the next person'; 'Sharing your sticker swaps with your sister'; and 'Not burping after you've drunk Coke'.[8]

It is important to give children an opportunity to discuss 'good manners' and to be critical of social conventions. Behaviour that is 'polite' or customary in a culture is not arbitrary, but part of a society's historical and social development. Some aspects of courteous behaviour are merely curious relics of past customs, like shaking hands, which demonstrated that you were not holding a sword, or saying 'goodbye', which is a condensed version of 'God be with you'. But some people feel that other forms of politeness reinforce and perpetuate archaic and oppressive social customs. For example, children are often expected to use courtesy titles (Mr, Mrs, Miss) when talking to adults, although adults call children by their first names. It is only when an adult is a close friend of the family that a child is allowed to use the adult's first name, and even then it is often qualified in some way, so that even unrelated adults may be called 'Auntie Mary' or 'Uncle George'. When children are called by their first names but have to give courtesy titles to adults it is a sign that they are socially inferior. The use of courtesy titles was challenged by the founder of Quakerism, George Fox, who said that it contravened the idea that everyone is equal in the sight of God. In Quaker schools today, children are encouraged to address teachers by their first names.

While many forms of politeness are harmless social niceties, which help oil the wheels of social intercourse, others are more problematic. The traditional deference which servants were supposed to show towards their employers would be considered unbearably servile and humiliating today. More recently, the courtesies traditionally extended to women – opening doors for them, offering them seats on buses – have been challenged as symbolising women's social powerlessness. This can lead to very real confusion as to what, in a particular context, or with a particular person, it is in fact the polite thing to say or do. We need to consider what our forms of politeness symbolise, how they reflect and perpetuate certain patterns in our society, and whether we want to reinforce those ways of behaving.

MANNERS AND MORALS

But when mothers talk about 'being good' they do not only mean having good manners. The second meaning of goodness is being aware of, responsive to, and considerate about, people's feelings, and behaving towards others in a caring and fair way.

In this respect, codes of behaviour have changed dramatically amongst both children and adults. The Romans amused themselves by keeping dwarfs, hunchbacks and physically deformed children in their households and laughed at their afflictions. They also found the sight of Christians being mauled to death by lions very amusing.[9] The famous philospher Cicero would entertain friends in his Corinthian dining-room opening on to the sea, discussing with them high moral questions about the nature of honour, the calm of their conversation occasionally pierced by a scream from the servants' quarters where a slave was being branded with a hot iron upon the face.[10] In the Middle Ages public executions were very popular and there is a record of the citizens of one town buying a condemned criminal from a neighbouring town so that they could have the fun of quartering him themselves.[11] In the eighteenth century the rich could amuse themselves by visiting insane asylums and taunting the inmates. Slavery was not only accepted as natural by Aristotle but slaves were kept in America, and Britain was still active in the slave trade well into the nineteenth century. Until comparatively recently terms like 'nigger', 'gyppo' and 'wog' were common and considered socially acceptable in white middle-class conversation. None of this behaviour is generally considered socially acceptable today. Our level of social awareness has changed dramatically. Perhaps we are exchanging some of the more ceremonial forms of courtesy for a more broadly compassionate approach to other people, and a concern for their human rights.

While the niceties of politeness and good behaviour rely on *conventional* rules, being kind and considerate is part of a *moral* rule, which is more fundamental. We can probably all think of someone who is 'polite' and well-mannered but whom we do not really like. The smile is just painted on, the pleasantries are empty, devoid of any real meaning, and although this person may 'never put a foot wrong' we don't really trust them, we don't know what lies beneath the charm. Conformity with conventional rules of politeness does not make someone a moral person. On the other hand, there are people who flout conventional rules, but do so out of a deep sense of moral conviction – like black people in segregated America who refused to sit at the back of the bus, allowing white people to have all the front seats. Good manners and morals are very different things.

Even young children understand the difference between conventional manners and morality. By the time they are ten they show a very clear awareness of the distinction. One developmental psychologist read a story to a 10-year-old in which a teenager cheated an old man out of money and he asked him whether or not taking the man's money would be wrong if no rule prohibited cheating and if everyone agreed it was all right.

I think that would still be wrong.
Why?

Because you're still cheating the old man. It doesn't matter whether he's stupid, rough or not, and it's not really fair to take the money.
What do you mean, it's not fair to steal?
It's not nice to do it, because maybe he needs it too.
What if the rule were changed about calling people by their first names so that everybody could call their teachers by their first names? Do you think it would be right or wrong in that case to do it?
I think it would be all right then because the rule is changed. Right? and everybody else would probably be doing it too.
How come the two things are different?
Because it's sort of a different story. Cheating an old man, you should never do that, even if everybody says you can. You should still never cheat off an old man.[12]

In fact this awareness of a difference between conventional and moral rules develops very early – by the age of 4 or 5 in many children. The same psychologist asked children in a pre-school group whether certain acts were wrong. Some of them were breaches of conventional rules (not hanging a coat on the 'right' hook for example). Children were asked if these things were wrong, and if they said 'yes' (which most of them did, because they knew the school rules) they were then asked whether or not the act would be wrong if there were no rule in the school about it. Eight out of ten said that it would be all right if no school rule forbade it. Other kinds of behaviour the children were asked about were breaches of moral rules (like hitting another child). When asked whether it would be okay to hit another child if there was no school rule forbidding it, more than eight out of ten said that it would still be wrong because it is always wrong to hurt people.[13]

Caring about other people's feelings, understanding how things appear from their perspective, is an important part of this second meaning of being 'good'. Many women who spoke to us stressed kindness, altruism, unselfishness, helpfulness and empathy. One mother says: 'I try to encourage Beatrice, just 4, to help her brother and sister, to share her things, and to understand when the little ones get cranky.' The mother of a 2-year-old makes an important point:

> I would very much like my child to be caring, kind and unselfish, but I do not see these as goals in their own right, i.e. something to be insisted upon as of high importance in any one context as my parents did. I see my child learning these as an *offshoot* of her own maturing personality and conscience, the respect she is given and the example she is given by others.

Children are generally given mixed messages about sharing. As Ruth Pennebaker points out, in her humorous guide to parents, written as if by a disgruntled toddler, 'Grownups have double standards. You never see either of them lend their clothes or cars to anyone, do you? But they're always pushing you to let that dorky kid next door play with your best toys.'[14]

Living in the UK or the USA children learn materialism and acquisitiveness from the television ads urging them to buy the latest doll's outfit or game, and mothers are often worried by this. 'It is the "me, now" approach to life that, more than anything else, causes people to trample and grab,' writes one woman, who argues that it is important to teach children patience. (Fewer than one in ten respondents in a British Social Attitudes Survey thought that patience was a quality that should be taught to children, and not a single woman who talked to us emphasised its importance.) An old man reminiscing about his childhood says glumly: 'When I was young the children ran around barefoot. Now it's their hearts that are bare.'[15]

In spite of these gloomy judgements, children often show empathetic, caring, sharing responses from a very early age. If they don't behave in a caring and helpful way as they grow older, perhaps that has something to do with the messages they get from adults. The ability to empathise may even be present at birth. Babies respond to the crying of other babies with distressed crying of their own, but don't cry if they hear computer-synthesised 'crying', or even if their own crying is played back to them on tape. It seems as though babies have a specific response to the sound of another human being like themselves who is in trouble.

Some children less than 2 years old offer their favourite toys to a crying child, hold and stroke a weeping adult, and bring their mother to help a friend in distress. An 18-month-old may react helpfully to someone else's distress about once in every three times. But children of this age vary greatly in responsiveness – some fail to respond at all, while others respond almost every time. Psychologists have found that mothers who frequently use explanations linking the child's behaviour with its consequences for the victim have children who are more likely to respond in a helpful way when they cause harm to someone. These mothers might say, 'Tom's crying because you pushed him' – a clear but neutral explanation. Even more effective are explanations accompanied by strong emotional overtones such as, 'You must never poke anyone's eyes' or 'When you hurt me I don't want to be near you. I am going away from you.' Children who are smacked or physically restrained, or who are never offered explanations of why they should not hurt someone are least likely to give help to people in distress.[16]

Children's ideas of 'helping' are applied first to special individuals and are only later generalised. If you ask a 4-year-old, 'Which people do you think you ought to help?', she will tell you the members of her immediate family – her mother, sister, baby brother. As she gets older, the range is widened to include other children she plays with or meets in school. Later still she will name groups of people (babies, old people, poor people in Ethiopia), but not until the age of 9 or 10 will she be able to generalise to say 'anybody who needs help' or 'anyone who has less than other people'. At 11 or 12, children generalise even more widely: 'You should help anyone who needs it; that's everybody I suppose, we all need help at one time or another.' During the teenage years there is a more mature appreciation of the difficulties and conflicts that arise in putting such a general principle into practice. A teenager may say, for example, 'You should help everybody, even burglars and murderers – I don't mean you should help them commit a crime, but you've got to try and help them to be better.'[17]

But in spite of talking about helping others, many people, much of the time, do not give help when it is needed. In the 1960s a young woman called Kitty Genovese was murdered by a man who first beat her up for a full half-hour in front of dozens of people. Nobody even rang the police. This incident prompted a flood of research by psychologists into what became known as 'the by-stander syndrome'. They wanted to find out why people often don't intervene when others are in pain or danger but just stand by and let things happen.[18]

One common finding is that people are uncertain how to behave because they are unsure about what they are seeing. Emergencies are rare events which usually happen suddenly and unexpectedly. How can we know that it is a real emergency, and not a prank, a game or a film being produced? The safest thing is to sit tight and pretend it isn't happening. A friend told us how she rushed out of the house late one evening to help a woman who was running down the street and screaming 'rape, rape!' Her intervention was not appreciated by the young woman who was enjoying a chasing game with her boyfriend. It is fear of making an inappropriate response in ambiguous situations that often stops people from taking action. Children who are punished, or subjected to severe disapproval when they behave inappropriately, are *least* likely to offer help in an emergency.

In one study, children were asked to wait alone in a room. They heard the sound of a falling chair, followed by crying and moaning from a young girl in the next room. Older children were *less* likely than younger ones to go to her aid and when questioned many said that they were worried about being told off if they left the room in which they had been told to wait.[19] Children from strict families, where obedience to conventional rules is emphasised, are most likely to fear disapproval or punishment and least likely to offer help. Those who have been encouraged to be more independent and autonomous and to question rules tend to take the initiative and give help in these situations.

Just *telling* children always to help others isn't enough. They are altruistic, compassionate and actively helpful when adults have acted in this way towards them. Psychologists put 3 to 5 year old children in a real situation in which they could be kind and helpful. Each child was invited to visit a baby, and while the child and a teacher were waiting for the baby to be ready, a basket of spools and buttons 'accidentally' fell off the table. Would the child help to pick them up? Then the baby's mother left the child alone with the baby for a few minutes while she went to get juice and crackers. Would the child retrieve the baby's toys that had fallen outside the playpen? Children with 'nurturant' teachers – teachers who help them, offer praise, sympathy and support – are much more helpful than those with teachers who are not nurturant. Even though both 'nurturant' and 'non-nurturant' teachers teach children that they should help others, if they are not themselves nurturant their message does not translate into action. Children who are taught principles of behaviour by non-nurturant adults give the 'right' answers when asked how they would respond to other people's distress, but in real life they often do not act on these principles.

Children are most likely to respond to the needs of others if people respond to *their* needs. Isabelle remembers how, when she was a child, her mother used to 'take whatever I was playing with and hand it to my sister in an effort to encourage unselfishness'. This just made Isabelle feel resentful and possessive of her toys. She encourages her son to share things, but she doesn't insist, and acknowledges *his* feelings too.

Children can also be helped to think constructively about the best ways of helping other people. The maxim 'do as you would be done by', which was taught children for generations and popularised in fiction by Mrs Do-as-you-would-be-done-by in *The Water Babies*, doesn't work because not everybody wants or needs the same thing. This is sometimes hard for children to understand and learning to see things from other people's perspective is a part of growing up. Gwen Raverat's recollection of an incident from her childhood illustrates this vividly:

I took the Christian precepts to heart too, and tried to carry them out, quite literally. 'Do unto others, as you would that they should do unto you': it seemed right and fair. So I gave

23

the kitchen-maid a copy of Milton's *Poems* for a Christmas present because I wanted it so much myself. She thanked me most politely, but I somehow felt it was not quite a success (poor kitchen-maid!) And I can remember saying helpfully to a new-made widow, aged about thirty-five: 'Never mind, you'll soon be dead, too' because I thought I should want to die if I had lost my husband. I recall very clearly the startled expression of one of her blue eyes, looking at me over the edge of her pocket-handkerchief. I always supposed that my feelings were exactly like other people's; it was much later before I noticed, with surprise, that they weren't.[20]

One way of helping children to understand other people's perspectives is to play 'the Sherlock Holmes game'[21] with them. Choose a friend or relative, discuss their likes and dislikes, and try to work out what you would have to do to make that person happy.

A 'good' child, then, is not simply passive, submissive and obedient. 'Goodness', in this sense, is hard work – it means taking responsibility for your actions, trying to imagine what someone else might be feeling, and being willing to act. A child who has been trained to be good in the sense of always being polite and obedient finds this other form of goodness much more difficult to achieve because it involves taking the initiative and, like the child in the waiting-room research already referred to who heard the crash of a chair followed by a girl crying, it sometimes means *disobeying* orders. Helpful, altruistic, compassionate children are those who feel secure and happy themselves, whose own needs are fulfilled, and who are willing to risk being wrong.[22]

BEING NAUGHTY

If parents are not sure what 'goodness' is, at least they are clear about 'naughtiness' or 'badness'. Often it means anything that adults find inconvenient. Children are 'naughty' if they are unhappy, tired or desperate for adult attention. Within a family, children may acquire an image of themselves as either 'good' or 'bad' children. If one child has already taken the role of 'good' and dutiful child, or set standards which another feels unable to meet, the other may become 'bad' to establish a different role for herself and so get attention. A mother's reaction to 'badness' often reinforces this identity, by singling a child out as 'the naughty one'.

A doctor who works with children tells the story of Charles, aged eight, who was a middle child with a capable older brother and a 'good' younger sister. He describes him as 'a holy terror'. He lied, stole and had set fire to the basement twice. He daubed all the walls with his crayons and his mother complained there was nothing she could do with him. She went for counselling and was advised to treat all the children 'as a unit', responsible for their own and each other's behaviour, and not to single out Charles in any way.

Two weeks later she came back and said he was like a different boy. He had crayoned on the walls once and she had asked all the children to clean it off together. In fact, Charles didn't help, but he had not crayoned on the walls again and when asked about it said, 'It's not fun any more. The others have to clean it up.'

The doctor's interpretation is that Charles decided that there wasn't any sense in bad behaviour if it didn't start a fight and force his mother into lengthy negotiations with him.[23] (All the same, we hope Charles could express himself in other ways, and that he had a wall for himself on which he *was* allowed to draw.)

Children are sometimes 'bad' because their own personal moral standards are different from those adults try to impose on them. Many 9- or 10-year-olds feel passionate loyalty towards their peer group and 'telling on' a friend is considered a terrible moral offence. Children who have been ordered to apologise to an adult for a misdeed sometimes refuse because 'I don't feel sorry, so it would be a lie.' They want to be true to what they feel rather than to uphold adult niceties of behaviour. Many adults can remember times in their own childhood when they confronted the distinction between the values adults tried to impose on them and their own set of internal values. Gwen Raverat describes the adult set of values of Badness and Goodness, which she calls 'System A', and says that this only partly coincided with her own private set of values: System B. She was always troubled by the confusion of trying to reconcile the two incompatible codes. She gives an example:

The grownups pretended that it was what you did *on purpose* that mattered. This was, and is, quite untrue. No one ever really regrets doing a Badness on purpose. For instance, if you were rude or disobedient to Miss X, a governess you rightly despised, you felt rather pleased with yourself afterwards; or if you paddled without asking leave, anyhow you had the paddling, and no one could ever take it away from you again. But if you were unkind or rude by mistake to someone you loved – Ah, then you just wished you were dead.[24]

Another writer, in his autobiography, describes how, by the age of 7, he had made the same distinction between adult versions of 'goodness' and his own internal code:

Good is obeying, wrong is disobeying the Voice Inside. What I hear there, in my heart, is the only judgement that counts – counts in my heart. Grownup views of bad and good are not without importance, if only because transgressing them might have unpleasant results; and their categories and catalogues will have played a main part in shaping mine. But good which Voice declares for is the only good I attach full moral value to.[25]

When his mother talked to him he thought she called this voice 'Constance':

'You can always know what is right,' concluded Mother, 'Constance will tell you ...' Queen Constance was always right; she *was* righteous. Human grownups were sometimes wrong. When reproof came down which Constance and I both thought unjustified, I ignored it and made a deaf ear while Mother delivered her homily, managing, while appearing to listen, not even to hear her words, at least in my heart.[26]

Instead of labelling children as 'good' or 'bad' and then rewarding or punishing them, we can consider how their behaviour relates to their own moral code. We can help them to articulate their own values. If we don't like their moral code, we can explore it with them, and try to persuade them, as we might adults with whom we disagree, that a different one might be better. But children's own concepts of right and wrong will always influence their behaviour more than our concepts can, and instead of lecturing them about ours, we need to listen and engage with theirs. Children are not blank slates on which we can write the morals we choose. They are active participants in their own socialisation – selecting amongst the range of values presented to them. We can help them construct their own beliefs about right and wrong.

CHAPTER
3

FOOD

Food is a metaphor for everything that goes on in the relationship between the mother and child in Western societies. This is so from birth, and her sense of success or failure as the mother of a newborn derives from the confidence she has in giving the breast or bottle. If the baby is difficult to feed, refuses the gift, brings back milk or cries inconsolably, it is as if the child is rejecting her. If she is breastfeeding and does not have enough milk she feels inadequate and impoverished, not only in terms of what her breasts can produce, but as a mother, and may fear that she will never be able to give this child enough of anything.

When a baby is obviously uncomfortable or distressed a major part of all the advice that floods in from other people consists of suggestions about how to improve feeding. When the giving and receiving of milk does not go well and the mother loses confidence, it may form the basis of subsequent conflicts about food with older children.

In those early weeks, too, the mother develops an idea of her child's personality, often reinforced by nurses and other advisers, which stems from the characteristics of feeding. The pattern is crystallised as the child grows. This affects children's self-perception and is an important element in the moulding of their behaviour. Mothers are told that babies are 'slow', 'greedy', 'lazy', 'stubborn', 'angry', 'impatient', and sometimes 'tyrants'. A baby may be called 'the king', 'the boss', or 'a little madam'. Women come to believe these things and to communicate them to their babies.

So it is not surprising that when asked about the values they want to instil in their children they often refer to food – even when the particular quality they are describing seems to bear little relation to feeding. We did not ask any questions about food directly, but found that women often referred to it and to their attempts to get children to eat certain things and avoid others, or to change their eating habits and behaviour at meals.

Conflicts about food symbolise the obstacles in the way of getting children to accept our own moral code, and represent the external influences on children to absorb what is unsuitable and refuse that which is good. We want them to take in, to digest and make their own those values which are important to us; instead they spurn us, spit them out, or gobble up quite different values instead.

Children's table manners – or lack of them – probably always posed a problem. In the fifteenth century, etiquette books like *The Babees Book* and *Urbanitatis*[1] instructed children not to lean their elbows on the table, not to speak with their mouths full, not to pick their noses, not to ask for a second helping or snuffle and spit, and to avoid blowing their noses in the tablecloth. The *Book of Nurture* written in the sixteenth century says that children must not spit across the dinner table, stretch their arms in a loud yawn, or burp. Erasmus, writing in *De Civilitate*, published in 1526, told little boys that if bored they should not fidget, nor glower at everyone, and that they should drink quietly 'and not make a noise like a horse'.

In Western cultural tradition, sitting at the table to eat is symbolic of the unity of the family in place and time. The child is supposed either to sit quietly or, especially in Jewish families, to make intelligent conversation. The observation of table manners – in the USA left hand under the table, right hand manipulating the fork; in German households both hands on the table; in the USA and Britain 'no elbows on the table and sit up straight' – is evidence of the child's consideration for others, so that meal-time becomes an occasion for the expression of family cohesion.

To refuse to come to meals, to make reference to food likes or dislikes or behave in a disorderly manner, to announce 'I'm full up' or 'I'm stuffed' instead of the English, 'No thank you, I've had enough' or, as in the US southern states, 'I've had a sufficiency', or to get down from the table before everyone has finished or without permission, disrupts family unity.

Though we should not assume that food is equally a metaphor of relationships in all cultures, even in societies where people live at subsistence level, and where production of food is the responsibility of every individual, the way food is eaten is an important element in morality. It has to do with sharing, with the careful regulation of consumption, often with ceremony, and with the basic means of surviving in conditions of poverty, drought or famine. Indeed, motherhood itself may be represented in terms of food. There is a Vietnamese folk poem which describes an elderly mother who is deeply loved as like 'fragrant bananas, sugar cane and the finest sticky rice'.[2]

The relationship to food is a major element in gender differentiation, too. Among the !Kung Bushmen of the Kalahari Desert children learn early in their lives that to become a man is to be a hunter, but that one must kill only that which is necessary in order to eat. To be a woman is to be a nurturer and provider of food, and the hearth on which food is cooked is sacred. Myths and legends reinforce this morality.[3]

Through food children are introduced to the essential values of a culture as babies. In Southern India a Toda father carries his 3-month-old son to the dairy and then to the herd of sacred cattle, where he lifts the cloth from his face for the first time in the open air. A mother carries her baby daughter to the spot where women receive buttermilk for cooking from the dairy, and then uncovers the child's face.[4] The Hopi mother of North America raises the blanket from her baby's face in a similar symbolic act at twenty days in order to introduce the baby not only to the neighbours, but also to the corn and to the sun that ripens it.

The eating and sharing of food is ritualised. The idea that 'primitive' people just grab a hunk of meat when they can get it and fight over who siezes the biggest piece, is wide of the mark. Food expresses the values of the society – the divisions of caste and class, differences of status and power. In African cultures, for example, the division of food between the clan members is minutely organised. Subtle shades of distinction in status are expressed through variations in eating etiquette – the correct way of talking at meals, how to request or decline food, and the people with whom it is shared. In subsistence level cultures when there is not enough food to go round it is women and children who usually go short, and in many cultures, men eat first and women and children afterwards.

Special foods may be prepared to celebrate the birth of boys. In the Arab world, a pudding made of ground rice, sugar, caraway, fennel and aniseed, decorated with almonds, pistachio nuts and cinnamon, is eaten to welcome the birth or circumcision of boys, but when a girl baby is born:

> When they said, 'It's a girl!'
> that was a horrible moment.
> The honey pudding turned to
> ashes and the dates became
> scorpions.[5]

In Nigeria almost all the severe malnutrition cases seen by one British doctor in the period following the Biafran war in 1970 were female children. She wrote that

> if food is scarce, the boys are given what little there is, leaving
> the girls to starve. It was not uncommon to see whole families
> of girls with severe kwashiorkor (a protein deficiency disease)
> whilst the son and heir was fit and well.

In one such family, the 2-year-old girl weighed 12 pounds while her 5-month-old brother had reached 18 pounds.[6]

In Europe, baby girls are breastfed less often, and for briefer periods, than boys, and are weaned earlier. An Italian study found that 8-week-old babies were suckled for an average of 45 minutes if they were boys, but only 25 minutes if they were girls. Mothers stopped breastfeeding girls three months earlier than boys.[7]

Watching a friend's son, who is told to eat up all his food 'like a man,' the German writer Mariane Grabrucker muses that 'no-one has ever thought of telling Anneli (her daughter) that she should eat up her food like a real woman'. When Anneli is 2½ years old Mariane Grabrucker has prepared pancakes for lunch for Anneli and her friend, Schroschi:

> I divide the portions on to two plates and notice that one is a bit bigger. Who do I give it to? Schorschi, of course, thinking that as a boy he is probably hungrier and will eat more than Anneli. I am transferring my expectations of masculine eating habits to a 2-year-old boy. Having realised this I then pay attention and realise that Schorschi's portion is too much for him by just the extra amount I have given him and that he is no longer enjoying it. But at least I don't encourage him to eat it all up as I would probably otherwise have done, being of the opinion that I had given him the right amount.
>
> Why do I think males always have to have more than females? Because my grandmother always gave the larger portion to Grandad and my mother to my father.[8]

A few weeks later, Anneli announces after breakfast: 'Now I've eaten so much, now I'll get fat and then I'll be a man.'

In the United States, 80 per cent of 10-year-old girls say they are on slimming diets[9] and it is young women who make up the majority of anorexics throughout the Western world.

FOOD AND LOVE

It is not just the physical health of girls that is undermined in this way. They also suffer emotionally. The giving and receiving of food represents love. When mothers give their children food they give their hearts. There is a Czech children's story, *Zuzanka Discovers the World* which tells of a princess who offers to cook a meal for her prince and sends the servants away. But when she goes to the kitchen there is only one egg, which breaks on the floor. She has nothing to offer him and weeps, thinking how she would give her heart for him. At this point her heart flies out of her breast and straight into the frying pan. So she cooks it and serves it up to the prince for dinner. But afterwards she is horrible to him, because she has no heart.[10]

When food is spurned it is as if love is rejected. Many mothers, like the princess, put their heart into cooking for those they love and then get angry because they have given too much. The giving of food involves sacrifice. The love that a child should show for a parent who is very ill was expressed traditionally in China by making soup in which a cooked piece of the child's own flesh floated.[11]

Mothers who talked to us often stressed the relation between sharing of food and generosity, between jealousy and withholding of food. Speaking about how she intended to bring up her baby, Katy, one of the women who talked to us, was critical of the way in which mothers may use food as a weapon to represent the withdrawal of love and was determined not to do this with her own baby:

> Our pastor's wife has four adorable little boys. At meals she'd say to her 5-year-old, 'Eat your peas or Katy won't love you anymore!' And she'd say this about other people too – all for the sake of peas! That's dishonest. Parents use food as emotional blackmail.

When a new baby is born, an elder sibling's sense of loss may be expressed as wanting to be cuddled every time the baby is fed, asking to suckle, or demanding a drink the moment the mother picks up the baby. Mothers are very concerned about sibling jealousy and often described the first signs of it when they were feeding a new baby. A French mother says of her little girl:

> She is jealous of the baby. At two weeks, when I was feeding him, she came on my knee and tried everything she could to take my attention away from him. I told her I had to feed him because he couldn't do anything for himself. I said I loved her and had given her milk in the same way.

They want to reassure the older child that love has not been withdrawn and to avoid sibling rivalry. They would like their children to co-operate, be friendly, to play happily with other children, and to share toys and food.

Almost one in ten of these women classed *unselfishness* as the quality they most hope their children develop. With small children, being unselfish invariably manifests itself in sharing playthings and food with others, especially brothers and sisters. Madeleine, for example, has twin daughters who are nearly one year old, and says: 'Unselfishness is essential for twins! At the moment they are very young to "teach" much but have learned to share food and toys.' Another woman describes her embarrassment when she took her 2-year-old and baby out to tea and the toddler seized some biscuits from the table – and then how her discomfort turned into delight as he offered them to his baby sister who was unable to reach them.

Conflict about values with other people or outside the home is also often expressed in terms of the giving or withholding of food, the consumption of certain foods to the exclusion of others – which are designated 'bad' or 'good', and the use of gifts of food to symbolise love and to replace or steal love or authority from the person to whom it is rightly due.

Children sometimes choose food their parents dislike – or think disgusting – as an assertion of independence, or as a demonstration of bravado to impress, shock or frighten their friends as well as other grownups.

> Nobody loves me, everybody hates me,
> I'll go into the garden and eat worms,
> Great big, juicy ones, little squiggly-wiggly ones
> Golly how they wriggles and they squirms . . .[12]

Perhaps this is why Australian children consume large quantities of multicoloured killer-python sweets and in Britain 3,000 tonnes of sticky, slimy, jelly creepy-crawlies are sold every year, including 'wriggly worms' and 'spooky spiders'. Woolworth sell a Pick-n-Mix selection of repulsive creatures – worms, toads, spiders and white mice.

Children themselves interpret food as proof and evidence of love, too. A gift of food may represent a way in which they are valued, and deprivation of food, the withholding of that love. Thus food can become a major issue between divorced parents, one of whom has visiting rights, or when children move between two households. One parent insists on home-cooking, the other takes the child to Macdonalds; one serves salads and whole foods, while the other allows junk food; one demands table manners, while the other lets the child 'eat whatever he likes and run wild'.

Between children, the provision of exactly equal quantities of food may symbolise fairness. A mother says of her three children: 'I thought they should be treated absolutely equally. Actually, this brought out competitiveness in them, and at meal times they sat looking at each other's plates to see if anyone had a quarter of an ounce of potato more than the others.'

As the child grows and develops food likes and dislikes, food can also be the occasion for a battle of wills between parents and children – one that, as we have suggested, usually started long before, in the feeding relationship with the baby. There is a good deal of historical evidence recording conflict over food in diaries kept by parents and in autobiographies. For parents were often convinced that children should eat whatever was placed before them. Frances Boscawen's little son aged three had been ill and indulged for six weeks, but now she was determined to resume discipline, and wrote to her husband in 1755:

How perverse and saucy we are, and how much we deal in the words won't, can't, shan't, etcetera. Today he would not eat milk for breakfast. The rod and I went to breakfast with him, and though we did not come into action, nor anything like it, yet the bottom of the porringer was fairly revealed and a declaration made by him that indeed he could not but say it was very good milk.[13]

Half a century later, across the Atlantic in the nonconformist environment of America, Susan Huntington explained how she did not believe in depriving children of cake and sweetmeats, which was the usual tactic when children were disobedient, because 'these are chiefly directed to the selfish principles of our nature ... I should rather aim to cherish ... the pleasure of being loved.'[14]

In the Old World, views had not become liberalised in the same way. In her memoirs of a child living in the first years of the twentieth century Elizabeth Grant recounts the terror of 'the milk rebellion' by children who most likely suffered from lactose intolerance, and tells how it was crushed by their father:

In his dressing gown, with his whip in hand, he attended our breakfast ... that disgusting milk! He began with me: (*she was 9 years old*) my beseeching look was answered by a sharp cut, followed by as many more as were necessary to empty the basin: Jane obeyed at once, and William after one good hint. They suffered less than I did; William cared less, he did not enjoy his breakfast, but he did take it. Jane always got rid of it (by vomiting). She had therefore only hunger to endure; I, whose stomach was either weaker or stronger, had to bear an aching head, a heavy, sick painful feeling which spoilt my whole morning, and prevented any appetite for dinner, where again we constantly met in sorrow.

They were served greasy mutton, but 'the stomachs which rejected milk could not easily manage fat except when we were under the lash, then indeed the fat and the tears were swallowed together'. She had the bright idea of constructing little paper bags which the children hid on their laps and into which they dropped the fat, throwing them away in the river when they went for a walk. Unfortunately, they were unable to dispose of spinach, a vegetable which made Jane vomit, in the same way. If she would not eat it at one meal it was served cold at the next, and she went hungry until she ate it, and then vomited during the night. 'Fancy a young child kept 30 hours without food and then given poison!'[15]

Even today many parents insist on children eating everything that is put before them and see the discipline of eating as basic to self-control. The child's rejection of food then becomes symbolic of a developing struggle for independence and autonomy. When children have strong food preferences and hatreds today's mothers are anxious that they are not having enough protein, calories, vitamins, minerals or whatever. Food becomes a moral issue which is also perceived as a major health issue, and agony aunts in magazines for parents are faced constantly with answering letters from mothers concerned for the health of children who will not eat meat or green vegetables or eggs, who refuse milk, or insist on raw food or food which has not been 'mixed up'.

Many children go through a period of not wanting to eat meat. The Vegetarian Society found that parents are much more tolerant of this if a child objects to the taste of meat than if she expresses concern about the suffering of animals.[16] Children are allowed to have likes and dislikes, but must not express moral values at variance with their parents.

Other parents are more accepting.

Nathaniel, age 4, watched intently as I cut up a fryer for dinner one night. He asked: 'Where is the wing? What happened to its head?' When I commented that he didn't seem very hungry, his eyes filled with tears, and he responded, 'It was mean to kill it. It got cold without its feathers. I don't like dead chickens.' The following nights there were more questions about the meat I served, and his portions were untouched. There seemed no point in pushing the matter. After a number of weeks he timidly started eating meat again, although a friend of his stopped for good.[17]

Sheila went through a similar experience of uncomfortable questioning when she was 9 and learning biology at school. An increased awareness of the place of human life in the spectrum of all created things, coupled with laboratory lessons in which pupils were required to classify dead insects, to cut up a worm and to examine rabbits and mice preserved in formaldehyde, led to a resolve to become vegetarian. My mother was herself radical – and had many friends in pacifist circles who were also vegetarian. She accepted my decision that I did not want to take life unnecessarily and my right to make it. I remember that she served my favourite dish – roast chicken – that weekend, half hoping I suspect, that I would be tempted so that shopping for food, cooking and meal preparation – jobs she detested – would be less complicated. But the temptation came when my resolve was still strong and I could resist it. I became a vegetarian and have remained one since then. She had communicated the value of life – something that was basic to her personal philosophy and her work for peace. My vegetarianism was another way of expressing her belief.

SELF-DISCIPLINE

When mothers worry about what they see as their children's 'food fads' and say 'you must eat everything on your plate', it often becomes for them a moral imperative. In this they pass on to their children aspects of their own relationships with their parents as expressed through food. Sometimes it is a matter of repeating elements in a relationship which they felt was satisfactory, as it is with the woman who says of her two sons aged 5½ and 3:

> Not eating was one of the problems but they have to eat what is put on the table. The values we are trying to communicate to them are not very different from what my parents taught me. I had a very good family life.

When an adult has suffered deprivation as a child, or looks back on childhood as a time of abnormal stress, food may become a major issue in the relation with children because they seem unfairly privileged. A father who is the child of German-Jewish refugees told his children:

> You can have either butter or jam, not both. Until I was five I never had a whole egg. I used to think I was very lucky when my father allowed me to eat the top of his boiled egg. When I was at school I used to stand at the grocery counter at lunchtime and eat a crust of bread and just *smell* the cheese. You children just don't realise how lucky you are!

Sheila remembers taking her children to lunch at the home of a millionaire who had risen from humble origins. With the two families seated round the vast table laid with crystal and silver she hoped that her children would be on their best behaviour. But one of the host's own children turned up her nose at something because it had 'little black beads' all over it. 'All I had to eat most days when I was a child was potatoes and spinach, and I had to eat everything on my plate,' our host said. 'I always insist on them having a bit of everything,' demanding that the child eat up her caviar immediately.

Many parents tell their children that they should eat what is put before them because other children in the world are starving and they ought to be grateful for what they have. So food is also related to the moral virtue of *gratitude*. Jessica, for example, has two boys of 4½ and 18 months and a full-time job as a nurse. It is difficult for her to make time to cook, and when she does so, she wants meals appreciated. Of her older son she says: 'He is sent to bed for not eating at meal-times. It makes me feel better. I've spent an hour cooking his meal and then he doesn't eat it.' The implication is that the child does not acknowledge how hard his mother works, and that this will teach him to be grateful.

When mothers try to get children to be thankful for what they receive they may also want them to become aware of poverty and famine in the world, and of their own privileged position. These mothers want to teach their children to be socially aware. But in selecting food as the occasion for this teaching they are on difficult ground, not only because food is essential to physical health and because conflicts about it may mean that the child is deprived of essential nutrients, but also because of its complex symbolic elements, and its function as a metaphor of the whole relationship between child and mother.

Deborah spoke about her childhood in the United States during the Depression, when food was scarce. Her family never 'fussed' about food because they were only too glad when it was available. Certainly there was no question of using food for rewards and punishment. Yet once married to a college professor and with her own family, the discipline of what she saw as appropriate eating played an important part in her relationship with her children. On Sundays she planned the week's menus. On Mondays the children discussed it with her and stated what they did and did not like, and she made changes accordingly. On Tuesday she shopped. After all this care and forethought she still found that when she put a dish on the table the two children recoiled in disgust and exclaimed 'yuk!' Eventually her daughter announced that henceforth she would eat nothing but chapatis and rice.

For every adult who states 'I'm glad I was made to eat my spinach. Now I can eat *anything!*' there are many others who describe the negative effect of forced feeding:

> My mother was a dreadful cook. The only thing she could cook was *gefulchte* fish. She made me eat everything in front of me. She'd stand over me and say 'Eat! Eat!' It's strange, but now, however much I am enjoying a meal, I can never finish what is on my plate. The memory of my mother forcing me to eat always prevents me enjoying it to the end.

This man (now divorced) looks back to his unhappy marriage and comments:

> Every meal-time we fought about what to do when the children wouldn't eat what was on their plates. We both insisted they eat it all up, but when they didn't, she would allow them dessert and I told her that was wrong and they shouldn't get any dessert.

Messages about eating and not eating communicate values about the importance of self-control, self-discipline and will-power. A child is expected to overcome personal desires, to use her will against her body, to control her bodily wants and needs and to battle with her own body. In this way food becomes an arena in which physical cravings are pitted against the power of the will, and the child learns to respond to her own hunger, her own desire and her own pleasure, by ignoring, governing, or even destroying it.

Later this is reflected in her body and her sexuality. It is the old Christian doctrine in which the spirit wages war against the flesh and resulting guilt when 'the spirit is willing but the flesh is weak'.

In cultures where it is believed that children are born evil, the moral education of the infant starts with the inculcation of strict food habits. Though many Irish women today would neither recognise this description of rural Irish child-rearing – because they were brought up very differently – nor contemplate rearing their own children in such a way, traditionally in Irish peasant families there is strict discipline concerning food. An anthropologist describes how, from the first years of life, country children in western Ireland are taught to control greed, sloth, gluttony, anger, jealousy and hate – the 'fleshly' passions – since the sacrament of baptism reduces but cannot eradicate them. 'The devoutly religious mother acts as though she was obligated to ignore her baby's response for sucking, stroking and rocking and to view these human *needs* as unnecessary *demands*.'[18] Breastfeeding is both sexually shameful and makes children 'soft' and overdependent on their mothers.

> Training in proper food habits is an important first lesson for the Irish toddler, as eating (like sexuality) is an aspect of physicality which carries connotations of anxiety, guilt and shame ... Even small children soon learn to share in the adults' depreciatory regard of food and eating.[19]

The child who asks for food may be sent away from the table with nothing. When food is there, it must be eaten quickly, with no comment made about it.

DIETS

Adults who are overweight, and who fight a losing battle with the desire for food, sometimes tell how their parents insisted they clear their plates. If they did not they would get no dessert. So sweet things became the favoured food and prize. Others tell of the misery of enforced dieting, constant comments about their weight from adults, and taunts of 'fatso' and 'piggy' from children. Boys as well as girls are subject to this kind of pressure, but for girls it can be unrelenting. We live in a society that judges women by our appearance and in which thin equals beautiful – a society that hates fat people.

Knowing the costs involved for women in being fat, women try to protect their daughters by helping them lose weight, and by encouraging them to stay slim. Daughters often learn to fear and distrust their own developing bodies. Tina Jenkins, now a member of the feminist Fat Women's Group, remembers being put on a diet when she was seven. Her mother promised that when she lost weight she could have a whole new set of clothes for Christmas. As her mother was a dinner lady at Tina's school she was able to enforce the diet strictly and told all the other dinner ladies what Tina was allowed to eat. Tina says now:

> I still have so many resentments against my mother because I thought of all the things that were good about me and all the things I was, as I was, which included me being fat. They didn't count with her because what counted was being thin.[20]

Other women restrict their children's food by putting them on exclusion diets intended to cure hyperactivity, and this too is often experienced by the child as a punitive measure. The active, demanding child who is hard to control is readily classified by modern American and British parents as 'hyperactive'. The treatment is to cut out all foods containing additives and in particular substances such as tartrazine – most processed foods are stuffed with additives, preservatives and colourings – together with foods often linked with allergy; wheat (bread, cakes, biscuits, pasta), milk and milk products (cheese, butter and yoghurt), eggs, chocolate, sugar in all its forms and citrus fruit.[21]

However well-intentioned or health-conscious the slimming diet or the exclusion diet, it may sow the seeds for later guilt and obsession which extends well beyond food into other areas of the child's life. Some women describe feeling that their parents were embarrassed by having a fat child, and preferred not to take their daughters with them when they went shopping or to visit friends. Others say they felt they had to choose between being fat and being loved.[22]

Susan remembers stealing biscuits from the kitchen when she was nine and her mother had put her on a slimming diet.

When Mother discovered what I had done she screamed at me that I was disgusting, greedy and weak-willed. She said I had no self-control, and how did I ever expect to get anywhere in life if I had no will-power and couldn't control myself.

Few mothers can teach this consistently. Tina Jenkins says her mother felt 'a bit guilty and a bit sad that I was allowed one roast potato for Sunday dinner' and used to sneak her extra food from time to time. Alison, whose 'hyperactive' 8-year-old is on an exclusion diet, says: 'I know it's for the best – he's much calmer and we get on better together now – but I still feel as if I'm depriving him and being a lousy mother.'

Thinking back to her mother's explosive outburst when she stole the biscuits, Susan says:

My mother always weighed more than she wanted to and was on and off diets all through her life. She was never able to stick to them. I think she was angry with *herself* for what she thought of as her own lack of self-control and will-power. Her anger came out at me but was really anger against herself.

Susan is determined not to treat her own children like this. She doesn't allow her three daughters to eat biscuits or cakes for health reasons and is a health conscious wholefood vegetarian, but she makes sure that they learn to *enjoy* food. She wants them to take pleasure in preparing and eating food, and to discover that desire, pleasure and physical delight can sometimes be indulged.

Her children enjoy helping to bake bread, kneading the dough into animal shapes with currants for eyes; they sprout beans for salads in a muslin-covered jam jar, go with her to Pick Your Own farms to gather fruit in season, make home-made yoghurt, and roast chestnuts over an open fire.

I was taught to think of food and my desire for food as my enemy. Food would make me fat and ugly. I want my daughters to enjoy food, to take pleasure in it, and to have confidence in their own desires.

GRANDPARENTS

Many conflicts women have with their own mothers find expression in disputes over the rearing of grandchildren, and a large proportion of these are also focused on food. It is as if food, having been the symbol of the daughter's relationship as a child with her mother, then becomes an equally potent symbol in the interaction between three generations.

In societies where a couple go to live with or near the husband's parents, or where they come to live with the young family, similar conflicts tend to take place with the paternal grandmother. A Japanese woman in Tokyo lives next door to her husband's mother. The mother-in-law has looked after her grandson (now 7 years old) since he was a baby. She says:

I breastfed for three months, but during that time I had a lot of stress because she wanted to take care of him (and that entailed switching to artificial feeding). She claims 'the baby is like my son – not at all like you'. She spoils him. She gives him everything he wants. Sweets, toys and TV programmes.

Women especially criticise their mothers and mothers-in-law for wooing their children with sweet things and unsuitable foods. They see them as doing this out of ignorance, because their values about nutrition are different, or – and this is the dominant theme – as trying to buy their love, and so steal the child from the mother. The older woman is perceived as seducing the children like the witch in Hansel and Gretel, who lived in a gingerbread house, lured the children to it, imprisoned them, and then fattened them up to eat.

Typical comments are:

The dispute over sugar in diet causes arguments with grand-parents. They consider sweets as showing love. I do not. I like to control how much sugar they eat. It could lead to blazing rows, but I try to keep a happy atmosphere, especially with my husband's parents.

This woman sensibly asked her own mother if she would substitute fruit as a treat, which she did.

Other women say:

The grandparents speak disapprovingly of the way I bring my children up, and undermine my authority. They fill them with sweets.

I have gone to some length to explain to grandparents, baby-sitters etc, that I do not give my son sweets. But he has learned to eat sweets from them, something I find very annoying. They think I am depriving him.

For a woman now aged 40, who had been a teenage anorexic, food is still a powerful symbol in her relationship with her mother:

My mother looks after the three children while I am at work – and there is always conflict. But I can't afford child care. We're barely on speaking terms, yet she thinks the world of my children. One of the greatest areas of conflict is diet. We come to blows about it.

She sees me as rejecting her treasured beliefs. She is an ordinary omnivorous eater and I am a whole-food vegetarian of ten years duration and have recently become vegan. She thinks that's freakish. She can't see the difference between that and my anorexia nervosa which I had when I was 15. She thinks that I'm polluting my children. They come home and say, 'Nanny gave us sweets and chocolates!' and when I ask her about it she lies and says she didn't. It worries me that the children are exposed to these conflicts.

Another woman describes similar conflicts with her mother:

> My mother totally undermined me on sweets. She came out
> with bags, giant packets of mini-Mars bars. She'd say, 'Let
> him have one a day.' She wants to buy favours with her
> grandson.
>
> When he was 9 it all came to a head as we were getting into
> the car after visiting her, and we found her slipping a couple of
> bars in his back pocket, telling him not to tell Mummy. When
> he was in the car he said 'I didn't know what to do. I had to
> take it from Nana, didn't I?'

Many people who give sweets to their grandchildren as a treat
grew up during the Second World War or immediately after it when
sweets and chocolate were scarce or rationed. Their daughters, on
the other hand, are nutrition conscious, in a manner characteristic
of the 1980s, and have often read magazine articles and books
about nutrition. Some limit their children's diet to bulky, high-
fibre, low-fat foods which may fill them up before they have had
enough calories or protein, and which may inhibit absorption of
minerals such as iron, zinc and calcium. Their children are at risk
of what has been termed 'muesli belt malnutrition'. So it is not
really just a question of sweet treats. Grandmothers may be really
anxious that their grandchildren are not getting enough 'good'
food.

Food can also serve as a link between generations – a symbol of
family unity and cultural continuity in the face of hostility from
without. This is especially true for families who have emigrated
from their home country, or whose country has been colonised.
Many expatriate British people ask visiting compatriots to bring
them tea or Marmite to their country of exile. In sharing 'British'
foods with their children they reaffirm their allegiance to the
country of origin.

For Asian and Afro-Caribbean families in Britain, food can be a
form of defiance in the face of cultural denial or oppression. The
banana fritter, the couscous, the dahl, become implicit symbols of
resistance. The importance of food as an affirmation of cultural
identity and political resistance is sometimes so powerful that

certain foods are outlawed. Palestinian cooking uses a great deal of wild thyme which, with toasted sesame seeds and olive oil, is a popular breakfast dip on the West Bank. Under Israeli rule the picking of wild thyme is punishable by military edict, although the ordinances do not explain why.[23] The food we encourage children to eat reflects our – and their – cultural heritage, and its values are absorbed along with each meal. Class-based values, too, are transmitted in this way. When someone rejects their culture or their class background, part of that rejection involves repudiating the foods of their childhood.

Thus food is a highly charged symbol of relations in families. It is used as a weapon by both children and adults. It is a tangible currency of exchange. It is proffered as a physical token of love.

Eating, refusal to eat, the quantities and kinds of foods consumed, and the sharing of food between children, are often perceived by parents as moral issues. Children use food as a way of asserting power over others.

The baby in a high chair who grabs the spoon from you and shoves the cereal in his ear is saying, '*I'm* going to do it, not you. I'm *me*. I want to find out how to do it.' This determination, this zest and energy, is an essential element in all learning. When we want to discipline children's eating it may have long-lasting consequences for their health and their whole attitude to food, though the outcome may be very different from that which we hoped.

In using food as a metaphor to express other issues in our relationships we may be failing to acknowledge and discuss other important questions. Instead of trying to analyse the child's behaviour, it is often more helpful to look back at the part food played in our relationship with our own parents, and so begin to understand the significance food has for us. We may not be able to change a child's behaviour, but we can at least change our own attitude to that behaviour.

CHAPTER
4

OBEDIENCE AND AUTONOMY

When her 2-year-old son started to become disobedient a mother, who was a sergeant in the Soviet army, took him to work with her one day. He was so impressed by the fact that grown men should salute her, ask her permission, obey her orders and jump to attention at her every command, that she never had any problems of disobedience again.

For most mothers this is not an option. Few of us wield that kind of power outside the home, and children are more likely to see us as power*less* in relation to their fathers and other men. Few of us, anyway, would feel comfortable with military style discipline and rigid obedience in the home.

In the West, attitudes to obedience have changed dramatically over the past fifty years – a cultural transformation encoded in the fictional representation of the Von Trapp family in the popular film *The Sound of Music*. Maria becomes governess to the Von Trapp children, whose father blows whistles and issues orders which the children obey with military precision, standing to attention until the 'at ease' order is given. By the end of the film the family is transformed into an egalitarian, happy group of people who sing and dance together and are united in the face of greater dangers from the world outside. The story is, on one level, a representation and promotion of changing patterns of childrearing. In place of the rigid discipline and obedience of the past, the family is a haven of democracy.

This, of course, stands in complete contrast to norms of behaviour in extended families as in India and Pakistan. The family consists of a man and woman with their unmarried sons and daughters and the married sons and their families. The oldest male has responsibility for everyone in the household, or in a number of houses in which the family members live, and has to make all the important decisions. In such a social system, it is not only marriages that are arranged. Everything else may be too, and decision-making on the part of the children is out of the question, or, indeed for adults if their parents live into old age. Muslim women, in particular, must be obedient and the Koran says 'Men have authority over women because Allah has made the one superior to the other ... good women are obedient ... As for those from whom you fear disobedience, admonish them and send them to beds apart and beat them. Then if they obey you, take no further action against them.'[1] So children must obey their parents unquestioningly, women must obey men, and everyone must obey the senior male of the family.

Because of changing ideas in the West, many Western mothers today feel very ambivalent about obedience. The women who spoke to us want their children to co-operate with reasonable requests, but are worried about the dangers of obedience to the wrong people. Almost everyone says that she wants her child to be obedient, but few choose it as the most important quality for a child to develop. Most mothers are aghast at the idea of demanding total obedience and submission, and are careful to qualify their expectations. They hope for obedience 'within reason', or 'most of the time'. Some add comments like, 'I would not like him to be totally passive', or 'there would be something wrong if he *never* opposed me'. A mother of a 5-year-old says, 'My son does not have to obey blindly except in obviously dangerous situations, although even those have been discussed at a less critical time,' and many women emphasise the importance they place on giving reasons and explanations. 'I always try to explain to Laura why she must do as I say'; 'Although he is only seventeen months, I try to teach him by explaining *why* it is important to do as I tell him.'

Women often add that adults are not automatically entitled to children's respect, but must earn it. The mother of a 2½ year-old girl says:

> Attitudes to obedience and respect for elders have changed. They are still important, but so are the child's feelings. I explain all values to my child, rather than 'what I say goes'. Respect is important, but that includes respect for the child. My child is an 'important individual' in her own right.

Pauline makes her point very strongly:

> Respect for elders just because of their age? Wisdom can be encased in youth and folly in an ancient body. Also it is older men and women who are abducting these poor children. If you teach your daughter to say yes to a man just because he's older than her, you are inviting a catastrophe. I respect knowledge and wisdom, not age.

Chris says that her own mother 'made me feel like I ought to be in awe of older people, and I ended up with hardly any confidence through this'. She tries to teach her children that 'if they have an opinion, even if it disagrees with an adult, they have a right to put it forward'.

Almost all the women who talked to us felt that their approach to obedience was more relaxed than that of their own mothers. One woman who makes a special effort to give reasons to her children says that her own mother 'rarely explained a reason behind an instruction, and often hit first, yelled second, and reduced me to tears in a matter of seconds'. Other mothers were described as 'rigid and protective to the extreme', 'bullying', 'nagging' and 'expecting total obedience – you will do as I say, when I say, with no reasons given'. Lilian's parents were in their forties when she was born and were very strict: 'I think obedience encourages a "towing the party line" attitude', she says, and she wants her 7-year-old son to 'think for himself'. Charlene, whose parents were both in the army, was brought up to obey without question and she hopes that her 3-year-old will 'develop his own ideas rather than having to accept all of ours, as my parents made us'. Donna, with two boys aged four and five, says she is 'not such a strict disciplinarian as my mum was':

> However, nine times out of ten the children know exactly how they are expected to behave in a given situation and will be pillars of virtue. Then let them rip once home!! It is to be noted, however, that my mum could take my sisters and I anywhere and we were never anything but perfectly behaved at all times, i.e. *ten* times out of ten!!

Compared with their parents, women are also less likely to use physical punishment against disobedient children – or at least, they feel guilty if they do. 'My father hit us hard as children to teach us things,' says Paula, who believes that 'a gentle smack is occasionally necessary, but not as a method of teaching things. Words are better.' Sharon's mother would 'nag until something was done, but if it wasn't she would work herself up into a rage and punish when really cross by hitting my face'. Sharon only punishes after warning her children and then just slaps them on the bottom, 'and never if I am really angry'. Jenny's parents used to pull her hair and scratch by way of punishment and she wants never to use physical violence against her own child: 'He's 6 months old, he keeps biting when I feed him, and I slapped him. I felt terrible about it. How could I hit a little baby like that?'

Very few women say that their mother's approach to discipline was more relaxed than their own, though one said 'Mum told us to do things but would always give way if we made a fuss. I insist on being obeyed.' But some of these mothers believe that obedience leads to all the other virtues. The obedient child will also be kind, polite, honest, tidy and respectful. 'I feel obedience is the most important thing and all the other qualities stem from it,' says the mother of an 18-month-old: 'teaching NO is the main way he learns this'. Another, whose daughter is 6 years old, says that 'if a child is obedient they will grow up to be a stable adult. I teach this by making her listen to us as parents. If she does not, I take a treat, or something she likes to do, away from her.'

Grandmothers sometimes told us, with distress, that they had brought their own children up in a fairly democratic and relaxed manner, only to find that those children, now parents themselves, expect rigid discipline from their children: 'I asked Andrea, "why are you being so tyrannical with him? I was never like that with you," and she said, "at least he'll know I care".' It seems as though disciplining her own child has become a weapon for Andrea to use against her – a way of accusing her mother of not loving her enough.

For some adults children provide an opportunity to be in a position of authority that is denied them in their jobs or in the community. One man said:

I work all day and the man's always telling me what to do. Everyone's always telling me what to do, but when I go home, I'm the one telling what to do. And those kids better mind or they know what for.

A woman who is deprived of power outside the home may enjoy the power she can exert over her children. As one woman said, 'I'm in control there. I run the show – more or less. My husband's not around and so it's pretty much my show.'[2] For some parents the whole relationship with their children is seen in terms of a power struggle, with children using their power to refuse, to be contrary, and to provoke adult rage. These parents see obedience as very important because it establishes and reinforces their own power.

But Kate's experience is more typical, and reflects the ambiguity many women feel about obedience.

I don't believe my daughter should be obedient all the time, and I allow her to have her own way and make her own decisions. That's not how my mother treated me. I think I'm doing the right thing, but sometimes I feel cheated – trapped between a mother and a daughter both of whom expect to get their own way and sometimes seem to want me to indulge their every whim. I think I've missed out somehow.

Another woman says: 'It's ridiculous, but I have to admit that I'm sometimes jealous of my own children because I've given them the kind of upbringing I would have liked myself, and didn't have.'

In traditional societies, a mother repeats with her own children the patterns her mother used with her. In rapidly changing industrial societies we don't expect to rear our children in the same way that our parents did, any more than we expect to drive the same sort of car or wear the same sort of clothes. We believe in 'progress'. Even if we *do* bring up our own children similarly, we know that we are doing this, and that we could do otherwise, whereas in traditional cultures it is taken for granted and neither noticed nor commented upon.

BREAKING THE WILL

Historically, obedience has been one of the virtues most emphasised in childrearing in Britain and the United States. The spirit has to be broken, the child forced to subdue its own desires and submit promptly and unquestioningly to the authority of parents. The medieval poem, 'How the Good Wife Taught her Daughter' (in *The Babees Book*) counsels mothers:

> And if thy children be rebel and will not bow them low,
> If any of them misdo, neither curse them nor scold,
> But take a smart rod and beat them in a row,
> Till they cry mercy and their guilt well know.

The fifth commandment ('Honour thy Father and thy Mother') was much stressed. In a seventeenth-century book, *A Family Well Ordered*, Cotton Mather (1699) declares that

> The Heavy Curse of God will fall upon those Children that make Light of their Parents ... the Curse of God! The Terriblest Thing that ever was heard of. Children, if you break the fifth Commandment, there is not much likelihood that you will keep the rest. Undutiful Children soon become horrid

Creatures for Unchastity, for Dishonesty, for Lying, and all manner of evils.

An early American statute in force in New Plymouth stated that if any child above 16 years old 'shall Curse or Smite their Natural Father or Mother he or they shall be put to Death'. The historians who discuss this piece of legislation suggest that 'this should not strike us as extremely tyrannical since the Puritans believe that "by the laws of God an incorrigibly disobedient child deserved death".'[3] According to the Calvinist doctrine of 'infant depravity', the child was believed to be born sinful, a creature of insatiable and fierce impulses which, if not vigilantly curbed, could easily grow beyond control and lead to ruin. Only through enforcing absolute obedience to adult commands could the child's salvation be secured. The aim was to 'break the child's will' and the techniques to be used were widely discussed. Mothers must be ceaselessly vigilant, and wage a battle against the child's appetites. Overeating in infants, for instance, was seen as a constant danger, and masturbation and thumb-sucking were both evil impulses. As late as 1938 in the USA a cuff was marketed designed to hold the child's arm stiff at the elbow and so prevent thumb-sucking.

Nineteenth-century American childcare books typically counselled mothers to leave their children to cry. Too much prompt attention would lead to the baby making constant demands and becoming a tyrant in the family: 'The very infant in your arms will sometimes redden and strike, and throw back its head and stiffen its little rebellious will.'[4] Parents sometimes deliberately withheld reasons for their requests on the grounds that the child should be taught to obey without question. When Augustus Hare was three, his mother noted in her journal that he kept asking 'why?', but she made a point of never giving any reason save that it was her will that he should do so.[5] Submission was considered necessary so that the child would accept moral virtues and religious truths before the age of reason.

Mothers often found it difficult to ignore their crying babies, and painfully hard to beat a naughty 2-year-old. They did it not because they were (for the most part) cruel and heartless people, but because they believed it was the only route to their children's salvation: 'To keep children in the proper state of obedience without having them stand in too much awe is sometimes difficult,' wrote one mother to another, in 1815; 'I have always wished that they should be afraid of doing wrong, but not afraid of me.'[6]

Fear of doing wrong was inculcated through nineteenth-century stories for children, both in Britain and in the US, which told of the horrifying consequences of disobedience. In one story Jane is told not to touch the fire while her mother is out, but tries to cook the dinner and badly scalds her little brothers and sisters.[7] In another, Softdown, a mouse, is caught in a trap and killed because he disobeys his mother. 'My very blood runs cold within me,' says Softdown's brother, Nimble, 'at the recollection of seeing Softdown's blood as it spirted from beneath the monster's foot; whilst the craunch of his bones almost petrified me with horror.'[8] In the 1820s version of Little Red Riding Hood, the wolf entirely devours her, and the moral at the end of the story reads: 'It is plainly seen, in this little story, how wrong it is of children not to do as their parents bid them, and what misery and suffering they bring upon themselves, even by trifling errors.'[9] The standard approach to obedience is reflected in a children's rhyme:

> Do as you are told to do
> By those wiser far than you.
> Do not say
> What the use of this may be
> I am sure I cannot see
> Just obey![10]

Sheila's grandmother used to tell her a story about a little girl who disobeyed her mother by going out in the rain without her galoshes. She caught pneumonia and died as a result of this disobedience. I was fascinated by this story, but not quite sure what galoshes were, though I loved the sound of the word. It didn't teach me anything about obedience but it did teach me about my grandmother's fear and about her anxious belief in a God of vengeance lying in wait to destroy us if we took one step wrong.

Despite all these stories and rhymes, and despite punishments for disobedience that included whippings, being locked in dark cellars and being deprived of food for days at a time, children, then as now, disobeyed their parents' commands. One nineteenth-century father, in a letter to his wife when he and his son, Frank, are away from home staying with friends, complains that 'Even if I speak to him in the gentlest way to ask him not to do something troublesome (as throwing about his big ball with a great noise in the dining room) he at once does it all the more ...' The letter ends, 'Frank has just smashed a window in the drawing room by his violence, not intentionally. It is very tiresome. You have no idea how dispirited I feel about it.'[11]

Novelist Alison Uttley remembers how she felt as a child, and her desperate need to save face. When she was 2, her grandmother ordered her to pick up a slipper which she'd thrown on the floor:

It was most important to her that I should be taught obedience at the earliest age and she pitted her will against mine. Over and over she said to me in a low but stern voice, 'Bring that slipper to me, baby' and I stood very still waiting too. At last I stooped down, and covered the offending slipper with my pinafore, and picked it up with the muslin around it. Then, keeping my fingers from touching the leather, I carried it across to her. Without a sound I deposited it on her lap. Happily she was satisfied, and I, too, was relieved that I had had my own way and not picked up the slipper ... There was an implacable overwhelming feeling about a grownup person's will constraining one's movements, compelling one to actions which were repulsive.[12]

Like Alison Uttley, children try to avoid humiliation by pitting their will against that of adults, or by stratagems which allow them to believe that they didn't 'really' obey the order. Some children convince themselves that they *want* to do whatever it is they are being *ordered* to do, so that it becomes a choice they make, rather than obedience to a command. One little girl, punished by being made to stand in a corner, replied, when told she could rejoin the family, 'thank you, but I prefer to stay here'. Another would unfailingly make her bed and tidy her room as long as her mother never referred to the fact: reminders in advance or 'thank yous' after the event were met with strong resistance and the words, 'I do it because I *want* to, not because you make me. If I didn't want to, I wouldn't do it.' 'Enjoying' or 'choosing' to do what one would otherwise be forced to do removes the sting of humiliation. The child performs the act, but refuses to submit her will to that of another.

Contemporary childcare books contain plenty of advice about how to avoid humiliating children, how to help them feel like human beings worthy of respect. Mothers are counselled to offer children choices ('would you rather wear the green hat or the red one?') instead of dishing out orders ('put your hat on'), and to offer alternatives to prohibited actions ('no, you can't pick the garden flowers, but there are some daisies on the lawn you can pick'). Other books recommend allowing the *child* to remove the forbidden object from sight and temptation, instead of confiscating it. One magazine article points out:

> A steady stream of 'no, you're too little', 'don't touch that, it's dirty', 'sit still' etc, etc, is bound to produce a difficult, rebellious child who is no fun to be with. You won't be much fun to listen to either, so ask yourself before you speak, 'Do I really have to prohibit that?'[13]

Letty Pogrebin[14] says that an act of correction occurs between mothers and their 2-year-olds on the average of once every three minutes. She points out that an easy way to make your child more obedient is to make fewer demands for obedience. Others suggest that the child's 'no' reflects the need to be psychologically separate and autonomous, a need which can be allowed expression in other ways. Respecting a child means acknowledging her feelings about what is demanded of her: 'I bet you wish you'd never have to get in this hot, sticky car again'. These are all techniques designed to leave children's dignity intact.

But historically the aim was precisely the opposite. 'Breaking the will' required that the child submit, become conscious of her own inferiority and powerlessness. As Sara Coleridge, daughter of the poet Samuel Taylor Coleridge, wrote in 1835 about bringing up her own children:

> My aim is something far beyond extorting obedience in particular instances. Unless the wayward *will* is corrected, what care I for the *act* ... I really think that 'you shall be beaten unless you do it, or you shall be mortified and annoyed till you look and speak humbly' is a sort of external force which does not touch the heart.[15]

Yet in order to 'touch the heart', physical 'correction' was often considered necessary. A mother writing in *Mothers Magazine* at about the same time (in 1834) describes how she finally exacted obedience from her 16-month-old daughter, who had refused to say 'dear mama' upon the father's order, only by locking her in a room alone and then whipping her intermittently for four hours until she finally obeyed.[16] This may seem an extreme example, but even today worse 'punishments' are perpetrated upon disobedient children by their exasperated or frustrated parents. A father who split open his 9-month-old son's skull said, 'He thinks he's the boss – all the time trying to run things – but I showed him who is in charge around here.'[17] Nigel Hall, who tortured and killed his 4-year-old stepdaughter, Kim, said 'I was determined that she would do what she was asked to do. I was determined she would eat her food and if I told her it was time to go to bed she would – and things like that.'[18]

In the US, homicide has become one of the top five causes of death in children, with parents and step-parents responsible for a third of the killings.[19] Greg Dixon, the Indiana Moral Majority leader, has engineered a weakening of his state's child abuse laws because 'the Bible instructs people to whip their children with a rod'. Reverend Dixon believes that 'welts and bruises are a sign that a parent is doing a good job of discipline'.[20]

With the rise of the New Right and the so-called Moral Majority, views like this are on the increase. In their 1988 Annual Report, the British National Association of Head Teachers blames parents for not disciplining children enough. Some of their members called for a return to corporal punishment in schools.[21] The Social Affairs Unit produced a book claiming (falsely) that 'leading contemporary theorists in psychology adhere to the traditional original sin view',[22] suggesting that unless children are taught 'moral restraint' they will develop into 'habitual criminals and psychopaths' (p.40), and calling for 'the end of indulgence' (p.9). This kind of complaint about children's disobedience and calls to curb and restrain them are not new. In the seventeenth century, Lord Clarendon complained that parental authority had been seriously undermined by the upheavals of the civil war so that 'parents have no manner of authority over their children, nor children any obedience or submission to their parents'.[23] At times of social or political upheaval, children may be handy scapegoats for adults who feel bewildered by change and want to establish control over at least part of their world.

For some women who talked to us, obedience is important because they believe that children need to know 'what the limits are' if they are to feel safe. A mother of two children aged 5 and 8 describes herself as 'terribly strict' because 'it's very important to give children parameters. If you have a child who doesn't know where the parameters are, they are beastly for ever.' She was educated at an A. S. Neill type school and says she 'saw so many people there who were utterly uncontrolled and uncontrollable. Children need to know how far they can go. That way they get security. My children know that after I've said no, there is absolutely no point in going on.'

In a chaotic world of international warfare, technological development, ecological disaster and constant change, mothers feel that rules and discipline are the only way to give security. The imagery is of 'boundaries', 'parameters', 'frameworks' and 'limits'.

It suggests the creation of a closed and protected world for children – the German 'children's paradise' – and is the psychological equivalent of the swaddling bonds in which infants used to be bound, unable to move arms or legs, also in the interests of 'security', and were thus made safe from outside dangers or from the damage they could do themselves from their own inner rage.

SELF-CONFIDENCE

Many women whose mothers tried to protect them at all costs describe the experience in very negative terms. Instead of feeling 'secure' they felt 'sheltered', kept in the dark', even 'suffocated' by mothers who exhibited 'a tremendous overprotective anxiety'. 'My mother did everything for me,' says one woman, adding, 'she was very suffocating.' 'My parents didn't tell us what the world was like,' says another woman. 'It was as if we were in a cocoon. Then when I was seventeen something terrible happened and I discovered that life was different. We were overprotected.' Barbara's mother 'gave me no self-confidence in myself by allowing me to do nothing for myself or to use my brain and make decisions, or speak out for myself. She over-ruled me completely – the dominant mother!' Another woman, who chose 'independence' as the one quality she most wanted to encourage in her children says her own mother 'never allowed independence as she always did things for me and sheltered me from experiences which she felt unsuitable, but which would have given me self-confidence'. Isabel felt 'very protected and safe as a child' but 'as I got older I just couldn't speak up for myself and was far too dependent on others'. The mother of a 7-year-old who wants to encourage her son to 'think things out and make his own decisions' says that her own mother 'kept me in the dark and I was very vulnerable and dependent upon her'. Helen was the only child of elderly parents

very good and loving parents whose only real fault was to overprotect me and make me timid. I have largely learned to overcome this, but it is contrary to my nature, an act, rather than natural, and I have always envied people who have an easy self-confidence. If you believe in yourself I think it helps you to love other people and to find your way in life. It helps you in every situation.

One woman describes feeling 'a fake sense of security' as a child, and says, 'I found it very painful to discover that adults are not infallible.' Sharon's mother who 'had done everything to protect me from the big bad world' died when she was 12: 'I am teaching my son to be a responsible person in his own right, and not to depend on me for everything – although he knows I will always stand by him if things get tough.'

More than one in three of the women who replied to our question-naire chose self-confidence or independence as the most important quality they wanted their children to develop. Often this is because it is something they long for themselves. 'I want her to have self-confidence, because I lack it and know how crippling this can be,' says one woman. 'My own lack of self-confidence has led to periods of depression,' says another, and a third, who was brought up in a children's home, says sadly, 'I have no self-confidence, so have very few friends and never go out. I do not want this lonely life for my child.' Anne feels that she has 'often allowed chances to go by in my life due to lack of self-confidence' and Carol says:

I grew up with no self-confidence at all and I ended up an outcast at school, a shy girl who dare not speak to anybody or do anything, and who other people had an opportunity to belittle and make fun at. I am trying to make my little boy mix and speak to others without being shy.

Another mother, who says she 'gets frightened easily and feels the world is full of danger', wants her child to 'be able to cope better than I do and so have more energy left to actually enjoy himself'. Nora, too, is trying to encourage her 2-year-old to develop confi-dence by allowing him to take decisions and make choices about his life, but my mother says I should *not* give him a choice – a mind of his own at his age, whereas I would like him to have his own ideas even down to what he wears and how much he wants to eat.

She wonders, betraying her own 'lack of self-confidence', 'I really don't know if I am right or wrong about this.'

Other women stressed how important self-confidence and independence are for girls, especially when they felt that their own upbringing encouraged them to develop the 'feminine' virtues of dependency and lack of confidence in their own abilities. 'I want her to have independence and courage,' says Vera of her 7-year-old, stressing that 'this is so important for a woman in this "man's world".' Many other women echo this view.

I was brought up with very stereotyped female expectations and limitations, and self-confidence, independence and courage were not encouraged in me or my sisters. I hope very much that in bringing up my daughter I can encourage her to develop these qualities.

I hope to encourage my daughter's self-confidence by encouraging her to do her best and letting her know that, whatever she's done, her best is always good enough. I think my mother's attitude was the old-fashioned view of women being very much inferior to men, and she tended not to lend too much encouragement to develop self-confidence and she didn't see its importance to her daughters.

Barbara's 6-year-old son has a severe port-wine birth mark and she, too, emphasises the importance of self-confidence because,

I don't want him growing up believing that this will stop him from doing what he wants in the future. If you believe in yourself your goals seem much more attainable and friendships are easier. If he believes he can be whatever he wants to be, then that's half the battle won!

In encouraging children's self-confidence and independence, these mothers encourage them to think for themselves, make their own choices, and discuss actions rather than insisting on unquestioning obedience.

DANGERS

Some women stress the practical, rather than the moral importance of obedience. This is especially true of women with large families. A mother of seven children says she doesn't have time to give detailed explanations or engage in negotiations with them: 'They've had to learn that if I said "do it" then that's it: no questions, no argument. If not, it's a smack on the fanny.' Harriette points out that obedience can be a life-saver: 'Fatal accidents result from disobedience, something which I personally do not want to happen to my son.'

No one wants a child to run into the road in front of a car, stick a screwdriver into the electric light socket, or put baby brother in the washing machine. But the best way to ensure that a child does obey in these sorts of situations may be to put less emphasis, not more, on routine obedience. Think of all the times you have walked past buildings in which a burglar alarm is ringing and have done nothing – because you know that these bells go off all the time and can usually be ignored: they are false alarms. Children who are expected to obey *all* orders promptly and unquestioningly may become unable to distinguish between the less important orders (things you want them to do for your own convenience), and the really serious and life-saving instructions. Sharon, whose daughter is 2½, says

> There are very few times when I order her to do things. Usually we discuss things, and I allow her to make her own decisions. When I *do* issue an order (usually to do with physical safety), she is so surprised that she takes it very seriously and obeys instantly. I think this is because I don't bully her about every little thing, and only demand obedience when it's really important.

Many women point out that *obedience* can be dangerous too. Some talked about toddlers who obeyed older children who led them into dangerous situations, and children who so wanted to conform that they went along with the crowd – a particular worry in the teenage years, with the threat of drugs, glue-sniffing and sexual promiscuity. Many women are desperately worried about child sexual abuse. It is common for abusers to moralise at their victims, telling them to 'be a good girl,' 'always do as Daddy says,' and 'obey when I tell you to do something'. Children who have been taught to obey adults at all times, and never to say 'no' to them, are especially vulnerable to abuse. Meg, whose own mother 'thought that adults should be obeyed directly' is bringing her daughter up very differently: 'I want her to be able to protect herself against any adult infringement of her person, so she must not learn blanket obedience. We have very few rules – concerned with safety mainly – otherwise things are negotiated.' Rosie was brought up 'never to interrupt adults speaking, never to ask for a drink in a relative's house but to wait until offered, to do as I was told at once, never to argue ("be cheeky") with an adult'. She wants her own daughter

> to learn how to think for herself. If I expect strict obedience from her, how can I separate this from other adults and teach her to say 'no' to sexual abuse, lifts in strangers' cars etc? Other adults seem less trustworthy these days.

Stephanie too was 'brought up to obey without question my parents, other family members, neighbours, teachers etc.'. She is determined to 'treat my son with more respect and allow him to feel that he is equal to his parents, although still in need of guidance. It's important for children to know they can say "no" to adults – less risk of sexual abuse.' A woman who was sexually abused as a child says, 'At 28 I'm now trying to fight against being the well-behaved little girl'.[24] Thinking back to her childhood, Becky describes herself as 'everybody's idea of the ideal child. I was completely obedient, and always did what I was told. I was a very *good* child.' She was sexually abused by her father from the age of 5 until she finally ran away from home when she was 15 and pregnant with his child. Now she is 23 and her 7-year-old daughter is 'completely different from me – determined to do things her own way, very bolshie. And I'm glad. I don't want her to be a victim the way I was.'

Many mothers are particularly keen for their children to be self-confident in the presence of other adults, and contrast this with their mothers' attitude. A woman says she is teaching her 2-year-old 'to be able to express herself well to adults even at an early age. Mother's approach was that children should be seen and not heard in the company of other grownups.' Alison was brought up like this, and says

I am trying to raise my child to feel confident to speak up and to speak his mind in a reasonable and polite way. I have often been unable to say what I really mean or think for fear of upsetting someone else.

She adds that,

When Martin is very direct and straightforward, although my instinct is to quieten him I make sure that I don't and allow him to be open and honest. In my own experience, 'damping down' kills a child's self-confidence and makes it difficult for them to express true thoughts and feelings except in an angry way.

LEARNING TO QUESTION AUTHORITY

Developmental psychologists say that an important part of growing up is learning that rules and laws are made by other human beings and can be changed. According to the famous Swiss child psychologist, Jean Piaget,[25] children under 7 typically see rules as deriving from the semi-mystical authority of older children, adults and even God. They see them as sacred and unalterable. From about the age of 10, children are more clear that rules are invented by people and could be changed. Learning that rules can be altered, and that obedience to laws or rules is not always good, when the laws are wrong, is an important part of moral development.

Children are most likely to develop an understanding that people invent rules and laws, and that people can change them, if they are able to contribute to rule-making and decision-taking. In order to encourage children to make their own decisions, some mothers encourage occasional role reversal. The mother of a 3-year-old girl says she will sometimes 'let her tell me what I must do and she pretends to be Mum'. Another mother of a 9-year-old son calls this 'boss time': 'The rules are that during this period he initiates conversation and suggests activities and I follow, paying him as nearly 100 per cent attention as I can.' She sees this as a way for him to 'imagine what he wants to do at a particular time in the future, to become inventive and to develop personality; and to feel more autonomous'.[26]

Involving children in family decision-making is recommended by mothers of children as young as 3:

When I was young parents decided almost everything and made it quite clear that they resented any attempts by children to make anything more than trivial decisions within the family. We try to teach self-confidence by encouraging decision making and going along with the child's decision, rather than always deciding for her, or contradicting her. If self-confidence can be maintained through mistakes and failure as well as success then I am confident that my child can face the world and cope with it.

The parents of a 13-year-old allowed him to choose the new family home conveniently near his school: 'As two working adults we depend on his ability to get around on his own', says his mother.[27]

Many women try to foster self-confidence by expecting their children to try to do things for themselves, praising them when they do well, but not scolding them when they make mistakes. Sensitive handling of failure is stressed, and here again they complain about their own mother's attitude: 'My mother only seemed to comment if we did something wrong or looked awful'; 'My mother always seemed to run me down'; 'My mother used to criticise me and put me down and discourage me in anything I wanted to do'; 'My mother used to always call me an idiot because I never did as well as my sister'. So with their own children, women want to behave differently: 'I try to be aware of her feelings and not laugh at her when she makes mistakes,' says one woman, whose parents 'were never aware of how it affected me when they laughed, and I picked up on their laughter when they tried to hide it.' The mother of a three year old says that her approach involves 'lots of praise, encouragement and acceptance of what my little girl is and has every right to be. My mother criticised me directly and indirectly all the time (still does even now!) and was, I think, embarrassed by me'.

They encourage their children to keep on trying. 'When I fell off my bicycle it was taken away for good,' says one woman, 'whereas my little boy is encouraged to get back on and try again. We encourage him to do things himself and praise him when he manages to do them.' The mother of a 5-year-old describes how she hopes to create an atmosphere 'where he is expected to try to do things and/or cope by himself, but help is always available before frustration point is reached'. She tries to 'gently push him to cope in new situations without letting him be overwhelmed or frightened'. Alice gives her 3-year-old 'lots of praise for achievements and I teach him to do tasks in very small steps so that success is more frequent than failure'.

I aim to teach Jennifer that if she helps by doing something around the home, for example, even if it isn't done well at first, she will receive praise and gratitude for attempting to do it, and hopefully she will gain confidence in herself. My mother used to say, 'Oh you can't do that properly, it's a waste of time, I will do it myself'. Or sometimes if I did do something for her she would inspect it and if it wasn't up to her standard I would have to do it over and over again from scratch until I got it right. I feel that this made me very unsure about tackling situations that others perhaps wouldn't think twice about.

I have very little self-confidence, resulting from constant criticism of all my activities as a child. My mother always knew how to do things best and would always show me the 'right' way. I let my daughter try her hand at anything, and I don't interfere. If the results are disastrous we discuss them. Our daughter is praised realistically for achievement and not made to feel 'small' if she doesn't manage things. I try to explain that we're all different. A lot of people will be better than her at some things, and a lot won't.

For another mother the word 'self-worth' best sums up what she wants for her 4-year-old:

It doesn't matter whether he's clever or good at sport or whatever, as long as he feels he's 'worth' something. I've tried to teach him this by praising things he does, *never* telling him he's 'stupid', and helping and encouraging him with things he finds hard. I also never compare him detrimentally with his peers.

Independence, a quality closely associated with self-confidence, is encouraged by many mothers as vitally important, and this often centres around the learning of practical skills. 'I encourage independence by teaching them to tidy up, help clean up, ironing and washing,' says the mother of two boys under 5. 'My mother always said it was easier to do it herself, but if my children ask to have a go I let them, and they feel so proud of their little selves.' Margaret wants her 4-year-old to be able to become as independent as possible: 'She uses her own ticket in the library. She has a purse and occasionally buys items for herself while I stand back with the pram. She "helps" me cross the road by showing me what to do. She dresses herself and chooses what she will wear every day.' Erica says her daughter at 20 months is 'already very helpful – she can load the washing machine more or less unaided'.

The ideal today, reflected both in the words of the mothers who spoke to us, and in childcare books, is not unquestioning obedience. Instead children are encouraged to discuss and negotiate moral questions, to think for themselves, to develop a sense that their own opinion matters, and to become independent and self-confident. The shift from the earlier emphasis on total obedience to the more recent stress on questioning and autonomy came about in part as a result of the Second World War. Nazi Germany offered many examples of people who respected authority and obeyed orders without question. They were SS men who rounded up Jewish families and sent them to concentration camps, and guards who shot children in their mothers' arms and packed living human beings into gas chambers and crematoria. These were otherwise civilised people who listened to Beethoven and read bedtime stories to their children, but who were prepared, under orders, to torture, persecute and murder Jews, gypsies, homosexuals and mentally handicapped people. When brought to trial for crimes against humanity, they said they were only obeying orders from their superiors. In the face of evil, it is people who refuse to obey who are the moral heroes.

As information about the Nazi atrocities became widely known, psychologists and educationalists in Britain and the USA began to change their minds about the desirability of obedience. Instead, they started to look at ways of encouraging independence of judgement and moral integrity. The best known research from this period is Milgram's[28] work on obedience. He wanted to know whether ordinary Americans would give electric shocks to strangers if he ordered them to do so, and how severe a shock they would be willing to inflict. He recruited people through advertisements in a local newspaper for what was described as an experiment in learning. Each time the 'learner' made a mistake, the subject was to pull a lever to give him an electric shock, increasing the voltage each time. (In fact, the lever was a dummy, and the 'learner' a confederate of the experimenters who acted his response.) After a few shocks, the 'learner' started shouting and asked to stop the experiment. Later he screamed with pain and pleaded to be released from the chair into which he was strapped. Later still, there was only a deathly silence. If the subject said he wanted to stop giving shocks, the experimenter said only 'the experimenter requires that you continue' – no threats or incentives to go on, just the order. Under these conditions, over half of the forty subjects delivered the full range of shocks, proceeding through and past the set of levers marked 'Danger: Severe Shock' to the last three marked 'XXX'.

These people were not sadists or psychopaths. They were ordinary people who believe that you shouldn't hurt others, and who disliked what they were ordered to do. They almost all complained to the experimenter and asked for permission to stop giving shocks. But when ordered to continue they did so, because they believed that authority should be obeyed.

> With numbing regularity good people were seen to knuckle under to the demands of authority and perform actions that were callous and severe. Men who in everyday life are responsible and decent were seduced by the trappings of authority . . . into performing harsh acts . . . A substantial proportion of people do what they are told to do, irrespective of the content of the act and without limitations of conscience, so long as they perceive that the commands come from legitimate authority.[29]

The mid-nineteenth century question 'How can we make children more obedient?' has changed into the mid-twentieth century question, 'How can we enable children to resist those who order them to do wrong?'

Children are more likely to refuse to obey immoral orders if they have confidence in their own abilities to think about questions of right and wrong, and if they come from families in which moral issues are openly discussed and negotiated. In homes where obedience is demanded, children are more likely to break rules when they think they can get away with it, and show both explosive outbursts and frantic efforts at control. They see the world as a dangerous or hostile place and are aggressive and dictatorial to those they consider their social inferiors. By contrast, children from more democratic homes are more thoughtful, tolerant and socially integrated, feel compassion for the underdog and want to protect the weak rather than tyrannise them. They are also more questioning, and able to resist orders from authority with reasoned arguments.[30]

Moral psychologists like Kohlberg emphasise that the only way to enable a child to develop an autonomous conscience is to encourage her to practise making moral decisions every day and to discuss them with her. Even very young children can understand the reasons behind many instructions if given the opportunity. One study showed that children less than 2½ years old were giving reasons for their own behaviour. They said things like, 'I'm hurting your feelings 'cause I was mean to you', 'I give a hug. Baby be happy', and 'Katie not happy face. Katie sad'. These children were almost all using the words 'good' and 'bad' and many used 'supposed to'. So children under three already have the language and the understanding of causality and other people's feelings necessary to understand the reasons behind many adult requests.[31]

When we discuss and negotiate, instead of issuing orders, we encourage children to think about the effects of their actions, help them to develop the language and concepts required for a more sophisticated understanding of moral issues, and enable them to learn more about the processes of negotiation, bargaining and compromise in personal relationships. We are also treating children with respect – as people who matter in their own right. 'I want him to know that he is just as important as an adult,' says one woman. 'What she thinks counts too,' says another. Respect for a child's autonomy can begin at birth, by feeding the baby on demand, trying to be aware of and to respond to a child's needs, avoiding interrupting a child who is concentrating on a task – even though it may seem trivial – and giving plenty of opportunity to touch and explore everything in an environment made safe for a child of this age and to discover her own body. 'If I treat my son with respect,' says Joanna, whose child is 14 months, 'I show him how I would like him to treat me, and I also encourage him to develop *self*-respect, which is the most important thing of all.'

OTHER CULTURES, OTHER WAYS

This emphasis on reasoning with children, and offering explanations instead of expecting instant obedience, is not only a relatively recent phenomenon; it is also specifically Western. In some other societies, instant obedience is demanded of all children from babyhood on. Among the Ainu of Japan:

> Implicit and prompt obedience is required from infancy; and from a very early age the children are utilised by being made to fetch and carry and go on messages. I have seen children apparently no more than 2 years old sent for wood; and even at this age they are so thoroughly trained in the observances of etiquette that babies just able to walk never toddle into or out of the house without formal salutations to each person within it, the mother alone excepted.[32]

Obedience is especially valued in agricultural economies, because it is important for the survival of the family unit. In countries where people live at subsistence level, obedience is particularly stressed. In Indonesia, the Philippines and Thailand, about three in every four mothers choose obedience as the most desired quality in their children, compared with only about one in every five mothers in the United States. And where independence and self-reliance are rarely selected by mothers in these cultures as important qualities for children, one in four of US mothers see them as important.[33] Mothers in many of these traditional cultures will not tolerate aggression against themselves and punish the child severely for such behaviour. The Nyansongo mother of a 5-year-old said:

> I only cane him if I find him becoming angry and hitting me. If he is near I would get hold of him and cane him, but if he runs away I would refuse him food for a couple of days more and he will learn himself what he had done wrong.[34]

In many traditional societies obedience is taken for granted and the child is taught to obey people credited with spiritual responsibility. In many African cultures, the tribal elders are believed to be in touch with the ancestors of the people and obedience is due to them not because of their individual superiority but because they are the carriers of tradition, speaking on behalf of the ancestors. (In fact, this is not so very different from Western childcare books which insist that 'our children should understand that their duty is *not* to obey our *personal wishes* because we happen to be their parents, but to obey eternal laws which we represent and expound and enforce'.)[35]

But there are also traditional cultures in which implicit obedience and subservience of children is neither demanded nor desired. Many American Indian tribes reject the ideal of the submissive child. The aim in childrearing is to arouse in the child the desire to share responsibility in adult life. The Crow Indians boast about their young sons' intractability, even when it is their own orders that are flouted. 'He will be a man!' they say, and are baffled at the idea that a child should show behaviour which would make him a poor creature in the eyes of his fellows if he used it as an adult. When the son of a Mohave Indian struck him, and the white mother said that the child should be punished, the father asked, 'But why? He is little. He cannot possibly injure me,' apparently unaware of the notion that a child should be obedient and respectful. If his child had been docile, he would simply have judged that he would become a docile and passive adult – which he would not have wanted.[36]

Contemporary Western cultures typically expect very different behaviour from an individual as a child and as an adult. In childhood the person is supposed to be reasonably obedient and to comply with the wishes of parents at least most of the time. As Letty Pogrebin[37] says,

> as a society, we love children only when they are *under control*. We hate children who defy us. We fear children who want democracy for themselves, children who are independent, quirky, free-thinking, nonconformist, idiosyncratic, superior or critical of adults.

The adult person by contrast, is supposed, at least in theory, to be a responsible member of a democratic society. Unlike the passive and obedient adult desired by totalitarian regimes, adults in a democracy are, in principle, actively contributing to the process of government, and are willing to take responsibility for the condition of the society in which we live. Obedience in adulthood is a virtue peculiar to prisoners and the armed forces. Behaviour we admire in a child is not behaviour we admire in an adult, and unlike many other cultures who follow a similar pattern of acquiescent childhood followed by autonomous adulthood, we have no special ceremonies and rites of passage to mark the transition. This is one reason why adolescence is often such a difficult time.

The family is where children first learn about power and authority and how it can be wielded. What we teach them in terms of obedience, or independence and autonomy, will later be transferred to the political sphere. What kind of citizens do we want our children to be?

LIES AND SECRETS

WHAT KIND OF A LIAR ARE YOU?

What kind of a liar are you?
People lie because they don't remember clear what they saw.
People lie because they can't help making the story better than
    it was the way it happened.
People tell 'white lies' so as to be decent to others.
People lie in a pinch, hating to do it, but lying on because it
    might be worse.
And people lie just to be liars for a crooked personal gain.
    What sort of a liar are you?
    Which of these liars are you?[1]'

Lying is a normal part of a child's development. We all – adults as
well as children – lie at times, when it is more convenient to do so,
or if we are pushed to the point where something we value highly is
set in the balance against truth. Children also lie because they have
vivid imaginations. They lie because they do not *want* to have done
what they did. They lie to make someone act differently. They may
lie to summon attention. They lie because a lie promises fulfilment
of a wish. Sometimes they lie because adults will not accept the
truth. They lie because they are powerless.

Children often tell the truth. But they quickly learn that truth is
not valued. They get punished for being truthful. What they are

trying to say is suppressed because it is discomforting to other people or reveals family secrets. Or they are simply not believed.

In research on children's perception of unfairness in schools, Celia found that one reason why children develop a burning sense of injustice is that adults often refuse to believe them when they tell the truth. These experiences of not being believed are so painful that they can remain with someone for life. One woman, now 50, described an occasion when she was punished for allegedly slapping a little boy despite saying, truthfully, that she had not. She says:

> I could hardly believe it could happen – for I had told the truth! And children are taught that if they tell the truth everything will be all right and justice will prevail!
>
> At the age of 7 I learned a hard lesson. Truth and justice do *not* always prevail, and little girls with pretty faces and fair curly hair (the real culprit) are more likely to have an easier path in life than plain little girls with straight dark hair and glasses (myself). I've never forgotten it.

Children often *do* tell the truth, and feel belittled and humiliated when they are not believed.

When children lie, when they will not reveal the whole truth, when they keep secrets from you, they are exploring, experimenting and proclaiming their autonomy. They realise that they can control events, and start to feel their own power. In the process they begin to learn about loyalty and betrayal, what it is to share knowledge and to be excluded from it, and about trust, negotiation, and how to stand firm.

Yet parents are usually very disturbed when children lie, or deceive them in any way. It was reported in the *New York Times*[2] that a couple beat a boy to death 'to correct his habit of lying'. The attempt to get children to tell the truth and be absolutely open with us stems both from our desire to control their behaviour and what they are – and we can do this only when nothing is hidden from us – and from our wish to produce honest and trustworthy members of society.

BEING HONEST

Many women answering our questionnaire selected honesty as the single most important quality they would like their children to develop. They believe it is the basis of relationships in which there can be trust. 'If one is honest,' Grace says, 'one can be trusted – the most important aspect of any relationship, and of love.' Other women say:

People know they can trust and respect you if you are honest.

My greatest concern has been to bring the children up basically honest, with a great respect for the truth, and honest in their communication between people.

You'll never be trusted by anyone and you'll lose all credibility if you never tell the truth.

A dishonest person is not worth knowing.

No-one loves a liar or a cheat or a thief.

If someone is honest they can never be all bad, and having to admit things will make them check their actions and their conscience.

Lying is seen as infectious. Other people's habits of lying cause conflict about values. One mother says that a lot of her son's friends 'have a secret from their parents. My child tries to copy them.' One man says that his ex-wife, when she has the children to stay, 'lies to them and they lie back'. And another woman reflects on the difference between her approach and that of her mother:

I have a tremendous sense of innate honesty which seems to bemuse my mother. She is more subtle – she loves secrets . . . I find it impossible to lie to my kids, which creates awkward situations, but I feel they are better equipped to handle life, and they seem to appreciate a straight answer.

For some parents honesty is connected with religion and is part of a specific religious identity. This is how Rachel sees the relation between honesty and being Jewish. She says of her 4-year-old son,

> I want to teach him a sense of identity. The majority of his friends are not Jewish and we want him to understand that he is different. One way we are doing this is by teaching him honesty ... It's not that I want him to be a Rabbi, but I'm reading him lots of stories about honesty.

Shirley is an Evangelical Christian and says: 'He should always tell the truth. Jesus is his friend and He is watching him. I tell him He knows whatever he does.'

Most women, however, stress the value of honesty in social relationships, without reference to religious beliefs, believing that honesty forges strong links between people so that they can trust each other. It is part of the acceptance of social responsibility.

Many women consider honesty so vital that they do not punish a child for a misdeed if the child has told the truth about it:

> I never punish him if he tells the truth first time.

> I never punish her for being 'naughty' if she has been honest with me.

> I usually punish lies more than any other form of bad behaviour. On the rare occasions when he does lie, he is not punished for the behaviour which he feels obliged to lie about, only for the lying.

> It is important for a child to be able to tell the difference between being honest and dishonest. I have tried to teach my son the difference which has meant that sometimes he has been praised for telling the truth even though he may have told me something he has done naughty.

> Honesty to me is most important and if my children reflect my priorities then I will have no worries. From when he could

understand when he had done wrong, honesty was most important. He began learning. If he'd knowingly done wrong I'd have got him to tell me no matter if I'd be angry, rather than find out later, which would make me twice as angry.

When a child is dishonest and lies, cheats or steals, parents may try to help the child correct the action. Amanda tells how she dealt with her 2½ year-old son's occasional lies and spontaneous pilfering:

If he tries telling untruths I correct him. If he picks up a packet of sweets in a shop I have taught him to give the lady the pennies *before* he eats them. He had tried to bring his friend's cars home, and once has actually hidden one in his pocket. I sat him down and explained that the car was his friend's and reminded him how upset he was when his toy bus was stolen. He quite happily walked back and took the car back to his friend.

Mothers also try to teach honesty by personal example – by being scrupulously honest themselves:

If I have acted unfairly I will say so quite honestly, and if I don't know the answer to the question they ask I will admit it and we will all, for example, go to the library and find the right answer together.

I never make promises I can't hope to keep.

I'm always honest with my children and reward their honesty.

At the same time, no parent is entirely comfortable with children who reveal outside the family all that happens within it. Some parents keep secrets from their children about the family. One woman describes not knowing that she was Jewish until her teenage years. Another remembers how her parents, who were not married, kept the fact of her illegitimacy from her, and how she grew up knowing that she was being excluded from some family secret without ever discovering what that secret was.[3] Parents also want their children to learn tact and consideration for others, and not blurt out their observations of other people in a clear, childish treble: 'Look at that fat lady!'; 'That man's only got one leg!' or show their dislike at the present they have been given. So they are also concerned to teach children discretion, tact and the art of 'white lying', a lie 'so as not to hurt people's feelings'. Since black people might object, quite properly, to this term, and Sheila's Rastafarian friends call insignificant lies 'black lies' and whoppers 'white lies', let us call them 'well-intentioned lies'.

From early in their lives children receive complex education in the minute distinctions between blatant dishonesty of word or deed and the conventional social duplicity of well-intentioned lies in order to make the wheels run more smoothly. They learn that their parents say 'It's so nice to see you!' to boring Aunt Agatha and 'It's lovely!' about things they know they dislike. One woman describes as her 'first deception' a time when she was four or five years old and feeling miserable because the family had just moved to a new house. Her father said, '"Smile Kay," and I smiled.'[4] Children are sometimes more sensitive than adults to this sort of duplicity. Many people can remember being ordered to apologise to an adult, and refusing 'because I'm not sorry and why should I tell a lie!'

In teaching children not to lie, we also have to face up to the fact that parents lie frequently. Some lie in an attempt to protect the child, such as warning one who is near the river that a giant lives in it who eats little boys for dinner; they lie to placate, as when they tell a child who is about to have a wound dressed that 'it won't hurt'; they lie to protect themselves, when they promise ice-cream to a child screaming in a supermarket in order to get her outside where she can be given a good walloping; they lie to threaten a child into good behaviour: 'If you're naughty, the policeman will come and take you away.' One mother told her children that the ice-cream van was an ambulance in order to avoid conflicts over whether or not the children were allowed ice-cream.

The mothers who talked to us stressed that they tried to avoid these kinds of lies and wanted to be honest with their children. And by 'teaching children to be honest' they meant much more than training them not to lie.

For many the meaning of honesty is complex. It does not merely relate to avoiding deceit, the Old Testament 'Thou shalt not bear false witness' and 'Thou shalt not steal', but means an open approach to life and openness between parents and children. It is a comprehensive expectation, born of humanistic psychology and the human potential movement, that children will be able to acknowledge and express their emotions and to share an emotional life with others. It corresponds to the more general statement made by one mother that she wants her children to grow up

> with the seeds of self-awareness – self-knowledge, of growing consciousness of what they do and what effect it has on others. It is the beginning of 'know thyself'. The older you are when you start on that road, the harder it is. I want them to begin now.

Mothers wish to have completely open relationships with their children so that they can have insight into their minds and help and guide them effectively. Many look back on relationships with their own parents and the misunderstandings that arose, at failures of communication, punitive attitudes and at punishments unfairly meted out:

> I want my child to feel that I won't get too angry or critical if he does wrong, so he can be more honest with me than I felt I could be with my mother – something I still cannot fully be.

One woman said that her mother never explained the reasons for being honest, although she was often punished for lying: 'She just went crazy if I did lie. I want to be more open with James . . . to discuss things. I don't want him to have any reason to lie.' Others say:

> As Zoe gets older I want her to be able to talk to me openly and not keep things to herself.

> I want to know that they will always feel able to bring their problems and troubles to me without fear.

I try to encourage my son, aged 5, to talk about his feelings and not to keep things to himself.

Psychology supports this approach to inculcating honesty. A loving relationship between a mother and child nurtures the gradual development of conscience, and children who have this inner voice are better able to regulate their own behaviour.[5]

On the other hand, it is wrong to suggest that the warmth of attachment between a mother and child is correlated with the child's level of honesty. In psychological experiments which tempt the child to cheat in tests, when the mother's expressions of warmth and approval are contingent upon a successful performance, a child is more likely to cheat. Where there is pressure to succeed, 'warmth is used inadvertently by the parent to shape deception'.[6]

THE MEANINGS OF LIES

The child's lying and deceit may tell more about the character of the adult than that of the child, for lies may be a way of holding back the truth, concealing the whole story, to outwit adults, so evading punishment or buying freedom. In his autobiography, Geoffrey Dennis[7] describes how lying, which headed the official category of sins in his family, was called 'story-telling' and says:

One told stories to avoid punishment, hide a misdeed, evade consequences. No chastisement and there would have been no lies; or fewer ... You hear good old-fashioned parents talk of thrashing the truth into a boy. What they do is thrash it out.

For the young child lying often means 'I did not *mean* to do it'. It is used as denial of bad intention rather than denial of the facts. It is as if the child is saying, 'I did something naughty, but I'm not a bad *person*'. A great deal of bad behaviour in children is impulsive. It is not planned. A child may know that something is wrong but act without deliberation. They realise they've done wrong, but have not yet learnt to delay gratification. They want everything *now*.

In dealing with lies like this it helps if an adult can separate out the misdemeanour, the act that caused harm, and emphasise that it was wrong to do this, rather than ascribing naughtiness to the child. Instead of 'You are being a naughty boy!', we might say, 'When you take money from Mummy's purse and don't tell me, I don't know how much money we have to buy nice things'.

Children learn to behave in a more self-controlled way when adults explain things and reason and discuss their values with them, and when they also give time for listening to the children's thoughts and feelings rather than 'laying down the law'. When a parent is herself concerned about other people's perceptions and feelings, a child starts to make moral judgements based on a similar concern and caring.[8]

Nancy Hale, in her autobiography *Secrets*, tells how her school teachers were suspicious of her because she 'told lies': 'I had insisted way back in Kindergarten that I had, at home, a cat that could read and write. I was then known as a liar.' Her mother, on the other hand, encouraged fantasy, and she asks: 'Could it be my parents were the wrong kind to have?'[9]

Children's lies are often only 'tall stories' of this sort, boasts consisting of fantasies of themselves or family members – 'I ate six ice-creams one after the other' or 'Daddy went in a rocket to the moon'. What they really mean is 'How exciting if it were really true!' An adult should recognise this for what it is and in a light-hearted manner make it clear that she understands the wish. It can be useful to distinguish between 'true-true' stories and those that are 'true-false' – ones you wish were true, but aren't.[10] There is always the danger, though, that you are belittling a child's real experience. One grandmother, now in her sixties, remembers being taught about Florence Nightingale in primary school:

During the course of the lesson I put up my hand and was eventually asked what I wanted to say. Bursting with pride I announced that my father had been to tea with Florence Nightingale. I was soon put in my place and told that he couldn't possibly have done so. I was called a liar. As a punishment I was made to stand on the seat of my desk for the rest of the lesson.

Of course I cried and cried when I got home. The following

day, father donned his best suit and stiff white collar and with great dignity arrived at school and confronted the teacher. Quietly and calmly he told her that he did have tea with Florence Nightingale and that Ruth was not a liar. She apologised to him but not to me!

She explains that her father, born in 1890, belonged as a boy to the Church Boys' Brigade; as they lived quite close to Florence Nightingale's home in Derbyshire, they were taken to see the great lady. 'They were all given a drink and a biscuit whilst the old lady sat silently on her chair.' Some 'tall stories' are true!

Another normal kind of lying is the 'instrumental' lie by which reality is bent to conform to children's wishes. This sort of lie is employed freely in what Kohlberg has labelled stage 0 of moral development – the pre-moral stage.[11] Instrumental lies are used to achieve a desired end or to avoid a bad one, sometimes because it seems easy or quicker to do this than to exert effort, and young children in the pre-moral stage do not see anything wrong with this if the outcome is good. They may, for example, manage to put the blame for their own naughtiness onto someone else or to avoid a task:

One morning when Matthew was 4, I found him still in his underwear fifteen minutes after I'd reminded him to get dressed for school. Spying an open comic on the floor I said, 'Matthew, have you been reading this comic?' He admitted he had. 'Well,' I scolded. 'You *should* have been getting dressed as I asked you to!' 'Hmmm', he said, 'I should have told a lie!' It obviously didn't occur to him that I would frown upon lying as a way out of his predicament.[12]

To teach children truthfulness we have to show them that we value honesty, but even when we say this they may at first see our comment only as reflecting a peculiar adult quirk of mind.

In Kohlberg's next stage of moral development – stage 1 – children acknowledge that lying and cheating are wrong, but only because they get disapproval or punishment for doing so: 'You should never tell a lie because somehow the brains inside grown-ups' heads are so smart that they find out.'[13] Then, at about the age of 6, children start to challenge you: 'It isn't *fair*', and to assert their rights and their independence from you. This is the stage at which there is a lot of what one psychologist calls 'spit and vinegar'[14] as they come to terms with a world in which grownups are the bosses.

From this point, if you are doing your job well and the atmosphere is tolerant and harmonious, the child tries to live up to the standards you are setting and to please you. This corresponds to Kohlberg's stage 3 of moral development, an important phase which may last until the onset of adolescence.

Persistent lying in older children may be a sign of deep unhappiness or of a difficult family situation. Miriam is an inveterate liar and cheat who 'sets parent against parent, siblings against each other, child against parent'. Described in an article in the *Guardian* written from the point of view of the embittered mother, she is said to have 'always been a manipulator, a user of other people; anyone can be turned into her cat's paw':

'At the age of 5 she was carted home by Mrs Jones who said "That child will get you hung one day." Miriam, smelling baking, had gone to Mrs Jones' door, wept copiously and said please could she have some food, her mother never gave her anything to eat . . .' She steals pencils and sweets at school, tells her teacher that her parents hit her, and whispers 'evil things' to her brother and sister like: 'Daddy says you shouldn't have been born, you were a mistake', 'Peter doesn't like you any more' and 'Debbie's always been Mummy's pet; she gets everything'.

Daddy, stressed at work and increasingly so by Miriam's behaviour at home, has a heart attack and dies. The family mourns. But not Miriam. She stares coldly if anyone weeps; one horrified teacher says she has never known such a cold child, she has no feeling.[15]

It is interesting that in this account of Miriam's behaviour as a small child the things the mother describes are those that many children do. Yet they were intolerable to these parents. It is common for children to complain that they do not get any food at home, to steal pencils and sweets and to say exactly what Miriam did to siblings. Readers' reactions were prompt. Some wrote in that their daughters were like this, too, and asked, 'Where did I go wrong?' Others pleaded for more sensitive awareness of the child's needs and feelings. One anonymous reader said: 'Child abuse can take many forms. Children can be raped. Or beaten. Or subjected to unbearable emotional stress.' She went on to say that as a small girl she was just like Miriam: 'I was not being "manipulative"; I was reacting with terror to a home situation in which I had been made to replace my mother as emotional support for my father.' Following this stress throughout her childhood, she had a mental breakdown at the age of eighteen and only found freedom in this way.

When a child lies, or cheats, or steals, it seems that some parents quickly seize on this as evidence of criminal tendencies. Images of children as 'evil', possessed by the devil, or as changelings from outer space, planning to invade and conquer the earth (*The Exorcist, The Bad Seed*) reflect women's feelings about the unpredictable strangers who have taken over our lives. These images are the other side of the coin of the angelic child 'trailing clouds of glory' who brings peace and love into the parents' lives. Both images reflect some part of the complex reality of childrearing, but neither can substitute for perceiving the child as a child and understanding the motives behind an act of dishonesty. For many of the women in our study honesty has to do with a two-way flow of communication between themselves and their children and it also entails *self-awareness*. They want to really know their children. They want nothing to be hidden.

This longing for openness about thoughts and feelings is in many ways far more demanding than the kind of truthfulness required of Victorian children. Contemporary children must also learn to be honest with *themselves*:

It's important to be honest, not just with others, but with one's self.

If he's honest with himself he will perhaps stand by decisions that he makes later in his life. We try to teach him this by getting him to say what he feels about everyday family life.

Being honest touches all aspects of our lives, not only the obvious ones (i.e. not stealing). I want them to say truthfully how they feel.

It also involves being honest about matters which in the past have been taboo – sex, for instance, and death – the last taboo. Parents are concerned to explore, explain, canalise, to take off all the old dust sheets, unlock doors, disclose all mysteries.

PROTECTIVE LIES

This new emphasis on the importance of honesty around sex is not always reflected in honesty about politics, which remains one of the most problematic areas for many mothers. One woman who told her daughter that 'the government won't let anyone drop a bomb on us' says, 'I don't really believe that – but what else can you say to a nine year old terrified of nuclear war?' Rebecca, who is Jewish, has avoided telling her children about the Holocaust: 'They're still too little,' she says.

I want to protect them from knowing that people could hate us that much, and could do such things to us. They'll find out soon enough. Until then, I want to give them enough self-confidence and sense of their own worth, that when the knowledge does come, they'll be able to deal with it.

Telling children the truth about the oppressions which directly affect them is a painful and difficult task. The black mother who tells her son that he too can be a lawyer just as easily as his white friend is not being entirely truthful. The white mother who tells her daughter that when she grows up she can choose to be an engineer, or a builder, just as readily as a secretary or a nurse, is talking about her own hopes and wishes but not about the reality of sex discrimination and unequal job opportunities. It's much easier to talk about our ideals of equality than it is to discuss with children the reality of oppression and how they might challenge that.

Women often yearn for relationships in which nothing is hidden: no subterfuge, no disguise of the truth, no deceit, no guilty secrets. They want children to be able to tell them everything. This includes sexual aspects of children's lives. The mother of a 6-year-old says that she wants her son to be quite open about his masturbation, for example, and to discuss it with her. The honesty required of children amounts to a complete revelation of self.

We are a long way from the enclosed world of the Victorian nursery where children were more or less separate from the life of adults in the family, who were in turn isolated from the children, though they might pay regular visits to the nursery, as the children made regular visits to the drawing-room. In the post-Freudian era children, it seems, must not be encouraged to withdraw to their own private worlds. Their parents want to know what they are thinking and feeling, and to keep anything hidden smacks of dishonesty. There may be a price to pay for this openness. We have taken away from children the possibility of privacy and of secrecy, and thereby, in the modern two-child family, the opportunity of co-operative intrigue in the face of the adults' powerful world (the kind of dreadful things that Nurse Matilda's charges got up to) as well as the invention of make-believe, the secret castles and treasure islands of children who conduct much of their everyday lives in a private space for children only, which is barred to adults. Instead, there is a social group consisting of one or two adults and one or two children whose thoughts, feelings and actions are, to parents conscientious about child-rearing, under constant scrutiny. There is little room for dishonesty of thought or deed – even, perhaps, little room for fantasy.

Some of the best adventures of Sheila's own childhood happened after dark, when my brother and I were able to escape adult protection in a nursery at the top of an old house, from which we climbed out of the window and on to the roof-tops. We balanced precariously until we could see the signal lights on the nearby station and hear the thunder of monster trains in the night. This was our private world. I cannot remember if we ever lied about it because no one ever asked us if we did it. But we certainly would have if called upon to do so because I'm sure they would have stopped us.

A man who is now a composer tells how his secret world consisted of playing piano when his parents were out at work. He knew that if they discovered that he could play they would insist on music lessons with a teacher in the same street whom he realised was very bad. He only ever played when his parents left the house. They never found out, so he was never required to lie.

Nancy Hale remembers that as a child she appreciated secrets 'sensuously', 'like a ripe plum bitten into, or rather like the surprise chocolate peppermint, allowed to dissolve upon the tongue'.

> The secret of secrets, as every child knows, is one that involves a receptacle. Thus when Jinny Welch and I discovered a secret drawer in the mahogany high boy in our dining room during Easter vacation one year, we gave each other one long, intense look and within minutes had formed a secret society.[16]

It is not only that children revel in secrets. The knowledge which they protect is precious for them, too, and they should not have to guard their secrets with lies.

Children in a psychiatric hospital who were never allowed to be alone – even when they were in bed at night or in the bathroom – devised different ways of misbehaving in the hope of being put in an isolation room, so desperate was their longing for some privacy.[17] Commenting on this, the philosopher Sissela Bok says: 'Where ordinary forms of withdrawal are forbidden, circuitous or disguised methods take their place, even in persons who have nothing to hide of a discrediting or personal nature.'[18] The diary hidden at the back of the drawer, secret treasure and hiding places, secret personal identity, a secret friend, the secret society with special codes and language and mysterious practices, the mysteries of Narnia and the magic of *The Secret Garden* – all express children's longing for solitude and for boundaries beyond which adults do not go.

Celia and her sisters once secretly owned three guinea pigs they named Salt, Pepper and Marmite so that they could talk about them in front of Sheila without disclosing their existence. Fits of giggles would accompany a request to 'Please pass the salt and pepper' or 'I'd like some Marmite on my bread'. This gave them a secret world to which their parents did not have access – as well as thrilling ownership of something which they had been forbidden to have.

The child whose secret world is assailed by adults may resort to lies to preserve it. So lies may be used as protection against parents who intrude too much on a child's thoughts and feelings. Being able to have secrets is an important part of personal and social development. The child who has secrets has a sense of autonomy and power. Edmund Gosse describes in his autobiography *Father and Son* how when he was 6 years old he suddenly realised that his father was not omnipotent and that he was a separate individual who had the power to withhold or to give information, and could influence the behaviour of others. The little boy had broken the pipe intended to carry water to a fountain being built in the garden and did not tell his father: 'There was a secret in this world and it belonged to me and to a somebody who lived in the same body as me.'[19]

'To realise that one has the power to remain silent,' says Sissela Bok, 'is linked to the understanding that one can exercise some control over events – that one need not be entirely transparent, entirely predictable or . . . at the mercy of parents who have seemed all-seeing and all-powerful.'[20]

Being able to have secrets and to be secretive is rooted in the child's developing consciousness of self, the growth of autonomy, the ability to act independently and take responsibility for these actions. It brings the tension of choice between concealment and revelation. The experience of having secrets teaches discretion, awareness of when to hold back and when to reach out. It confers power. Part of the maintenance of secrets may entail lies. They are used to bar the intruder, and also to conceal mistakes. But later on, Sissela Bok says: 'Children may learn to cope with the responsibility without needing to conceal mistakes. But this learning only comes through repeated experience with secrets kept and revealed.'[21]

IMPOSED SECRETS

But there are bad secrets, too – secrets imposed by adults on children, the keeping of which is rewarded by gifts and bribes, and the breaking of which is threatened with punishment. Indeed, for the child who is the victim of sexual abuse in the family, the whole of life becomes a lie, and secrets must be kept in a terrible conspiracy in which the child is overpowered by the exploiting male.

Historically in Western society it has been accepted that family secrets are inviolate. Wife-beating and violence against children have been treated as a matter of domestic quarrels. The nineteenth century saw mounting shocked concern about the violent abuse of children resulting in their maiming or death, and there are newspaper accounts of terrible injuries inflicted on children in the name of discipline.

Yet what went on within the family remained essentially private. One of the profoundly shocking things about Nazi Germany, Stalinist Russia or Chinese Communism to Western ears was that children were required to denounce their parents. The English image of the secrecy of the family was, in a way, crystallised in the portrait of the investigating Roundheads behind a great oak table and a little Cavalier boy in front of them, brave and straight, who, when they asked him, 'When did you last see your father?' answered truthfully, 'Three days ago, sir,' because the child had had his eyes closed as he lay in bed as his father kissed him before he fled. The child is expected to preserve the secrets of a family and an essential part of the morality taught to children is the command 'honour thy mother and father'.

In a paper called 'What is meant by "telling the truth"?' Dietrich Bonhoeffer wrote that it must mean something different according to the situation. The child 'should reveal ... everything that is hidden and secret to his parents'. They, on the other hand, cannot be expected to reveal themselves to the child, while the child should not, have to reveal family secrets to others outside it. He gives an example:

> A teacher asks a child in front of the class whether it is true that his father often comes home drunk. It is true, but the child denies it.
>
> The teacher's question has placed him in a situation for which he is not yet prepared. He feels only that what is taking place is an unjustified interference in the order of the family and he must oppose it. What goes on in the family is not for the ears of the class in school. The family has its own secret and must preserve it.
>
> The teacher has failed to respect the reality of the institution. The child ought to find a way of answering which would comply with both the rule of the family and the rule of the school. But he is not yet able to do this ... As a simple no to the teacher's question the child's answer is certainly untrue; yet at the same time it nevertheless gives expression to the truth that the family is an institution *sui generis* and that the teacher *has no right to intervene*. (our italics)[22]

In totalitarian states, parents who resist the system often have to impose secrets on their children. There is no other way. A Polish couple discussed with us their concern about what they see as 'state indoctrination' of their children at school. At home, the children are taught the parents' version of the history of their country, but warned that this dangerous knowledge cannot be shared with their teachers. Children in lesbian households, where ex-husbands are trying to get custody, may be warned by their mother not to talk openly about her relationships. American children whose families were part of the underground railroad, helping black slaves to escape, were also enjoined to secrecy. When the values of the mother conflict with those of the society in which she lives, she can sometimes only share those values with her child if the child's commitment to secrecy can be ensured.

Yet adults often impose their own ugly secrets on children, drawing them into a conspiracy. This happens especially in families where there is child sexual abuse. The father or other adult man may at first be gentle and tell the child to touch or to suck his penis or allow him to fondle her because she loves him and she is his 'little princess'. He becomes more demanding, penetrating her with his penis, with a bottle, or any convenient tool, and then warns the girl to be silent lest she be severely punished. He may tell her that what she is doing is very naughty, so no one is to find out. He may threaten to kill her pet animal if she tells anyone, or to send her away, or may actually use sex as a punishment for misdeeds he has caught her committing, especially masturbation.

While the secret worlds of children are precious and their secrets should be inviolate, adults may impose on children an intolerable burden when they confide grown-ups' secrets and invoke secrecy in order *to protect adults*.

How, then, can we explore the subject of lying and secrecy with children so that they are able to make their own judgements? How can we support and reinforce their own moral values?

It is not a simple matter of wishing that they always tell the truth, or that a lie can be told in order to avoid hurting another person, for if the child who is being abused tells the truth to the social worker Daddy or Uncle may go to prison. Nor is it enough only to give children information about the risks of sexual abuse, and to tell the child this is wrong. An important part of education, in the home and in school, is teaching children to become aware of their own rights. 'A child should be protected against all forms of neglect, cruelty and exploitation,' the United Nations Declaration of the Rights of the Child declares. Somehow we need to help children recognise abuse and to recognise the potential situations of abuse. Most adults did not receive that education in their own childhood and have to learn new skills so as to communicate this to children. As when sex education was first introduced for little children, there is a struggle to find the right words and to create a language with which to communicate with them on the subject, and to provide the children themselves with language in which they can express their feelings and ideas.

The danger of sexual abuse does not come, for the most part, from strangers but from people they trust – those nearest to them, and especially within the family. Concepts of 'good' and 'bad' feelings and touch that is pleasant or confusing can be explored:

> Touching that feels good like hugging and rocking and cuddling ... touching that you don't like – like kissing, or touching in places that make you feel strange, touching when you're half asleep and pretending not to know, touching that someone tells you *not* to talk about.[23]

We can help children to trust their spontaneous feelings, too, and know that if something does not 'feel right' they should stop and think, and perhaps talk about it with someone who understands and who is not directly involved – mother, teacher, or other grown-up. We can teach them that it is all right to say 'no' to an adult when the feelings are not 'good'. And we can teach them about the tricks and bribes which may be used to induce children to keep secrets. We explore this subject in more detail in Chapter 6, and look more closely at some of the problems involved. The point that we are making here is that we need to accept both that obedience in children cannot be a primary virtue, and that in developing consciousness of self and in becoming responsible for their behaviour and their bodies children must be free to withdraw from us – and even from our tender care at times. There comes a time when a small boy being soaked in the bath tub puts his hands over his penis and says, 'That's mine!', when children lock the bathroom door and we do not know what is going on inside, when they want to be alone and safe in their solitude.

A woman remembers back to just after she had started to go to school, and her mother came into her bedroom one evening and sensed her embarrassment. Her mother took it as a signal to sit down and tell her that masturbation was OK and to give her a little homily about the beauty of sex. In fact, the little girl had been praying, something she had just learned about at school, and she knew that her mother wouldn't approve. Children seek their private space. For one small child it was the kennel of a much-loved smelly old dog. She crept in and no one, nothing, could get at her. It was the beginning of the sense that she could control what other people did to her. For other children it is a tree-house, the cupboard under the stairs, the garden shed, or the lavatory.

Much of the debate about child sexual abuse has consisted of arguments about 'who owns children – families or the state?' The conflict about the Cleveland case, when a number of chidren were taken into care in Cleveland following alleged sexual abuse, was largely expressed in the media in terms of 'Do the Social Services have the right to take children from their parents?' 'What are parents' rights over their children?'

It is an extension of the debate about whether fathers have rights over their children and whether mothers have any rights. In early nineteenth-century divorce cases in England fathers were acknowledged as having legal property rights in their children because it was their seed, their name which was being passed down. If a father died and his children had not yet reached the age of majority, he could name a legal guardian to replace him whose rights had priority over those of the children's mother. A mother had no rights over her children during their father's lifetime.[24]

For many women denied power in a society managed and run for the most part by and for the benefit of men, their only sense of power and fulfilment rests in their children. When they abrogate rights in their children, or when they are wrested from them, they are left completely powerless.

EMPOWERING CHILDREN

Yet perhaps what we should be acknowledging is that *children belong to themselves*.

A vital element in enabling children to resist abuse of all kinds is that they develop self-esteem and self-confidence. That means that adults have to surrender some of their power and have to allow children to choose between alternatives, to experience some self-direction in their daily lives, in play and in school work, and not be under the autocratic control of adults.

It also means that we must respect their choices. It entails encouraging in children a sense of responsibility for their own bodies, and that includes what they eat and drink, their personal hygiene and what they wear. Daily life may seem complicated enough with small children without letting them choose whether or not they clean their teeth or wear a coat when they go out in the cold. Yet these are important choices for them and it is possible to introduce elements of choice and decision-making into activities which relate to children's ownership of their own bodies, and thus develop a sense of self-direction and positive feelings of self-worth. Until we recognise that children should not be the possessions of their parents, that they are not owned by them, however benevolently that ownership is expressed, children cannot be really free to resist sexual abuse and exploitation of all kinds. The conspiracy of silence, the guilty secret that is guarded in many families, will persist.

Even when children have the courage to reveal sexual abuse they are exposed to a series of events over which they have no control. They are isolated from their families, medically examined and treated as helpless victims.

Ultimately it is not whether or not children tell lies, but the powerlessness of children, both in the family and in the larger society, which is the issue. Only when the empowering of children is achieved can they be free to speak the truth.

CHAPTER
6

SEX AND BIRTH

Andrew, aged 4, asked his mother, Anna, why she slept with Daddy instead of him. He had never before asked any questions remotely connected with sex. She did some quick thinking and said, 'I'm Daddy's teddy bear – like the teddy bear you cuddle when you go to bed.' Andrew obviously did not believe this. So she went on: 'At night I change into a big bear suit.' Having got herself into this situation, to add credence to her story Anna hired a bear suit so that when the children came into the bedroom one morning she could be seen wearing it. After telling this story, the author of an article in a magazine for mothers comments: 'The episode effectively deflected any further embarrassing questions', and she advises mothers to 'lie by omission', to 'bend the truth a little' because it is 'easier' and makes suggestions about how 'to be economical with the truth'.[1]

The women who told us what they believe would not have gone along with this. They try to be as honest as they can and usually found it easy to tell their children about pregnancy and birth. Many really enjoyed doing it. They felt they didn't have the hang-ups that their own mothers had often had when talking about these subjects, and were confident in discussing everything to do with making and having babies. Though from magazines and books which give advice to parents you might think that this topic proves a major problem, women often said that the subject came up spontaneously when they were pregnant and making preparations for a new baby. They say things like:

> I am pregnant at the moment and tell my 8-year-old son what I am feeling at any time. He cuddles my 'lump' often. Any questions I am able to answer confidently and without embarrassment.

> I explained and illustrated how pregnancy progresses by showing my 3-year-old my tummy growing and pictures in baby care books.

> We looked at pictures of naked ladies and we talked about my sister and the baby she is expecting and how when it moved my daughter (3 years) will be able to feel the baby in my sister's tummy. I told her how she used to be in my tummy and explained that babies are safe and warm until they are born.

> I used a balloon to show my son (7 years) how the neck of the womb and vagina stretch to allow the baby to pass through.

Even 2-year-olds are able to absorb a great deal of information. 'My child was interested in my pregnancy from about five months gestation and by the time the baby arrived he was well prepared.' They can feel the baby moving, listen to stories about what happened when *they* were in Mummy's tummy and when they were born, 'help' with their mother's antenatal exercises – even play with a rag doll with a rag baby tucked inside her and an opening between her legs for the baby to come out.

Discussion about the benefits and hazards of high-tech pregnancy apart, modern technology has contributed to the detailed information women are able to give their children. They often take an older child with them when they have a scan at sixteen weeks. Sandy says of her daughter aged 3:

> The arrival of a new baby was something that I dealt with well. We compared fat tummies, talked about breastfeeding, looked

at other babies, went for a scan together, and she got a photo of her new brother or sister!

For Ginny's little daughter, aged 4, that scan proved to be especially exciting: 'She was at the scan when we first found out it was twins, and was completely involved right through.' In fact, of all the values about which we asked women's ideas, birth was the subject which they felt they had dealt with most successfully.

Perhaps this came about as a long-term consequence of the so-called 'sexual liberation' of the 1960s, to which we now look back so critically. It probably owes a great deal to the rise of feminism, and to women's increased self-awareness and concern to 'reclaim' their bodies. Before then, a lot of worrying was done about explaining how a baby got 'in' and parents feared that accurate information would result in wholesale sexual experiment.

STORKS AND GOOSEBERRY BUSHES

Mothers used to put a good deal of effort into protecting children from all knowledge about sex and birth. In traditional farm households in Catholic Ireland, for example, childbirth was kept secret. If a woman was having her baby at home, when she started labour they were sent to relations. If she went to hospital the children were told she had 'gone shopping'. Even children as old as 10 and 11 believed that babies were ordered from a shop, and younger children thought they were found on the beach or came in a doctor's black bag. In the seventies an anthropologist writing about her field work in western Ireland remarks: 'Children and adolescents are sheltered from the facts of life, all mating of farm animals is kept from them, and they accept miraculous birth myths, often well into adolescence.'[2]

Back at the turn of the century, Western 'sex education' was based on religion. A poem called 'Angela's Birth' published in a book of *Songs for Little People*[3] has a refrain:

Angela came to us out of the flowers,
God's little blossom that changed into ours.

Evading the issue of *how* exactly little Angela emerged from the rosebuds, it represents one way in which an aura of romance and sentimentality shielded many middle- and upper-class girls from all knowledge of biological processes until they married, when they might be warned that men do 'horrid things' and that women have to put up with them for the sake of married status and having babies to love.

Jessica Mitford tells how she broke that taboo when she was 9 and attended a dancing class which met weekly in different families' houses, with little girls in organdie dresses and cashmere shawls, presided over by starched nannies:

> One fateful afternoon the teacher was an hour late, and I took the opportunity to lead the other children up to the roof, there to impart some delightful information that had just come my way concerning the conception and birth of babies. The telling was a great success ... Several weeks later my mother sent for me. Her face was like thunder; one look, and I knew what must have happened. In the dreadful scolding that followed, I learned that one of the little girls had wakened night after night with screaming nightmares ... Finally, her governess had prised the truth out of her ...

Jessica never went to the dancing class after that and was no longer considered a suitable companion for nice children. She says that years after, when a debutante of 17, she heard from an older cousin that two young men were still forbidden to associate with her.[4]

Even thirty years ago, women who *were* anxious to give their children accurate information about sex and birth felt very awkward about describing their own anatomy, dreading that the child might ask to see it. They wrote to agony aunts for help in finding words to explain sexual intercourse and make it reassuring. Women's magazines constantly ran features in which somebody discussed this problem. The advice usually given was to concentrate on the idea of love and stress that Mummy and Daddy 'cuddled', and above all to keep it simple. The uterus was 'this lovely warm place under Mummy's heart', the vagina 'the special opening', and sex was always firmly linked to reproduction: 'Mummy and Daddy did it to make you because they wanted a little baby.' Mothers who managed to get the information over in this vague way felt they had succeeded. It was a straightforward goal.

FINDING THE WORDS

This approach was probably never really satisfactory. Sex is obviously not just about making babies, and discussions about sex only in terms of reproduction run into trouble later when children ask questions about sexual activity which does not result in babies, and when they become curious about abortion or homosexuality. Baby-making is inadequate as an explanation of human sexual behaviour. Even mothers of 2 and 3-year-olds sometimes discover this: Miranda has two boys aged 5 and 3 and a baby of 6 months. She told me:

> They knew there was a baby in my tummy, but the older boy was worried about how the baby was going to get out. I showed him what happened with the help of your book. Then he asked: 'How does the baby get in?' And again with the help of your book he was satisfied about that, too. But afterwards, when Simon had his arms around me one day, he asked, 'What are you cuddling Daddy for? You've already got a baby!' Simon said, 'Mummies and Daddies need lots of practice.' I thought that was rather good.

On the other hand, she was uncomfortably aware that it was not a sufficient explanation and that she was going to have to think through more deeply the way she discussed sex with her sons.

The assumption used to be that every child of about three or four lived in a protective and loving home, with a nice Mummy and a nice Daddy. It was taken for granted that sex education at this age consisted merely of teaching 'where babies come from', though a pet cat or dog might produce useful illustrations about pregnancy and birth. Sexuality was communicated to children as part of domesticity, and – because of the tender, warm feelings aroused – it was assumed that it contributed to the welfare of all in the family.

We have come to realise that this cosy picture of the family is often an illusion, and that many children are sexually abused by their fathers and other men close to them in the family.

With the widespread publicity this has received, more children are aware of the issue of child sexual abuse and ask about it. The mother of a 4-year-old says: 'I find it impossible to answer her question of why some people wish to hurt children and how to enable her to distinguish safe adults from non-safe adults.' Another describes a conversation with her 6-year-old:

> I told him that people could want to touch him, kiss him or make him do things but he said he liked kissing. It is hard to tell him what people would do. I want him to be aware and yet not terrify him.

Judith Arcana[5] tried to explain rape to her 5-year-old:

> Anxious to the point of halting speech, I slowly groped for the words that could give him a sense of it, without that full charge of horror and pain no 5-year-old needs. And no adult either. I was fearful, should I be saying all this? Is it right? ... I had always assumed that we'd have these serious conversations when he was twelve. Labouring along, I was saying something like 'The man forces his penis into the woman's vagina, forces her into sexual intercourse,' when he interrupted. 'But I thought sex felt *good*, how could he hurt her by having sex with her?' [...] Daniel sat up in his bed next to me, leaning forward on one arm, looking into my face as I spoke. I leaned forward too, and stroked his arm gently. 'Doesn't that feel good?' I asked him. As he nodded yes, I struck out, hitting his arm and knocking it aside, pushing him over sideways. 'You see, your arm is the same arm, and my hand is the same hand, but I can use my hand to hurt you as well as to make you feel good. That's how a man can use his penis to hurt a woman in what isn't really sex, but rape.' I know that he understood. I had

seen the understanding move from me to him – through his body to his mind.

We need to talk to both girls and boys about sexual abuse. Boys must also learn that they should never use their sexuality against girls. For even in primary schools gangs of small Rambos drag girls into the boys' lavatories, dare each other to exhibit themselves in the playground, giggle together over soft porn and whoop it up to terrorise little girls.

We should be aware, too, that when we are talking to children about sexual abuse, they may *already* have been abused. Our ignorance of this and insistence that they can say 'no' can make them feel even more guilty. Nothing a child can do can provide protection from sexual exploitation. With this in mind, we should make it clear that whatever happens *it is never the child's fault*. Tell the children you are ready to listen whenever they want to talk, and that there are other people too, like those who work with Child Line, to whom they can speak on the phone if they need other help.

It sometimes seems that there is nothing we can say that is appropriate, and that fits every situation. We may say 'Nobody has the right to do anything to your body which you do not want done.' But what about if you are having an injection at the clinic? What if you don't want to wear your seatbelt in the car and somebody insists on fastening you in? Even talk about 'good feelings' and 'bad feelings' may suggest to a child that it is she who is 'good' or 'bad' rather than the feelings. So perhaps the best we can do is to say 'If you feel uneasy about anything someone wants to do, tell me, and we can find out whether or not it's sensible.' And we have to add, 'This applies just as much to friends and to people whom you like as to strangers or people you think are nasty.' Books can help us talk to children about sexual abuse, too, and we have listed some on page 303.

We may also have to explain other aspects of sex in relation to reproduction, such as miscarriage and abortion, in vitro fertilisation, surrogate motherhood, homosexuality and AIDS. Like Judith Arcana, mothers often find themselves having to discuss these issues long before they expected the child would ask questions about them, and maybe before they themselves have even sorted out in their own minds what they believe, and before they know the facts. They feel that discussing such issues with small children is to inflict adult problems on them, shattering their innocence. They may believe that in the past children grew up in simplicity and innocence in a world which was a mixture of Peter Pan and *Wind in the Willows* with a touch of Arthur Ransome thrown in. Such a world existed only for a tiny minority of upper middle-class children, but the myth of the 'golden age of childhood' is a potent one. And today it all seems much more complicated, with nine and ten year olds already into pop culture and using the explicit sexual imagery of groups like Pet Shop Boys or Bros. Children as young as ten and eleven have 'boyfriends' and 'girlfriends'.

Open the pages of Jackie, Hi or Blue Jeans and you get a dismaying picture of children under intense sexual pressure, caught up in a school life where fancying a boy or girl is taken to the point of obsession. Children's parties now demand a diet of pop music, even the Brownies have started their own discos. It's all a far cry from Enid Blyton and the Famous Five.[6]

Moreover the Government's AIDS campaign on television means that children are exposed to information about this from a very early age. The International Planned Parenthood Federation claims that primary school children may grow up as 'a generation of sexual cripples' because of the powerful images they see on television linking sex with gravestones, skulls and death. Many children believe that they 'can never get married and never have sex'.[7] The whole idea of sex has become ugly and dangerous – an odd concoction of a smash and grab raid, a groupie crush and a gamble with death. In school playgrounds even little children may hurl abuse at each other such as 'queers', 'tarts' and most recently 'AIDS-merchants'.

The intense social pressure towards even earlier heterosexuality, the fear of AIDS, and open discussion of child sexual abuse are the sort of problems that make many adults yearn to go back to the illusory simplicity of that 'golden age', when sex was something a mummy and daddy did when they loved each other very much and wanted to make a baby.

One in every three primary school teachers in England has seen children engaged in sexual activity or imitating sexual intercourse. They usually try to divert the children and rarely discuss it with them. A teacher who became aware of two 5-year-olds simulating sexual intercourse on the Wendy House carpet said briskly, 'I can hear the kettle boiling.' Another, faced with the same situation, said she knocked at the door and announced: 'It's Postman Pat. I've got a letter for you.'[8]

While some teachers cope with heterosexual activity by ignoring it or by diverting children's attention, many others react with shock to children who simply use words like 'gay' or 'lesbian'. Joanna, aged 4, trying to placate 3-year-old Sally who was sulking because Peter refused to play Daddy in the Wendy house, suggested 'Let's play lesbians instead.' Her outraged teacher demanded that Joanna never use 'that word' again, or talk about her home life in nursery school. Though some mothers share the attitudes of these teachers, many of the women who talked to us say that they don't want to deal with sex with their own children in the way their mothers did with them. They were often secretive and embarrassed and offered a romanticised version of sex and birth:

My mother's attitude was that any discussion of sex was taboo. Yet despite her beetroot cheeks she would try to give me the answers to my questions.

She said married people kiss and then a baby came. I really believed that kissing made babies. And I thought it was impossible to have a baby unless you were married.

She never told me how babies were conceived – only that a tiny baby grew out of love.

DISBELIEF AND CONFUSION

On the other hand, you can give children the facts but they may not believe you. The novelist Maeve Binchey, in her autobiography

A Portrait of the Artist as a Young Girl,[9] says that her mother had never had the facts of life revealed to her so she made up her mind to explain them clearly to her own children. She went into great detail about conception. But her daughter refused to believe any of it: 'I decided that this was absolutely impossible.' She thought her mother must be mentally ill and told her father so. When he suggested tentatively that there might be something in what her mother had said, she concluded that he was being 'amazingly loyal' to his deluded wife.

Children may rigidly resist any discussion about sex if the subject is left till an age when, perhaps under peer pressure, they feel embarrassed by it or see parental concern about giving sex education as an effort at indoctrination (which, of course, it may be). Val's two daughters are sixteen and fourteen and her son ten. She is now very open with them about sex, but remembers back to a time when her whole approach was more guarded: 'I once gave them a book *Where do Babies Come From?* – very tasteful, beautiful water-colours. They said, "Yuk! Why did you put this disgusting book in our bedroom?"' She is also concerned that they have negative ideas about birth: 'I don't seem to have got across to them the beauty of birth,' and she adds regretfully: 'They think I'm freakish about it. When I say I enjoyed having them they say they don't believe it, and that it must be terrible, terrifying pain.' She is aware that they think this because it is what all their friends at school believe, and consider her positive approach to birth just one of their mother's oddities.

Amelia told her son about pregnancy and childbirth when he was 6, an age before which it seems that most children have already asked questions about birth: 'He said that he didn't believe me as he had no wiggly things (sperm) in his willy. He wanted to see his Dad's.' She is pregnant and now he has been to see the scan and has felt the baby move, he says he supposes it *might* be true.

Children may be confused between urine and semen and between the anus, urethra and vagina, 'a spaghetti-junction of plumbing lodged within the female trunk', as one man remembers thinking of it as a 10-year-old at prep-school.[10]

Never having experienced an orgasm (an all-important Fact which is usually omitted from the explanations offered to children) I assumed that when the daddy had put his ... etc., he dispatched the seed on its voyage by doing a sort of pee inside the mummy. As a result, I would often stand in the 'bog' beyond the boot room staring with wonderment – and a little anxiety – at the stream of what I understood to be baby-seeds gushing wastefully down the urinal wall. I imagined them struggling blindly to fulfil their destiny while they drowned in the school's sewage system. I had been told that millions of them were produced at a time, and the spectacle of these numberless hoards of my children, dead before they were alive splashing twice or thrice daily down the cracked and stained channel of a common jakes was worrying, though I marvelled at my inexhaustible springs of fertility.

If children don't get the facts at the right time they develop their own ideas about how babies are conceived and born – the commonest being that the mother ate something which then grew into the baby in her stomach. They may think that her stomach has to burst like a balloon, or that the baby is cut out, or born through her umbilicus or anus. Little boys do not know about the existence of the vagina unless they are told. Little girls may know, and have probably explored their vaginas, but need to be assured that the vagina opens up and gets bigger so that the baby can slide through. It is also important that children are given the word 'clitoris'.

Even after 2 and 3-year-olds have had it carefully explained to them that, 'Daddy put a seed in a special hole' and that the womb is a different place from the place where the food goes, they may continue to believe that the baby entered through the mouth and is in the stomach, because this process relates to their own experience of eating, feeling full, and having a big tummy.

When children are not given accurate information the imaginative child, curious about what is happening, tends to invent birth stories in which fanciful explanations provided by other children or adults may be incorporated. Such explanations may involve modern technology: 'Babies come from the frozen food counter in the supermarket, just like TV dinners. All the Mommies do is warm them up when they want them.'[11] They may justify the doctor's role: 'Mommies just get in bed with a big stomach like a balloon. The doctor makes her tummy go down. He hands the baby to the Mommy and says, "Here's your baby."' They may be imaginative guesses because other explanations have been rejected as false: 'They come parcel post, like things from Sears and Roebuck. My Mommy tole me that storks bring 'em. But I know that isn't true 'cause we have lots of babies around my neighbourhood . . . but I haven't seen *one single stork*!' Children sometimes continue to hold on to birth myths long after they have been given accurate information.

Ronald and Juliette Goldman interviewed children between 5 and 15 in different countries and found that they created their own stories and explanations on the basis of inadequate sex education.[12] Before the age of 7, children often knew that babies grew in their mummies' tummies, but also might believe that they opened their mouths to feed every time the mother ate, that when she watched TV the baby could see, too, through a little slit in her navel, that when it was time to be born the navel opened up, and that afterwards there was a long thing called a 'young Billy Cord' that had to be cut. By the age of 11 they said things like, 'The egg and the squirm, when they meet, they kind of fight it out. The bossier one wins. If the egg wins, it's a girl. If the squirm wins, it's a boy.'

The Goldmans call for accurate and detailed sex education 'with warm feelings and positive attitudes'. Children are capable of understanding procreation by the time they are five but are often given only snippets of information. This is irresponsible behaviour on the part of adults.

Nor is it enough to tell a child about conception and birth once and think, 'That's it, I've done it.' Children at 2 and 3 years old understand things like this best when they are part of a story often repeated which is related to the child's own experience and life-story, such as 'what happened when you grew inside my womb' and 'the story of the day you were born'. Anne's daughter is 2 and she told us: 'I conceived her on the pill. Now I'm writing a book for

Alice in which I tell her everything, why she was conceived and born and how I was feeling.' (She was unmarried and went through a lot of heart-searching.) Angela says when she was pregnant her two and a half year old talked freely about the baby in the womb and how it would get out: 'Even now (she's four years old) it is a story she asks for again and again at bed-time – how *she* was in my womb.'

Sheila's book, *Being Born*, with photographs by the Swedish photographer Nilsson, can provide the vivid words, phrases and visual material on which such personal accounts can be based. Pregnancy can be described as a journey which the mother and child shared, and birth as an adventure they experienced together.[13]

There is a tendency to offer children the facts about birth either in terms of 'nuts and bolts' anatomy and physiology – about what is put where – or in behavioural terms of what happens when a baby brother or sister is born – with the main focus on the arrival of a sibling. Both approaches are necessary for a small child. But this other aspect of birth, presenting the story as part of the child's autobiography, is an important element in sex education because the factual, emotional and behavioural elements are fused. It becomes a story which has personal meaning for the child, one which she can take and make her own. When we do this we create a unity between biology and culture, integrating the facts with discussion of relationships, and enabling further exploration of values.

If we neglect this we are still communicating values but in a way which either indicates that sex is just biological – nothing to do with feelings – or that we are telling this story anxiously only in order to minimise the child's jealousy of the new baby.

Once mothers have told children how babies get out, it seems that some are happy to leave further sex education more or less to chance. This happens particularly with boys. Abby says: 'When he was seven he asked me how babies were born. I told him, "The man puts his penis in the woman's vagina and they enjoy it very much." He became very quiet.' Then she left him to acquire the rest of his sex education from schoolfriends. He is now eight and a chorister at an English cathedral school. 'He gets his sex education in the old-fashioned dirty book way,' she told us. 'The older choristers all have girlie magazines.' In the USA the National Clearing House on Family Planning discloses that *Playboy Advisor* is the most widely read sex education source for boys. Like many other women, the same mother approached her daughter's sex education, however, with more concern. She gave her a cartoon book at the age of four which 'described all the functions factually.' Girls are seen as more vulnerable. It is girls who menstruate and have to cope with that – and girls who get pregnant.

It may also be that a mother talking to her daughter finds it easier to identify with her and to say, in effect, 'When you are older you will be like me. You will have periods. You can have a baby.' She may feel that male sexual experience is beyond her comprehension. Many of the mothers with adolescent sons joke and laugh about their son's sexuality as if it resembles that of a male animal in rut. Though some women expressed surprise about their son's sensitivity and tenderness with women, it seems that once he is adolescent a son usually becomes 'one of the boys', an alien creature, more or less beyond control.

Children have always picked up information about sex, babies and a host of other topics, from overhearing adult conversations. In Letty Cottin Pogrebin's perceptive book *Family Politics: Love and Power on an Intimate Frontier*[14] this is called 'eavesdropping on reality'. In many families there is a special coded way of speaking which carries with it all the mystery and excitement of conspiracy. It involves abbreviations and initial letters and evasive terms to mask the reality of whatever is being discussed in front of the children. Many children quickly pick up this coded language. Letti Pogrebin tells how in her family her parents always resorted to speaking Yiddish when the conversation was about sex or divorce. This was the only time they ever spoke Yiddish, and the children always pricked up their ears.

COMMUNICATING ATTITUDES

Women find that giving children the facts about how babies are born is only the beginning. Education about birth is not just a matter of telling the facts – and of what I have heard described as 'the valuable moment in the bathroom' (answering questions about nakedness, breasts, pubic hair, penises, putting in a tampon) – but of communicating *attitudes*. Children also need to be aware of and to grow to understand the emotions involved. That means being able to explore often complex feelings – of curiosity, excitement, fear, shame, guilt and rejection. It also entails exploring the significance of birth in terms of human relationships, and a transition in the development of these relationships – a child who becomes for the first time an older brother or sister, the mother's role with a new-born baby, and other people's interest and concern about these processes.

Most people today have grown up to see birth as a medical crisis and something which women are powerless to control. This view of birth is fuelled by the media. An analysis of American TV soap operas reveals that half of all the pregnancies in them result in miscarriage and 16 per cent in the mother's death.

In the past in many families children would quite naturally be around when babies were born at home. The thrill of preparations, the eager waiting, seeing what the mother did in labour and the meeting with the baby were all part of it. Though in some traditional cultures, as we have seen is the case in Ireland, children are excluded from birth, in many others small children have always been present to share in one of the most powerful events of human life. An anthropologist writing about field-work with the Seri Indians of North America remarked that at one birth she had counted sixteen women and children 'most of whom were sitting around in an aura of fiesta'.[15]

In fact, in many traditional societies not only are children present at birth, but older ones take an active part in giving the mother comfort. In South Africa, the Zulu have young girls prepare the birth hut and make it beautiful, and believe that it is good for children to be present at both birth and death so that they can understand the value of life.[16]

Even in societies where children do not witness birth, once girls are teenage it may be taken for granted that they have a place in childbirth. Though in Mormon polygynous households which

Drawings by children who were present at birth

Girl of 8 years 9 months who was present at birth. Mummy has just pushed the baby out on a bed with a flowery sheet. The whole family is there and everyone is smiling.

'The birth supper'

This is a birth party drawn by a boy of 5 years 8 months who was present at the birth. The baby has popped out and afterwards Daddy is in the kitchen cooking while smiling children are preparing for the celebration party.

112

Drawings by children who were not present at birth

'Just in case'

A birth drawing by a boy aged 10 years 6 months who was not present. Note the high-tech setting reminiscent of a torture chamber: 'things that hold her legs open', 'syringes and things' and 'air, just in case'. The mother is unsupported while the technicians concentrate on getting the baby out.

'The operating room'

This drawing is by a boy aged 10 years 3 months who also was not there. The mother is completely passive, with an intravenous drip in her arm, and the baby's head is being delivered by the doctor through a hole in a sheet. Though there is a nurse at the mother's head end her eyes are on the baby, not the mother.

conform to 'the Principle' young children are not present, once girls are married at the age of fifteen they join the group of women helping during childbirth along with the other sister wives who have not yet had babies.

Most children in modern Western society are denied the opportunity to learn about birth at first-hand. The result is that when a woman has her first baby she has little or no understanding of what birth was like for her mother, her aunts and her sisters and cousins. It is something which takes place outside the home, and instead of being part of the pattern of everyday life is an obstetric event conducted by doctors in a hospital.

In childbirth classes Sheila often asks women to think back to the meanings that birth had for them as children. They remember mysterious operations and then being parted from their mothers, visiting Mummy in hospital, encountering a strange baby in a cot, and all the frightened lonely feelings that this aroused.

Some women have no memories of birth except those of *trying to find out*, and getting snippets of information about the bursting of waters, bulging bottoms and haemorrhage. As the facts were revealed they tell of their disgust and horror that women should have to swell up, push a baby out like a bowel movement, split open, bleed, and be sewn up. They often describe half overheard accounts of obstetric difficulties as women mourned them in discussion together. Thus birth represents to them humiliation, danger, agonising pain, catastrophe. Above all, they learn of women's passivity and suffering.

WELCOMING THE NEW BABY

Keeping children away from birth, trying to shield them from knowledge about it, is a way of inculcating in them learned helplessness and fear in the face of a significant life event. Women who remember a young brother or sister being born at home have very different stories to tell. The emotions they describe, rather than being those of the isolated ex-baby, are those *shared* with others in the family. There was anticipation, waiting, mounting excitement, and then the wonder of the new baby and being able to hold her for the first time. Women who decide to have their babies at home often make this decision partly because they want their other children present. They consider it an important aspect of their education and a major life experience. Increasingly, those having hospital births are asking if their other children can be there, too. About twenty years ago fathers were admitted at delivery for the first time, often very reluctantly and with dire warnings from professionals about how they would feel disgusted, faint and never want sex with the woman again. When it is suggested that children watch their mothers giving birth professionals may react with shock and disgust. 'A sacred taboo is being broken.'[17] The ban on children represents the last bastion against family participation.

Talking to children about childbirth may start with facts about pregnancy and birth, but it is important to realise that a 3-year-old may understand the mechanics about birth and delivery and still have no inkling of the emotions that may be aroused, not only by the birth, but by the coming of the baby. Children also need to be prepared for the highly charged atmosphere and drama of birthing, the sounds and movements the mother may make, the boring interval when nothing exciting seems to be happening, for the appearance of blood – which to a small child invariably means injury – for the bursting or leaking of the waters, the actions of the midwife or doctor and the appearance of the new-born baby, who may be purple, blotched, bruised, with a squashed nose and a receding forehead. Once the baby has arrived it becomes the centre of attention. The ex-baby may have to cope with intense feelings of rejection, with the apparent withdrawal of love and attention, and with surges of hatred against this child who has replaced her and who causes complete disruption in the family.

A woman who wants to have her children present at birth has to face up to other issues, too. She needs to confront the implications for the child if the birth is not easy, perhaps of seeing her in pain and coping with crisis – even of the baby being in poor condition at birth, or not breathing. Women who decide to have their children with them at birth stress values of openness and honesty. They also emphasise the importance of this experience to reinforce relationships in the family.

But there is more to it even than that. The essence of the moral dilemma for parents is 'whether children should not experience all of life, whatever it brings, on their own terms'.[18] When we attempt to shield children from birth and death we often leave them with nightmarish fantasies about what occurred.

> Real things can be dealt with and can be growth-producing. Nightmares remain in the world of fantasy ... By restricting children's experiences we deprive them of the opportunity to take the reality of that experience and use it in ways appropriate to them.[19]

Sheila was watching a film of home birth in which two older children were present and where the mother wept with tears of joy as the baby slid out, and then continued to weep – shaken to the depths. When the film had finished, one of the women watching it with her commented, 'I'm not sure that I would have wanted my children there. It must have been upsetting for that little girl.' Immediately another woman said, 'But did you see? It was her daughter (about seven years old) who came straight to her and put her arms around her.' And we all realised what had happened. The father patted his wife on the shoulder and was looking at the baby. The midwives were busy. It was the little girl who responded to her mother and gave her all her attention, standing with her cheek against her mother's, wet with tears. The two hugged each other, close in a way different from any they had been before. Instead of being treated as a child who could not possibly understand about feelings, she was made welcome to enter and play her own satisfying and meaningful part in this essentially adult experience. To this child were revealed some of the deepest emotions an adult woman can have, and the two women shared this peak moment together.

In being completely open about birth and in having the older children present if they wish to be, parents give expression to their conviction that we have within us the strength to face reality in a practical way, and they hope to communicate these values to their children.

Some women also see the child's presence at birth as being one element in communicating the dignity and power of womanhood. They want their sons as well as their daughters to grow up aware of the strength and creativity of women's bodies, and not to think of birth as something that is done to women by doctors but as an active expression of life-giving power. Feminist midwives and doctors sometimes take their own children with them when they attend births for the same reason. They want to demedicalise childbirth for their children and welcome the opportunity of them being in a group of people who are helping and sharing in the birth.

This is the reverse of the view of parental responsibility as one of filtering all experience of the world through to the child, the German view of the *Kinderparadies* that keeps the child sheltered from reality.[20]

When adults try to cocoon children from profound emotions – suffering, striving, loss and other intense feelings – we deny them the right to experience them. The alternative is to help a child confront and deal with reality. Where there is pain or grieving, for example, the child can witness the force of human compassion and love, see how people reach out to help each other, and be part of that caring community. It is an important way of learning about human values.

But, of course, many births nowadays are virtually surgical operations. One in every four or five births in the United States, and one in ten or eleven births in Britain, is by Caesarean section. Children also need to know what happens in Caesarean birth. A mother whose baby was born by Caesarean section may choose to talk to her child about how she felt it important to be awake so that she could welcome her baby, and so had a pain-killer which did not send her to sleep. She may tell her how Daddy or a loved woman friend was there right through and saw her born, how he or she helped, and how everyone worked together. She will tell her child how she felt when the baby was lifted out, how she touched her – and why she believed it was important that she should be able to greet her child in this way. Or she may explain that a sudden decision had to be made to do a Caesarean section so she had to be put to sleep for a short while, and how Daddy held the baby and stroked her, and then she describes her first sight of the baby as she woke up, how she felt, how she reached out for the baby, and about all the people who helped her have the baby safely and later cared for them both.

As they grow older, children can also be told about the pros and cons of this way of birth and that many people today are concerned that there is an epidemic of Caesarean sections in the West. It is not enough to give a child the facts. By ourselves questioning the health care system, we encourage the child to question too. And there are vital questions to be considered here: Should this be so? Is this what we really want? Is it what we believe to be right?

In many hospitals nowadays older siblings can be taken to meet a new baby in the special care nursery, and instead of just viewing the baby through glass, they can touch, hold her hand, stroke and if she is well enough, even cuddle her. Children tend to be far less troubled by the technology – the tubes, catheters, ticking machines and winking lights – than adults. They see the *baby*, and questions about the electronic and other equipment only come later.

As with the subject of Caesarean births, parents can stress the caring skills and the love surrounding the baby. Our own beliefs about what it is right to do when a baby is severely handicapped or dying may be put to the test. If these have never been talked about openly between the parents themselves, if they have not explored their own moral values and shared their thoughts, it must be terribly difficult to know what to say to a child. Yet when a newborn baby is very ill or handicapped adults tend to ignore the issue from a child's perspective, and may withdraw into an adult world from which the child is painfully isolated. She can only watch their dependence on and need for each other, their sad faces, their tears, their hope and joy, as if through a translucent wall. To do this to a child is to shut her out from the possibility of sharing the experience and learning about values.

The reproductive revolution has brought other methods of making babies than the long-established flesh-to-flesh way. An estimated 20,000 babies are born in the USA every year following artificial insemination. For all these children the account 'When Mummy and Daddy cuddled each other . . .' does not hold water. As children grow and ask questions, parents need to be ready to discuss at least some of the implications of assisted reproduction, of in vitro fertilisation and embryo transfer, and the ethics of surrogate motherhood. There will be many occasions when we do not know the answers, or are confused. So we must be prepared to say 'I don't know.' We must also be willing to try and find out more, and – with the child – to acquire the knowledge on the basis of which they can make more informed value judgements. Television documentaries, articles in the press, news stories may add to the information. A good library can help. There are usually resources – institutions and individuals – in the neighbourhood who can help, too.

Women who have secondary infertility (those who have a child but become infertile subsequently) or who have miscarriages say they find one of the most difficult things about the experience is talking about it with their children. They sometimes say: 'My child is too young to understand about it, so I avoid the subject.' When the child asks questions they are evasive or try to distract her. A woman who cannot conceive or who has lost a baby through miscarriage may be in a state of permanent mourning. Every time she menstruates it is not only a sign of failure but like the death of an unborn child. So it is not surprising that talking to children about it is difficult and painful. It takes courage to explain to a child something of what you are feeling, and to be open about discussing painful personal experience like infertility and miscarriage.

CHILDREN'S SEXUALITY

It can also take courage to deal openly with children's own sexuality, particularly now that, with all the publicity about sexual abuse, any mention of children's sexuality becomes suspect – as though it offers men an excuse to abuse them because 'they were asking for it'. But children *do* have sexual feelings, even though these feelings are different from those of adults. We need to be able to talk about 'warm' and 'tickling' and 'excited' feelings the child

119

may experience and to reassure children that masturbation is all right.

Open masturbation, as we have seen already, is a special problem for many parents. Laura complains that her 4-year-old daughter masturbates openly. Rosemary's 4-year-old son,

> does understand that some parts of our bodies and some things we do are 'private' and not to be done or mentioned outside the family – in other words, he's welcome to play with his penis or talk about intercourse but in his own home and with us. Other adults treat these things as private and so must he, though he's not sure why – neither am I.

As recently as the 1920s children were forcibly restrained from masturbation. Childrearing experts recommended that they were tied up so that they could not reach themselves or – the more 'modern' experts – that they should simply be distracted because it was merely natural curiosity and was really nothing to do with sex. A letter received at the Children's Bureau in May 1927 (the Children's Bureau was the first advice centre for mothers in the US) describes how a baby girl, 10 months old,

> had gotten into the habit of crossing her legs and rocking to and fro and sort of bearing down at the same time, and somehow or other I can't seem to make her stop. I have taken her to two baby specialists and they call it 'Masturbation' and suggested putting a stick (or knee crutch) between her legs, but somehow or other it seems to do no good. I have even gone so far as to tie her legs to her crib and also to her high chair when she is sitting, but she seems to be able to rock and breathe heavy just the same. I am at my wits end, and feel that I cannot endure watching her any longer, as it is a most disgusting thing and is making a nervous wreck of me.

The 'modern' reply was that many babies go through such a phase and the mother should bring herself to the frame of mind when you can regard it impersonally. The danger to the child ... is in making the child self-conscious and in calling her attention to the habit in such a way that she becomes so impressed with it that she will not give it up. If you offer her a toy to distract her attention ... you may find that this will help.

Today's mothers may be equally disconcerted by evidence of children's sexuality and their uninhibited joy in it.

I'd started bathing with my infant son for sheer convenience, and we continued to enjoy the closeness of a shared bath. But one day, when he was almost 3, I was startled by the realisation that he was rhythmically thrusting his erect penis into my belly button. I hardly knew whether to laugh or cry. The innocent pleasure ended for me. I finished up the bath as casually as I could, knowing that life had pushed us forward on a path we couldn't retrace. It was our last bath together.[21]

Other mothers must have been similarly frightened off by children's exuberant sexuality. It seems sad that women should be so surprised and alarmed by it. Maybe this is because many people assume that children are not sexual.

It is understandable that this mother was upset. She wisely did not show her horror, finished the bath casually and made the decision not to bath with him again. That is, she drew boundaries around what she found was acceptable. Just as we make it clear that we will not tolerate being bitten or hit, though the child may be enjoying it, so we can make it clear that there are other things we don't like, too.

We owe it to children in the same way to get them to understand that though we may be quite happy about masturbation and their pleasure in their bodies, other people may react negatively to children's overt sexuality.

PERIODS

Though women find it easy to tell their children about birth, the subject of menstruation is more difficult. They are concerned that the thought of bleeding may disgust or frighten them, and some are embarrassed – perhaps even humiliated – when a child happens to come into the bathroom when they are changing tampons. When her two-year old daughter asked 'What's that?' one mother answered, 'chalk', then worried that her child might start pushing chalk inside her.

Martha said she told her 6-year-old daughter: 'I have a flow of blood to show I'm not pregnant. It means I haven't started a baby yet and it's getting ready for him.' But this woman is worried that: 'Blood still equals danger and pain in a child's mind, and I don't like her being there when I change a towel. I feel embarrassed.'

Many women have grown up thinking of menstruation as necessary but messy and somehow shameful. It is not something you have general conversation about in mixed company. It belongs with secrets about our bodies like emptying the bowels and sweating, matters concerning nasal mucus and earwax. It is all about *dirt*, and since women are the ones who menstruate we are stuck with this dirt. We are contaminated by it. Some women hate their bodies when they have periods. It is not just pain; they hate the whole filthy process.

One woman was shocked when her mother told her about menstruation at the age of ten and presented it as an 'unpleasant duty'. She was so disgusted at the idea of blood coming out that she felt faint and had to go and lie down. Her main worry was that her brothers might find out but she was reassured by thinking that if she did not know when her mother had her period her brothers would not know when she did.

In *The Wise Wound* Penelope Shuttleworth and Peter Redgrove present a contrasting picture, celebrating the regular cycle of fertility as part of the moon-rhythm in which women are in touch with the flow of nature.[22] Yet there is a paradox, in that feeling disgust and shame about menstruation is characteristic of many cultures in which it is also seen as a symbol of human power.

Jamaican women say that when you start a period you 'see your health'. It is acknowledgement of the vitality of a woman's body and her strength.

Because a woman's flow of blood is powerful, it is often thought of as dangerous to men, who will become ill if they touch a menstruating woman or even cross her path. Among the Thonga of East Africa, a girl goes to any woman she chooses – not necessarily her own mother – and tells her she has started her periods. Then three or four girls who all started at about the same time live together in a hut for a month where they are taught about sex. Every morning older women lead them to a pool to bathe, singing bawdy songs and driving away with sticks any man who appears in the vicinity. They say that if a man sees a girl during this month of seclusion he will go blind. After four weeks or so the girls go home and there is a feast.

A girl's first period is announced to all and sundry in some cultures because it is a matter of pride. In parts of Southern India the news is broadcast over the village tannoy system so that preparations can be made for the celebration that follows. It is also the sign that a girl is ready for a much more detailed understanding of sex. Traditionally in Japan it was the time when a specially knowledgeable woman came to the house and discussed subjects like sex and birth with her and her mother.

In some cultures the first period is the occasion for a stern warning against getting pregnant, and girls may be carefully chaperoned from then on, or may simply be given the cryptic message which perplexed one of Sheila's friends: 'Don't let boys *do anything* to you.' When she was in northern Thailand girls told her that their mothers lectured them about avoiding all physical contact with boys from then on until the wrist-binding ceremony which meant they were engaged to be married: 'We must not let even our boy cousins touch us. Our mothers worry that we will go to the night market and meet boys there, so they always watch us.'

Fifty years ago in Western countries menstruation was also a secret between a mother and her daughters, and it had to be kept from the men of the house at all costs. When a girl had her first period she was given a serious talk about the risk of pregnancy though she was often not told how this could result: 'From now on you must not let men touch you' or 'Never let a boy kiss you.' As a result girls were sometimes terrified that a kiss or cuddle would lead to pregnancy. One woman remembers:

> I was 11 years old when it happened. I was reading in bed and realised I was bleeding. I went into my mother to tell her. She wasn't a very nice person. (Because someone's a mother doesn't make them a good person.) She slapped me on the behind and said: 'Don't ever bring a bastard home.' I said: 'What did you do that for?' She said: 'It's the proper thing to do. It's traditional'.

After the Second World War a variety of leaflets, books and magazine articles appeared which could be left about casually so that a girl thought to be just about to start her periods could learn about how a body worked without the mother needing to have an embarrassing conversation.

The 1960s and 1970s were the age of a sometimes rather self-conscious sexual enlightenment, and saw the celebration of the first period in some families. Mothers sometimes greeted a daughter with: 'Congratulations! Now you are a woman!', even arranged menstrual parties, and fathers brought home bouquets of flowers to mark the event.

With improved nutrition during and after the war, now girls started to have their periods earlier, and some now start while they are still attending primary school. In the mid-nineteenth century the average age of puberty in girls was 16. By 1978 it was less than 13. Now girls have their first period when they are 10 years old or younger.[23] It is important to prepare girls *and* boys to understand menstruation and to develop positive attitudes to it by the age of 8 or 9. It is when this instruction is left to the last minute that parents act in a way which they may later regret, and that girls are bewildered and frightened about what seems to be a shameful disease. One woman who had no idea what was happening to her said:

I just stood and screamed and my mother called out: 'What's happening?' and came running. Then she sat me down and explained that this would now happen once a month – just a biological explanation.

I had big problems with my periods and was put on the pill to regulate them. Mummy mistimed it. It was ghastly ... My daughter is three and she already knows what a tampon is. She says, 'When I'm a big girl I can wear a tampon.' That must be because they are around and she's inquisitive. I think children should start to have that kind of information early enough so that it's perfectly normal ... If you can't talk to your mum about periods, you can't talk to her about very much, can you?

Another woman says she had been given a book to read by her aunt, but: 'Nobody had really prepared me for having my first period.' When she saw she was bleeding she was acutely embarrassed and didn't tell anyone for three days. She stuck her pants into corners, and remembers sitting in a concert wondering the whole time whether she had leaked. Her mother found the pants and said: 'Why didn't you tell me you *weren't very well*?'

That's how it was in those days. She was very affectionate, very sympathetic when I had painful periods, but we never talked about it at all. I was one of the first girls in my form at school to have periods and didn't like the fact that it marked me apart. I felt I was a child having to cope with something grown-up.

I have a daughter aged 12 and I've talked to her openly about these things ever since she was a little girl. I did work for sanitary protection firms when I had a job as a market researcher, and the house was awash with their products.

She reckons her daughter has learned about such things very easily.

Girls also need to be prepared for the changes in the consistency of cervical mucus and vaginal lubrication which starts *before* they have their first period. Many of them are anxious when they discover patches of mucus in their pants and believe they have contracted a disease – which they may feel has been caused by masturbation. In her novel, *The Radiant Way*, Margaret Drabble describes Liz at puberty:

> Her mother being mad, and madly fastidious, there was nobody to tell her anything about the onset of adult life, of bodily changes. She knew about menstruation from school friends, advertisements in magazines, and labels on discreet packets of sanitary towels laid sideways in the chemists. But nobody talked to her about the changes that precede menstruation. She convinced herself at the age of 11, 12, that she was suffering from venereal disease. She had only the dimmest notions of what this was, notions gleaned from small type-faced notices on the doors of public lavatories and from consulting the dictionary and *Pears Cyclopedia*. But she knew that it was shameful, too shameful ever to mention to another human being. And she believed it had affected her, as a vengeance for her wicked imaginings ... Miserably she had stared at the stains in her bottle-green regulation school knickers. She would try to wash them, surreptitiously, before putting them in the linen basket for her mother to inspect. She would crouch drying them before the bar of an electric fire, guiltily, dreading that Shirley would catch her at it, braving the strange, disturbing, wet, woolly, squidgy, sexual smell.[24]

Most of the women who talked to us are very clear that they want to be open and honest and to give their children straightforward factual information about menstruation whenever they ask questions about it. Becky's daughter is now 12 years old, but she says:

> When smaller she asked me about some tampons she'd seen in the bathroom. Basically I explained what they were, and since then she's asked more questions, often in more depth. Now she's 12 and her own periods have started she knows the 'mechanics' but still enquires about emotional aspects. I take it as a compliment that she brings her friends to me for a 'talk' if they are worried and can't talk to their own parents.

Children may at first be incredulous about menstrual bleeding and the way women deal with it. 'You're not going to push *that* up your bum?' one little boy asked his mother, disbelievingly. Boys have penises, but women can actually insert these things like tiny white mice inside their bodies and then walk around as if nothing has happened! It is a conjuring trick which men cannot emulate. Rachel says her son, eight years old, is always asking what Tampax are for: 'I caught him trying to "use" one. So I explained what a period was and why I needed them. He listened intently and just smiled.' She says he has told her that he understands, but one is left with the feeling that perhaps he feels deprived of something.

When girls already know about menstruation and understand that once they are ovulating regularly they can get pregnant, they often look forward to having periods with eager anticipation as a sign of being grown-up. There may be great competition at school, girls who have started forming little cliques in which they share adult secrets – and the rest feeling very out of it.

Mothers often find themselves caught in a double-bind in the values they communicate to children about periods. On the one hand they wish to present a positive image of womanhood, and the energy and power of a woman's body. On the other, they personally may suffer from pre-menstrual tension, feel bloated and in pain while their periods last, and want children to be understanding about this. So what they offer children is a mixed message. They do not want to talk about having periods as if it were a disability, but when they have periods they may *feel* disabled. It is all very well celebrating a girl's first period and telling her 'Now you are a woman!' but what happens when she has to cope with the discomfort and mess of periods or if she is doubled up in pain, and how do boys react to the experience. Is it 'yucky'? Is she trying to skive work? If having periods is so marvellous for a woman, why is she lying in bed curled round a hot water bottle? And why are they soaking the sheets to get the blood stains out?

The whole area of sexuality and reproduction bristles with topics about which adults have strong moral values and they want to impart these to children. North American women who are anti-abortion can give their children 'Grace the Pro-life Doll' who croons an anti-abortion message. She sings 'Jesus loves little children' and says 'God knew me even before I was born' when hugged.[25]

Abortion can be one of the most difficult subjects to discuss with children. Yet we may believe it is important for them to realise that women must be free to choose whether or not they have babies, that birth control is not 100 per cent effective, and that sometimes a baby starts to grow inside a woman when its birth would bring great distress and the child's life be miserable.

Homosexuality, too, raises strong and conflicting feelings. One woman said: 'My daughter watched a programme about homosexuality being a "normal" variation and how this should not bar such people from having custody of children. I believe this is not right and was annoyed at its portrayal.' In contrast, another mother told us:

We have a friend who is gay and has had years of torment, an unhappy marriage and a breakdown. We explain to our son that if society was caring and fair, none of this would have happened and our friend would have been judged on his merits as kind, funny and loveable, and not by a silly label.

When we talk about sex the opportunity is there to help children think about their experiences and how people can care for each other with sensitivity and awareness. Out of adults' openness and willingness to discuss these issues and to listen to children's thoughts and feelings, out of such sharing, human values of lasting importance in that child's life will grow.

CHAPTER
7

FRIENDS: THEIRS AND YOURS

Most moral rules in religions and codes of ethics all over the world are to do with how people should behave towards each other. Children are given instruction in these when they are considered old enough to understand them. It usually begins with inculcation of basic socially acceptable behaviour and ordinary politeness, with consideration for others and respect for parents and other adults. Formal rules apart, however, children actually learn more about morality through actively engaging in relationships and finding that their behaviour is approved or disapproved. 'No, you mustn't bite/hit/grab toys away from Judy. You should play *nicely* together'; 'Give auntie a kiss'; 'Say "ta"'; 'Be a good boy and do what your teacher tells you'; 'You really *love* your little baby brother. Share your sweeties and bricks with him'; 'It's not kind to copy that man who can't walk properly'; 'Take it in turns'; 'Be quiet so that Mummy can have a rest'.

Of a list of twenty-six kinds of problem behaviour in children drawn up by a psychologist, over half are directly to do with the child's relationships with others – things like 'refuses to be part of family events', 'speaks negatively about me' and 'shows off' – and all the remaining items in the list have an effect on relationships or are an expression of them, ranging from 'resists toilet training' to 'dresses inappropriately'.[1]

When mothers talked to us about the values they wanted to hand on to their children and about those the children picked up of which they disapproved, a great deal of what they had to say was to do with their children's friends and playmates and with suitable and unsuitable friendships.

MAKE-BELIEVE FRIENDS

The first friends in a child's life may be very elusive and hard to control. They are make-believe friends. Some children invent a make-believe friend from the age of 2 or soon after. This person is either completely invisible or takes the form of a stick, a bit of blanket, a teddy bear or doll. Up to one third of children have an imaginary companion like this and parents learn to adapt to the presence of this invisible child in the family.[2] Children find they can exploit this playmate's capacity for mischief and wrong-doing.

Maya Angelou describes the effects of her son Clive's invisible friend:

> Clive explained to all who would listen that he, Red Rider and Fluke were going to ride their horses to the moon and talk to God, who was an old Black man who played the guitar. Red Rider was a Western character from books and Fluke was Clive's invisible miscreant friend. Fluke made him laugh aloud at his mischief. He was able to do things Clive could not do, and Fluke did them with impunity. If a lamp was overturned and broken, it was because Fluke was walking around on the lampshade somewhere. When the bathtub ran over and turned the tiled floor into a shallow pool, Fluke had gone to the bathroom after Clive left and turned the spigot on.
>
> Vainly I tried to explain the difference between lying and making up a story, but decided it was more important that Clive keep his non-existent buddy to lessen the loneliness of an only child. I liked to listen from the kitchen as he told Fluke goodnight stories and when, in his morning bath, he laughed outright as he warned his friend against indulging in trouble-making antics.[3]

Fantasy like this is not simply escapism. It is a way of making sense of the world and preparing to handle the challenges it presents. Small children rehearse reality in imaginative play, internalising the moral rules laid down by adults and evolving their own. It enables them to practise behaving in morally variable ways; an imaginary friend provides the basis for an exploration in morality. They may, in a similar way, talk about themselves in the third person and comment on and criticise their own behaviour: 'Tom mustn't steal the chocolates' and, reaching out to take a chocolate, '*Naughty* Tom!' Tom 1 knows the rules, but Tom 2 can't resist temptation, does wrong and is then criticised – or even smacked – by Tom 1. Especially when children are solitary, a relationship with an imaginary friend or with themselves as if in the third person may continue for a long time.

CHILDREN'S REAL FRIENDS

Whatever problems parents experience with imaginary friends (and they can make life very complicated) *real* friends are often far worse. Women tend to attribute bad behaviour in their children, particularly swearing, to the influence of unsuitable friends – children at playgroup, kindergarten and school.

This parental disapproval of friends can increase their attraction for a child. As one mother says: 'It's rather like unsuitable boy-friends. Let's face it, the more critical your parents were about a particular boy, the more attractive and wonderful he became.' And another woman:

> Our eldest, Sarah (aged 9), became very friendly with a little girl who was virtually allowed to do exactly what she wanted. Not only that, but she had everything bought for her, too. It was very hard to cope with such a different way of life. We've always been very strict on things like pocket money and we sounded so mean compared with Donna's family, where money was handed out on request.'

This mother decided to stick to her guns, but was careful not to criticise Donna and her parents: 'Sarah accepts now that we're not going to change our views on things and that Donna's parents have just as much right not to change their's either.'[4]

Another child, aged six, became friendly with a boy at school who was being brought up 'in a very macho way': 'Things came to a head when Thomas brought his new penknife round to show Daniel and had all the blades open, stabbing a tree in the garden, only inches away from our 3-year-old daughter.' This woman spoke to the boy's mother about it and Thomas was never allowed out with the knife again.

Parents may discover that their children are watching horror films on video at another child's house, or are allowed to play outside in a dangerous street, or that there is very rough play unsupervised by adults. English mothers are often worried that their children are learning bad language and ways of speaking which are incorrect. Though there have been enormous changes since the 1950s, and radio and TV announcers are no longer plummy, the class system in British society is still strong. As soon as anyone opens their mouth to speak they can often be placed in terms of class. The Queen's English is seen by middle-class parents as oiling the social wheels and giving educational advantages.

Swearing is the most blatant demonstration of crude language. Children sometimes enjoy swearing because they know it shocks their parents. Most mothers say that they ignore it. Barbara's son, aged six, came home from school 'using bad language and singing rude songs.'

> I explained that I would prefer he didn't use (this language) in my presence or in front of his brother and sister. The fact that I didn't react shocked or in a more interested way took away a lot of the pleasure for him, and I feel he soon got bored with it.

Some women explain what the words mean and ask their children if that is what they really wanted to say, but others jib at this. One woman got rid of the TV set because her daughter, aged 2, 'started to notice the violence and bad language and that was enough for us, because it causes a double standard in the home'. Parents may feel so strongly about it that they put an end to children's friendships.

Outside the home children represent the standards of the home. A child who behaves badly is exposing parental inadequacy – and because mothers are held responsible for their children's behaviour is, in effect, announcing to everyone that he has a 'bad' mother. It is an act of social humiliation. Because parents have sole responsibility for their children's behaviour, and since it is usually the mother who is with a small child for twelve hours a day, it is she who must control bad behaviour and who is blamed for it. When an adult criticises someone else's child, the child's *mother* is usually being criticised.

It is very different in traditional societies. There any adult can scold a child because everyone is agreed as to what naughtiness is. Each child is under the watchful eyes of aunts and uncles, grandparents, neighbours and other village members. In contrast, an English mother describes how 14-month-old Oliver, her friend's child, pushed 10-month-old Jane down the stairs: 'As Oliver's mother didn't seem to notice Jane's wails, I removed Oliver from the scene of the crime and told him not to do it again. That was a year ago, and Oliver's mother still hasn't spoken to me.'[5]

This absence of community control and interest in the lives of children – no village police officer, neighbourhood shopkeeper, family doctor and district nurse who knows everyone, and often no local schoolteacher – can have far-reaching consequences throughout childhood. It is safer for adults to ignore children's bad behaviour – and even violence – in public and just to let them get on with it. To do anything else is to intrude on something which is not their business. In the West children are seen as the 'property' of their parents – and typically have very few relationships with adults outside their immediate family. When a couple divorce and remarry, each may resent the discipline imposed on 'their' child not just by the other parent but, still more, by the other parent's new spouse.

Bobby, 6, had been visiting his father, divorced from his mother and remarried. When he arrived back home he had crusted blood about his nose. His mother, quite concerned, asked what had happened.

'She slapped me and made my nose bleed.'

'What on earth for? What were you doing?'

'Reading my book to her.'

'Well, why did she slap you?'

''Cause I couldn't read a hard word.'

The mother was furious. What right did that other woman have to slap her child? That evening she called her former husband in a rage, and the following day she called her lawyer.[6]

Because they represent the standards of the home, children's behaviour and physical appearance are often a source of conflict. Parents are not really so anxious that children will catch their 'death of cold' in unsuitable clothing but are concerned that what they wear reflects on themselves. The children realise this and may use it as a weapon, older ones adding to the armoury by the way they do their hair, the cosmetics they use, T-shirt messages and badges of affiliation to groups of which their parents disapprove. Victoria Gillick is a prominent British pro 'Lifer' and champion of conservative morality. Her daughter Beattie rebels against her mother's conservative attitude to sexuality by wearing 'shorts that are too short and jeans that are too tight and not wearing a bra'[7] and finally embarrassed her mother when a tabloid newspaper obtained a photograph of her topless with her boyfriend on a Greek beach on holiday.

The way parents often feel is summed up by the columnist Erma Bombeck in the 'classic motherhood speech' of a woman whose daughter plans to pierce her ears:

Scene: Mother is seated at center stage, engaged in something domestic like reading the *American Journal of Tooth Decay* and making notes in the margin.

Daughter enters stage left.

Daughter: 'What would you say if I told you I was going to pierce my ears?'

Mother: (putting book down and marking spot) 'My feeling is that your body is your own and if a girl wants to punch holes in her earlobes with an ice pick, it's strictly her own business. After all, darling, we don't live in a Victorian age any more. This is ... (current year). Every woman is a human being in her own right and it is her decision to make, and if you are thinking of piercing your ears it will be over my dead body! I did not pump you full of vitamins and fix your feet to have some bungling butcher perform back-street surgery on my only daughter.[8]

Children are for their parents, in Goffman's phrase, 'a presentation of self in everyday life' and it is brave parents who are prepared to flout social evaluation of their parenting by willingly allowing their children to present to the world an aberrant image. Rosie says her friend cannot understand why she let her 10-year-old son cut off his gorgeous auburn curls in order to have a bristle-brush 'punk' style, with tufts of hair exuding like a growth of fungi from his naked scalp. It was not just a matter of aesthetics, but of the manner in which it reflected on his mother.

DIVORCE, SEPARATION AND NEW PARTNERS

While many women complain about the unsuitable friends their children make, many *children* dislike the friends their parents have round for a meal and to whom they expect to show them off. There is no reason why children should like *our* friends any more that we should always like theirs. The difference is that whereas the children's friends don't usually move in to live in the family home, adults' friends sometimes do. One in three of all marriages today involves one partner who has been previously married, and in many of these cases this partner already has children. Added to this are the increasing numbers of cohabiting couples that include children from past marriages or relationships which have ended. The child in this situation is confronted with a boyfriend or girlfriend of the parent moving in to the house, taking up a great deal of the parent's time and assuming certain rights over the child. The child may still be grieving for the parent she has lost and is expected to accept the new adult as a replacement parent.

Remarriage and step-parenthood are not new – and the problems of children in these situations have a long history. The likelihood of losing one's spouse before old age was much higher before the eighteenth century than it is today – at any one moment up to a quarter of all households consisted of widowed people, the great majority with children[9], and remarriage was very common. In the sixteenth century, one in every three marriages involved one partner who had been married before – about the same proportion as today. Men in this situation often remarried for the sake of the children – to give them a new mother. Gilbert Burnet, Bishop of Salisbury, took a third wife in 1700 in order, he said, 'to provide a Mistris to my family and a mother to my children'.[10] Not all women wanted to be stepmothers. In 1532 the widow Katherine Andrews told her suitor, a Norwich widower, that she would marry him except for one thing: 'I woll never be step moder, for I understand ye have children, and that shuld cause us never to agree'.[11] Most people at the time believed that remarriage was difficult and 'seldom so comfortable and peaceable as the first'. An important reason for this was the attitude of the children of earlier unions who disliked their new step-parent and whose undutiful behaviour caused 'much discord and dissention'.[12] Children's resentment towards step-parents, which sometimes broke into abuse or even physical violence, is amply documented in wills and records of litigation. Children were often sent away from home in order to avoid friction between them and their step-parent. Today around half of all British children are living in some form of step-family. In fact, in the United States there will be more of these 'blended' than non-step families by the 1990s.[13]

Some parents divorce 'for the sake of the children' and believe that to remain in an unhappy relationship is harmful for them. In the past couples stuck together for exactly the same reason, believing it important to put on an act so as to provide the children

Joint Custody

Love 40

with the security of a home. Traditionalists argue that in the past, as with toleration of adultery, it was acknowledged that:

> parenting was an investment which demanded protection and a great deal of self-control and self-denial. It also acknowledged that the home was an educational environment, where the adults' behaviour provided lessons for children in interpersonal conduct. The parents themselves may not have always been able to keep to the ideals they aspired to, but at least they endeavoured to demonstrate to the young how things *should be*.[14]

According to this moral code, parents have a duty to stay together for the children's sake.

It is clear that parents today, whatever they might or might not do for the children's sake, often get to the point when a relationship becomes intolerable. Many women find themselves single mothers even though they saw their mothering continuing in a conventional long-term partnership, but the man runs out on them. The outcome is either unplanned single parenthood – which in practice usually means that the woman is the sole parent – or a reconstituted 'blended' family following remarriage, with the children moving between two households. Patricia Morgan says of these that 'for most children there are really no such things as second or "reconstituted" families *since their own parents are irreplaceable*.'[15]

Children of these families have often experienced what can be called 'sequential variations' in parenting: two parents in a relatively stable relationship; two parents in an unstable relationship; one parent taking the major – or all – responsibility; a one-parent family with a visiting partner; and finally a blended family.

Children may feel responsible for the marriage breakdown. They often think it happened because they were naughty, or not clever enough. One father says: 'My son is convinced that his mother and I are getting divorced because he couldn't figure out how to make his model aeroplane.'[16]

It is vital to allow a child to mourn the lost parent – something which the children of lesbian or gay couples don't always have an opportunity to do openly. Ten-year-old Alison describes the problem:

> Sue's my best friend at school and last year her mother got divorced from her father, and everyone was really sympathetic and people understand that she would feel really upset. But when my mum stopped living with Barbara nobody said anything, or saw any reason why I should care. But Barbara is like a mother – she *is* a mother to me from when I was two years old.

Children may pass months – sometimes years – hoping their parents will get together again. They are likely to resent newcomers on the scene. They feel guilty because they believe they must be responsible for preventing their parents getting together, and they may be passionately loyal to the displaced parent – whom they see as the only acceptable parent. A girl says of her step-mother: 'I felt she was taking up my space. I felt she was taking John away from me.'[17] Another says: 'I felt like – dropped. And there wasn't anything I could do about it.'[18] A 13-year-old boy describes arguments with his step-father: 'I didn't know what to hit him with because adults have sharper words. So I'd use him being my stepdad, and say: "You're not my real dad – you can't order me around."'[19] And a girl expresses the same resentment when she says: 'He used to discipline me and set down rules, and I used to say, "You can't do that – you're not my dad."'[20]

While it is important to acknowledge a child's negative feelings, this isn't the same as giving in to them. Marie McShea remembers what happened when she objected to her mother's new husband:

> My last spontaneous display of anger was at age seven when my mother suddenly announced at a small celebration that she was going to get married to a man called Reg. I threw myself to the ground crying, raging against this man I didn't like, raging against his intrusion into my life . . . The celebration never got off the ground. Neither did the engagement. I was told that my mother had changed her mind because of my tantrum. I went

around for years afterwards with an uncomfortable burden of responsibility that my mother's life was somehow lessened because of this decision. I became afraid of showing my feelings . . . afraid of what happened when I wasn't nice . . . afraid that my mother would further ruin her life.[21]

Even childcare experts find divorce and remarriage difficult to handle. Dr Benjamin Spock admits openly that he did not do well as a step-father. It took many years for him and Ginger, his 11-year-old stepdaughter, to learn how to get on with each other. After the first year he, his wife Mary and Ginger went to a counseller who specialised in step-family problems. She told him he was living in a fool's paradise if he thought he would be accepted by a step-child within a year or two.

Writing about what happened, Mary Morgan says that her daughter felt that if she was at all kind, or even polite, to her step-father it would be a sign of disloyalty to her father. Her mother did not realise this and in her own emotional turmoil kept on criticising her ex-husband in her presence, so Ginger leapt to his defence. Sometimes when Ginger went to visit her father Mary took on the role of victim, and feels now that she abused her power over Ginger by expressing her jealousy and resentment.[22] This pattern of behaviour is very common. One study of children after divorce reveals that half of all parents at some time refuse access to their ex-spouses so as to punish them.[23]

When Mary's daughter came home and described a delicious meal her new step-mother had made, Mary felt that she was saying that this other woman could offer her better parenting: 'I had to realise that what she was really telling me was that she needed more nurturing and that this was the only way she knew to ask for it.'[24] She felt torn in two as her daughter and her new husband competed for her love. Ginger played them off against each other.

This playing adults off against each other is often a four-way process, an elaborate game conducted between the four adults involved. The more divided they are, the easier it is for children to do this. 'It's like espionage,' one girl said. An 11-year-old, talking about her parents' different rules and morality, says that joint custody is difficult for children because it puts these different moral judgements on the line. She describes her younger brother's behaviour:

> At my Dad's house Matthew had to do his homework right away, but he gets to stay up until nine and watch the A-Team because that's his favourite show. Mom doesn't want him to when we are at her house but she feels she has to give in because Matthew says: 'Well, Daddy lets me do that at his house.' He is learning to play them against each other . . .[25]

In the Spock-Morgan household Ginger's room was always in a disgusting mess – wet towels on her bed, and under them plates of mouldy food. Her mother says: 'I would constantly close the door in the hope of forgetting that that plate of garbage was really a symbol of what my child was feeling towards me. Ben, on the other hand, went in each morning and tidied up:

> She had him beautifully house trained and she knew it. He knew better but he couldn't seem to stop. I saw him walk to the door that I had previously closed, step back, and try to stop himself, but just be unable to. The power this kid had in this one act must have compensated for all the powerlessness she had felt . . .[26]

The price the child had to pay for this, however, was that he would 'persecute her' in the evenings and punish her by denying her some privilege. In Dr Spock's words later: 'The ultimate outrage – that this uninvited, unwelcome invader is now issuing orders or punishments.'[27]

So then Ginger became the victim again and attacked by throwing more wet towels on the floor, challenging her step-father to become persecutor. It lasted for five years.

The couple came to see that they had to discuss issues *together* before telling Ginger what she should or could not do. And they discovered that they should provide her with more options in the relationship with her step-father. They could not force her to like him just because her mother loved him. She had to have time and space in which to form her own relationship with her step-father *if* and *when* she wished. In fact, parents need to acknowledge that a child may hate a step-parent but that her mother (or father) – the step-parent's spouse – does not reject her for this reason.

Dr Spock suggests a regular family meeting for airing feelings and striving towards honesty and fairness, saying:

> This is new for all of us . . . We each have our own way of doing things (not necessarily good or bad, just different). It will take time and effort to learn how to share our values, handle our responsibilities and resolve our difficulties . . . [28]

He also believes that it is important to spend individual time with each child separately since everybody in the family is entitled to a relationship with every other person in it without having to be self-conscious about each other's reactions.

When families split and new relationships are formed, children are often passionately loyal, deeply angry and hurt, and the troubled behaviour that follows is an expression of these powerful feelings and a basic morality of unwavering loyalty. Parents should acknowledge this ethic and recognise that neither force nor seduction can destroy such loyalty. Only time and patience will allow the creation of new relationships which are equally, or almost, as strong.

While, as Spock makes clear, it is hard for men to be step-fathers, women who become step-mothers have to deal with a cultural stereotype of the 'wicked step-mother' of fairytale fame. Cinderella's wicked step-mother turns the girl into a household drudge. Snow White's jealous step-mother tries to murder her with a poisoned apple, and Hansel and Gretel's pushes them out into the woods. 'When she . says, "you're not my mother, you're my *step*-mother" it's true, but it also sounds like a terrible insult,' says one step-mother. It is also sometimes harder for step-mothers because, as women, they are expected to take more responsibility for the children and for the domestic details in the house. 'I like her now,' says Juliet, 'but she was awful when she first came to live in *my* house. She got rid of every single thing connected with my mother until I felt there was nothing left of her any more.' 'Mine refused to let us eat nice food,' recalls Diane. 'We wanted things like baked beans and white bread – things we'd always eaten – but she kept giving us this disgusting brown rice and lentil muck.' One step-mother remembers:

> I couldn't ever bring myself to use the term 'step-daughter' – I had all those appalling images of cruel, wicked witches. I think Jane, who was five at the time, realised I had this problem because one day she just said, 'I know you're not my real mummy but it would be easier if I called you mummy.' Knowing how much she loved her mother, I felt incredibly flattered. And after that we were much more loving to each other.[29]

We have gone into the Spock account at length because it is one of the most intimate published discussions of what happens when adult values are directly in conflict with a child's values within a reconstituted family. What the Spocks did not write about was sex – how a child feels when parents have new sexual partners. Many parents try to be discreet about this and hope to keep it, at least temporarily, secret from their children. Some children first discover that a parent has a lover only because another toothbrush appears in the bathroom. In intact families sexuality is more or less submerged and opaque. With separation and the arguments, accusations and counter-accusations that precede it, it is visible, and with the introduction of a new partner into the home it may become threatening.

A girl who was living with her mother[30] says she felt cheated when she discovered that her father had been remarried for a year without really telling her: 'Then I found the wedding photographs, and she was half-way pregnant. I felt awful – upset, angry, very hurt and betrayed that he hadn't told me.' Joanna says: 'I went through a stage of hating my Dad'.

When he and my mum split up he went off abroad and he only sent me two Christmas cards in several years. Then he came back and started wanting to be all fatherly. Then he got a girlfriend – I had a lot of shit with her. She was jealous. He had to ring me up when she wasn't there and he wrote me secret letters. It was like being a secret mistress.

Two sisters focus on the sexual nature of the relationship when they say: 'You feel like you're intruding. You have to knock on the bedroom door. I resent that.' And the other adds: 'You feel like you might be interrupting.' . . . and they laughed.[31]

Children feel moral outrage when their behaviour is corrected by an adult whose behaviour they themselves consider immoral and irresponsible. 'When they are alone, everything they do is for you. When they remarry, it's for themselves,' was one girl's pointed comment.[32] Some loathe the very idea that the parent should be having sexual relationships. 'Why do you need to have sex?' demanded an 8-year-old. 'You've got four children, isn't that enough?' Another snarled 'Oh yuk, disgusting, really gross, oh ugh, revolting' and left the room clutching his stomach.[33]

When a parent changes the gender of their sexual partner this can be a particular problem. 'You make me feel sick,' said a 9-year-old when his father told him about his love for another man. Another father describes his 10-year-old's reaction:

'I think all gays should be burned and killed,' my 10-year-old son would say, then look at me intently to gauge my reaction. Or, while dressing in the morning: 'I don't want to wear *that*. People would think I'm gay.'

I responded in as relaxed and lighthearted a way as I could, not being certain what this testing meant and not wanting to escalate things into a heavy number. In a couple of months he gave it up and now cuddles and loves me as well as ever.[34]

Fifteen-year-old Satya, whose mother came out as lesbian when Satya was four, describes the qualities she thinks you need if you have a lesbian mother:

'You have to be willing to be different, or at least accept it,' she says. 'You'll need an inner sense of being O.K. . . . You have to learn to trust yourself. You always have to think who you can tell and who you can't. You have to learn to not pay attention to what other people think. You have to not let what other people do hurt you.[35]

Social prejudice and discrimination against lesbians and gay men means that children whose parents become homosexual often find this very difficult to handle. But those who have been brought up from birth, or from a very young age, within lesbian relationships take them for granted and may feel shocked and betrayed if their mothers later enter into *hetero*sexual relationships.

Eight-year-old Mandy's mother describes herself as bisexual. She has been in a lesbian partnership for the last five years. Her lover gets on well with Mandy and the three of them have been to many lesbian concerts, workshops and conferences. But she has just become involved with a man:

I thought any new person would be difficult for her, but I suppose it didn't occur to me that his being a man would affect Mandy particularly. But she's taken it very badly and shouts lesbian feminist slogans at me, sings lesbian songs very loudly around the house, and has taken to wearing my lesbian badges whenever Pete comes round.

What is at issue here is Mandy's sense of betrayal and her outrage at the changes her mother is forcing her to accept.

Often, though, we underestimate children's capacity to deal with adult sexuality. Sara, who is 12, described how one morning, after sleeping at a friend's house, she came home earlier than planned.

Well, I just stormed into my mother's bedroom, and there was this guy in her bed – she was somewhere else, in another room. I started crying and everything, my mother tried to convince me she had slept on the couch. Now that I look back, it was pretty hilarious, but of course I don't care – I mean I understand about those kind of arrangements. In the beginning, when my father had a girlfriend sleep over, he didn't know how to tell me – he just sort of said, 'Oh, you're sleeping on the couch tonight,' because at that point I didn't have my own room at his house and shared the bedroom. It's still hard for my dad to level with me about this part of his life, but he's getting better. Anyhow, neither of them should worry about my getting upset, because I'm old enough to understand that grownups are allowed to have private lives, which includes other people. But if someone's going to stay the night, I think it's better and less awkward if I know about it beforehand, so I'm not taken by surprise.[36]

When a parent enters a new partnership often she or he is exposing the child not only to a new adult but also to that adult's children, requiring that they form a whole new set of relationships with them. Some lively competitiveness is to be expected between step-siblings – and sometimes grandparents consciously or unwittingly encourage this.

'Jillian's daughter is a good tennis player, but Andrew's daughter plays the clarinet. Jillian's daughter got six O-levels, but Andrew's daughter...' Here are two girls of the same age with different grandparents who are anxious that their particular grandchild should put up a good showing compared with the alien in their midst.

Children learn ways of manipulating, and sometimes ganging up, on parents. 'You treat Steve's children much nicer than you treat us,' etc. Jacki has two children and Lin three. They have been living together for two years: 'My children go to Jackie if they want privileges,' says Lin, 'and her children come to me. Both sets have sussed out that their mother's lover is the soft option.'

When China became Communist, women who had previously been expert manipulators within the extended family – especially the grandmothers – became the most politically active cadre members. Their education and activism had come from negotiating intricate relationships within the family. In the same way children, for better or worse, learn about human behaviour, and how they can influence it, within the family. It is possible that they learn this more readily, though painfully, in complex 'blended' families than in a straightforward nuclear family in which adults share the same values and always try to be consistent.

LEARNING TO LIVE WITH OTHERS

Friends, whether ours or theirs, can threaten personal loyalties and challenge accepted ideas in an uncomfortable way. For both parents and children, friendships may arouse anxiety because other people intrude like aliens on a close relationship, may seem to steal affection, and certainly represent different, and sometimes conflicting, values and standards of behaviour. Children may be torn between loyalty to their peers and loyalty to their parents. Adults may be torn in a similar way between a loving relationship with another adult and love for their children.

Yet the cosy, sheltered world which is often represented as the ideal of 'home sweet home', one in which doors and windows are closed on the outside world, and which is insulated from other values, does not prepare children for the real world, nor help us as adults to grow and learn with our children. Learning to live with and relate to others is an important element in family life. Our children's friendships, as our own, can widen the horizons.

CHAPTER
8

AGGRESSION AND VIOLENCE

'They are constantly bickering,' says the mother of three children, aged 6, 4 and 2. 'I can't leave them playing together for more than a few minutes without hearing screams and wails because Paul has thumped Thomas and Thomas has pulled Mary's hair and Mary bit Paul. I just don't know what to do!' Daisy says of her 6-year-old:

When she's tired she starts picking on the little one (aged 2) and snatching things away from her, and she can't see why she shouldn't. She comes and grabs a book or a toy. I try to explain what is fair and what is not. I think she's understood and it proves later on that she hasn't quite. You can't sit down and lecture her. She just carries on grabbing what she wants.

Alison's 8-year-old is in a gang of boys at school who rush round the playground shouting and beating up other children: 'I don't understand why he's like this,' she says.

Why do children resort to aggression and violence? Is it just 'natural', or is it learned – from parents, television, school, other children, the values of a violent society? And when we notice it, how should we deal with it?

CHILDREN IN THE FAST LANE

In industrial cultures physical aggression among adults has been largely replaced by competitiveness and the struggle to acquire power, wealth and status. Professional and executive parents in New York start their infants on a rat race almost from birth. There is frantic competition to get children into the best nursery schools and toddlers' classes which claim to increase their IQ. Mothers spend 'quality time' with their child, teaching Shakespeare-flash cards and educational games even before the second birthday. There are violin classes, and dance and fitness sessions and other after-school activities that lead to 'toddler burn out'. Three-year-olds must pass exams to be accepted at fashionable schools because 'going to the right nursery school is perceived as the way to get on the fast track to Ivy League colleges'.[1] This high pressure lifestyle produces a distinct kind of child who is highly competitive, egotistic and painfully self-conscious. Following a recent magazine article about the pressures on children in New York the following letter appeared in a subsequent issue:

Aren't we more highly educated, more sophisticated, more cultured, and street-wise at a younger age than other kids? We are like diamonds that must be polished over and over again for that perfect look. I think we are the best. (Tzinia Bohn, aged 10, Manhattan)[2]

Japanese children get forced into the same rat race. A woman living in Tokyo told Sheila she plans to leave the country for the sake of her children:

Japanese society is super-competitive. They put big stress on going to the best schools, because if you don't go to the best schools you can't get a good job. It is 100 per cent more competitive than anywhere else.

I want my son to be a person who has time for people. He doesn't have to be Prime Minister, or anything else.

The best times of life in Japan are either when you are very

149

young or very old – both times when you can do whatever you like. The reins are put on slowly until they are really tight when you are about 20 . . . Mothers never slap children or push them in the way they should go, but once they get to primary school at six the expectations are much greater.

A columnist in a Japanese newspaper warned parents that children are being treated like 'bent cucumbers' by shopkeepers who throw them out as unsaleable. Those who do not fit the standards are rejected by the school. These attitudes are transferred to the pupils who bully anyone who is different.[3] When children are under pressures like this they have two alternatives: they either become aggressive in an effort to be first in the pecking order or they simply give up. A 10-year-old in Miami, Florida, killed himself rather than face his father with a bad end of term report.[4]

It is not only in highly industrialised societies that children may be put under terrific pressure to succeed. A mother in China beat her 9-year-old son to death because he failed to score 90 per cent in school tests. He lied about the results, and when she found out she beat him for four hours, and he later died in hospital. His mother killed herself while in gaol, leaving a note expressing deep remorse.[5]

The same pressures are becoming increasingly evident in Britain. Many parents are concerned to help their children 'get ahead'. Private nursery schools are booming and parents who cannot afford them are looking for other ways of boosting their pre-schooler's performance through private classes in gym, swimming and music.[6] With the introduction of National Attainment tests for seven year olds, so that the progress of each child will be measured against established standards and so-called norms, the emphasis on success and competitiveness is likely to increase both in the home and in school as the teaching of 5 and 6 year olds becomes geared to exams.

More and more children of this age are being groomed for entry to independent schools, receiving extra tutoring to pass the entrance exams. To get into one top school in London parents must put their children's names down almost at birth. The head of The Hall, a prestigious prep school, is quoted as saying that the competition is producing 'an absolute epidemic of coaching' and the director of a tutorial centre says 'It's a competitive jungle and it's intensifying each year.'[7] All this goes along with 'creative' activities too – music, drama, sport as well as extra maths tuition. It results in long, tiring days for a child, with little time to play or just stand and stare. Judith Haynes, an educational psychologist, says that children may become restless, inattentive and develop headaches, tummy aches, tics and difficulty in sleeping.

The next hurdle is getting into public school. But parents may believe that putting their children under this pressure is better than exposing them to the state system. A mother of a 12-year-old who is having private tuition to get into an independent day school says she does this because 'he isn't assertive, he doesn't fight for his rights – he's been like that since a baby'.[8]

Like parents in the US and Japan, many British parents are concerned about these pressures to succeed at any cost. One woman who told us she was 'determined not to put emphasis on having to achieve' remembered that: 'When Simon went to primary school and brought home his report he was graded first in his class, and I was horrified. Why did they have to start making them compete so soon?' These parents believe that children are encouraged to compete soon enough without being forced to even when they are pre-school. A father writes:

Competition makes some children despair and give up – children who have important and vital talents and abilities that may never be developed as a result of this. In a co-operative environment the talents of each could be developed without conflict.[9]

Competitive sports have always been an important element in the English public school system – and one which has been taken over by the state school system. Many adults look back on school 'games' as miserable, painful and humiliating. Today there are children who are being groomed for success in professional competitive sports – rather like race-horses with many hours of intensive training and stretched to their limits of endurance. The tennis star Tracy Austin competed at Wimbledon when she was fifteen but had to retire from professional tennis before she was twenty because of injuries exhaustive training had caused. There is evidence that all competitive sports, bar swimming, delay menstruation in girl athletes and we do not yet know the effects of this.

When some schools scrap traditional sports day races and replace them with co-operative games which don't have winners and losers, people may react with outrage. A Conservative chairman of one education authority said she was 'horrified' because: 'It is a vital part of their education and development. How are they expected to get good jobs without being competitive?' and another writer described it as 'a disaster on the playing fields that could diminish us as a nation'.[10]

TEACHING AGGRESSION

There are other cultures – mostly tribes – that encourage overt aggression far more than we do, like the Kwakiutl warriors of Vancouver Island who put high value on aggression and systematically inculcate it through the family, and the Yanomamo Indians of Venezuela and Brazil where 'a high capacity for rage, a quick flash point and a willingness to use violence to obtain one's ends, are considered desirable traits'. In order to produce the appropriate adult behaviour, the Yanomamo encourage their children, especially young boys, to argue, fight and be generally belligerent.[11]

But there are also cultures in which all forms of aggression are restrained. When the anthropologist Malinowski asked Trobriand islanders why they did not use corporal punishment with naughty children they considered his suggestion 'unnatural and immoral'. Why should adults hit children?[12] Innuit parents around the Hudson Bay discourage aggression and anger by ignoring a child of two or three years who has temper tantrums and snatches and grabs things from other children. Aggressive behaviour in adults is considered shameful.[13] In religious communities such as that of the

Canadian Hutterites values of non-violence are also pre-eminent, and children are taught to respond to aggression with love.

Cross-cultural research has consistently demonstrated that the competitive and aggressive attitudes of Anglo-American children interfere with their ability to co-operate with others in problem-solving, even when such co-operation would be to their advantage.[14]

Children first learn about conflict and aggression in the family. They watch what happens when adults disagree, and see how their

153

parents resolve those disagreements. Aware that their children can sniff out conflicts between them – often as if with a sixth sense – many parents worry about how to handle such conflict and the often heated discussions about how to bring up the children or how to deal with their own parents. When a couple have a row should there be a rule that it is 'not in front of the children?' Ought all the bickering to take place behind closed doors and out of earshot?

Robin Skynner, a psychiatrist and family therapist, believes that 'a hidden form of trench warfare' or one partner's domination of the other without protest or argument is much more damaging to children than open argument because it results in a poisoned atmosphere.[15] Children need to learn that confrontation is not a disaster, that conflict can be resolved by listening to each other and seeking a solution together, and that it can have a good outcome. 'Even if an argument upsets children at the time, they will be far more disturbed by a constant atmosphere of seething anger, discontent and nasty sniping.'[16]

Children are often used as an excuse for not sorting out problems between a couple and for evading challenges to which they ought to face up. Moreover, being able to accept disagreements, be open about them, and seek positive solutions to conflict are important elements in being assertive – and children need to learn this. They may not like to hear their parents having a good row but can understand it because they know that they get upset with their friends, too, and can still like them after the row is all over. As one 6-year-old said: 'When my mummy and daddy are shouting I just say to them "Stop squabbling, you two!" Because that's what they say to me and my brother.'[17]

In some families, however, disagreements go far beyond this. Violence is the norm and then they become 'training centres for aggression'.[18] When a husband or boyfriend uses violence against the mother her children are often, if not victims of it themselves, at least witnesses to this violence.

In the Dobashes' powerful and perceptive study they show how children are sometimes called in to witness their mother's punishment as an additional degradation for her:

Oh yes, they've seen me be hit. He used to delight in lifting them up out their beds so that they could watch. And this was 2 a.m. and he sat on the chair and sat and told me everything he thought about me and he dragged the whole three kids out their beds and made them all sit. He lined them up against the couch and told them all what I was. He said to them, 'Now you see her, she is a whore.' And he'd say to Chris, 'See her, she's a cow.' And the bairn was only three months old and he'd say to him, 'See her she's nae good. She's dirt. That's what women are. They're all dirt. There's your daddy been out working all day and there's nae any tea ready for him. See how rotten she is to your daddy.' And all the bairns were dragged out of their beds for nae reason at all.[19]

In one Scottish city these sociologists found that of 314 attacks by men on their wives, nearly half took place in front of their children – who must have often heard what was happening even when they were not present. In another study well over half (59 per cent) of battered women said that their children were usually present during an assault. They usually stood by, screaming, fled and hid or pleaded with their fathers to stop being violent.

Donna used to get hysterical. The wee soul, she'd only be about six and one half, and she would say, 'Come on, Dad, you're going to be good and you're not going to fight with Mum tonight. Please, Dad, you promised.'[20]

Moreover, children may see this violence *legitimated* by social workers who 'advise women to appease a husband by not arguing with him or by satisfying his demands, in other words, to be a better wife and mother'. It is often also legitimated by police, who until recently have been reluctant to interfere in domestic disputes, by doctors, 'who rarely sought to discover the source of injuries unless the woman offered, and generally failed to acknowledge that violence had occurred', and by friends and relatives, who 'advised the woman to remain in the relationship and attempt to appease the husband'.[21]

Male violence, even when it is not directed towards the children, offers a model of aggression and provokes violent behaviour in boys. Boys are trained in the family to be aggressors and girls to be victims.

But it is not only a question of witnessing violence. Violence against children is common – as recent statistics on child abuse indicate. Women who talked to us often look back to their own childhood, are critical of punitive violence employed by their parents, and are determined never to have recourse to violence with their own children. They say things like: 'My mother hit first and spoke afterwards. I never want to be like that'; 'I was afraid of my Dad. He had a terrible temper and lashed out at anybody in the family when he got mad'.

Even so, John and Elizabeth Newson's research with 700 families in Nottingham in the 1960s revealed that 75 per cent of 7-year-olds had been smacked or struck with an implement, and that mothers smacked 93 per cent of their 4-year-olds and 62 per cent of their one year olds.[22] If things have changed they must have changed dramatically.

In hitting children we foster their feelings of impotence and inadequacy. Because conflicts between children and adults often end with the adult striking the child (in Sweden this is illegal), it is not surprising that conflicts between children also often end with one child hitting another. We are providing a model for violence.

BULLIES

Even if we never use violence against our children, they are likely to encounter it at school in the form of bullying from other children and aggressive outbursts from teachers (often in response to the bullying!). The British National Association of Head Teachers has made public its concern over disruptive behaviour and physical violence even amongst the youngest pupils. Giving evidence to the Government Enquiry into discipline in schools they stated that: 'Attack as the best form of defence rules the behaviour of a significant and growing number of pupils, especially in urban areas.'[23] They blamed the parents, the influence of television, the rapid turnover of staff, boring teaching – and the abolition of corporal punishment in schools.

Their report focused on the increasing attacks on *teachers* by children in infant and even nursery schools, and the inability of those in authority to do much about it. Parents may be more concerned that their children are starting out on school in an atmosphere of violence, one in which children who have been brought up not to hit out are exposed to taunts, threats, kicking and punch-ups in the playground.

A survey in the British magazine *Mother* published in 1988 showed that one in four primary school children was a victim of bullying by other children. A Norwegian campaign against bullying in schools was launched after three children who were victims of bullying committed suicide. The way to make a bully is, according to Norwegian researchers, to neglect a child and leave him more or less to his own devices, to be permissive of aggressive behaviour and to use physical punishment against him.[24]

Children often do not tell about bullying because there is a code of silence, and breaking it would expose the child to even more bullying. Even when a child does tell an adult, it can be hard to find words in which to express what has happened, or the adult may dismiss or trivialise the child's account, or simply not believe it – perhaps because we tend to idealise childhood and are often insensitive to the pain and suffering a child is enduring.

Many people believe that a bully needs 'a taste of his own medicine'. A Professor of Moral Education remembers seeing a school-teacher standing with both hands clutching a boy's head and banging it against the blackboard in order to stress each syllable as he said, 'If there's ONE THING I WILL NOT TOLerate it's BULLYING!' Research reveals that bullying is one of the most common offences to result in caning.[25]

Even when children are not themselves struck, the fact that other children *are*, and often in front of them, creates an atmosphere of fear and submission. One of us (Sheila) remembers keenly witnessing physical violence used repeatedly in her primary school by a teacher against boys who were cheeky or rough. There was one little boy – he couldn't have been much more than 6 – who seemed never able to do anything right. He was dirty, wore a grubby jersey that was unravelling, hand-me-down shoes that were too big for him and socks that concertinaed round his thin ankles. His face was constantly streaked with tears, his nose ran and his flesh was goose-pimpled with cold. The teacher's favourite form of punishment was to get this child to stand up in front of the class and then to hit him behind the knees with the side of her hand – with something like a karate chop – until he crumpled on to the floor. Then she stood gloating over him. I knew even then, at the age of six or seven, that she could never treat me like that – would never dare – because I came from a 'nice' home and was carefully brought up whereas his home was in the mean streets down by the railway. That child's suffering stimulated in me a burning anger against oppression and a determination that this injustice, this blatant discrimination and cruelty, should never be allowed to happen. I knew that my mother would be on my side in this and told her about it, and she went to speak to the head teacher. I remember that she occasionally asked me if it was happening again – but it didn't. He just had a lot of black clouds marked up against his name on the wall chart on which our stars and clouds were recorded for all to see. (He was the biggest owner of black clouds in the whole class!)

When corporal punishment is used in a school, even obedient children may be terrified that it will be used against them. Steve Roberts remembers 'a morbid fear of corporal punishment' from his school days. 'Not that I was ever hit by a teacher. I was almost pathologically conformist and well-behaved.' What frightened him was the regimentation, the stern discipline. 'The rules and punishment are still handed down from on high. It is the introduction to a hierarchy of fear, the teaching of submission.'[26]

Corporal punishment is now officially illegal in British state schools but violence against children by teachers still occasionally makes the headlines. A prep-school headmaster beat an 11-year-old boy with the sole of a training shoe for swearing.

Gritting his teeth and with his right arm held high, he hit the boy with all his force. After three blows the boy begged him to stop. He was screaming loudly but he was told to bend over again for the last three blows. The boy's mother was horrified when she saw the nine inch purple weals and bruises on her son at home that night.

He later beat an 8-year-old boy six times on his bare bottom with the same shoe after ordering him to write a 400 word essay on 'the whackings I have had' for doing poorly in French. This was because his essay was only 363 words long.[27]

Another deputy head hit a 15-year-old girl with a walking stick after he found her smoking,[28] and a music teacher hit and kicked children for 'insolence'.[29]

The headmaster of another preparatory school was exposed by a former teacher who said that he 'went to the extremes in a bid to get better exam results for the school'. Children were hit on the head and back, kicked on the shins, struck with a slipper and had their hair pulled. Another teacher said, 'I saw children in the classroom shaking, wetting themselves and crying. They were often bruised in the back because he would thump them at the base of the spine with his knuckles.'[30] Many parents never found out about injuries sustained by their children at the school.

In the United States corporal punishment – prodding, spanking, pinching, hitting and tying up children with rope – is allowed in thirty-nine states. Each year more than 1 million school children are physically assaulted by their teachers – legally. Thousands of them end up needing medical treatment. When one 10-year-old in Ohio didn't answer a question correctly, his teacher lost his temper, pulled out a handful of hair and scratched his face so badly that he needed a tetanus shot. Jamie Logan was hit so hard 'my lungs burned, my eyes saw stars and my ears hummed'. She now limps after sitting still for any period and has had countless visits to neurosurgeons.[31]

Research suggests that corporal punishment fails to curb violent children. In fact it has the opposite effect because it provides a model of aggression and triggers further aggression.[32] Parents who use physical punishment are more likely to have aggressive, hostile children.[33] We may lecture children about how 'two wrongs don't make a right', and 'just because he hit you first is no reason to hit him back', but our own actions often tell a different story. One four-year old said to her mother: 'You told me I mustn't hit anybody smaller than myself but that's what you're doing to me!'

A side-effect of continual physical punishment is that children develop an over-riding sense of shame and self-disdain, while other feelings are blunted.[34]

Even punishment which does not employ violence can stimulate aggression when it is based on techniques of what has been called 'power assertion' – threats, scathing verbal attacks on a child, forcing a child to be physically immobile in an uncomfortable position, locking a child in a dark cupboard or denial of food.[35]

TELEVISION

Women who talked to us were often anxious about the effect of violence in the media. They believe that aggression is fuelled by observing violence, especially on TV.

Analysis of TV serials in the United States reveals that seven out of ten stars of these programmes are involved in violence and that the hero is twice as likely to start it as the other guy. The victims are usually women or black people. In the eighteen episodes of *Miami Vice* the heroes killed forty-three people – 'five times as many as the entire Miami police force killed in a full year of real-life police work! Whereas TV cops fire their guns in almost every episode, the average Chicago police officer fires a gun once every 27 years.'[36] But the most violent TV programmes are cartoons designed for children's viewing. In cartoons for children screened in 1967 there was three times *more* violence than in programmes meant for adults.[37]

While parents have a lie-in on Saturday and Sunday mornings, children are fed a steady diet of cartoon violence, much of it conveying the Sylvestor Stallone moral code that 'so long as I have this machine-gun the rest of you can go to hell'. An analysis of Sunday morning programmes in 1969 recorded a violent episode at least every two minutes. These cartoons are also 'thinly disguised pieces of propaganda for American defence politics right through to

"Star Wars"'.[38] Defenders of the Universe simply zap anyone who stands in their way.

With some children the violence flows like water off a duck's back. They are not disturbed by it and do not admire or imitate it. Like the Keystone Cops or the flung custard tarts of the early days of cinema, they enjoy it as knock-about comedy or as fantasy and adventure which bears no relation to real life.

For other children the effect of TV violence is insidious and damaging. And it is not difficult to see why. By the age of 15 the average American child has spent more time watching TV than at school, and as a result has seen more than 13,000 murders.[39] If the child has access to pay cable TV or a VCR as well, the number goes up to 32,000 murders and 40,000 attempted murders and a quarter of a million acts of violence by age 18.[40] Children learn from this glamourised violence that violence *works*.[41] It seems that the more of it they watch, the less they react emotionally when witnessing aggression, and the less concerned they are about violence in real life.

In an American study of third grade children, half watched a baseball game, the other half watched a violent detective programme. Then they were given responsibility for 'babysitting' some younger children in a near-by trailer by watching them over a TV monitor. The third-graders were told to seek adult help if the children got into trouble. Here is a description of the behaviour of the younger children that the third-graders saw:

> Each began criticising the block structures that the other had built. After increased criticism the boy knocked over one of the girl's buildings. This led to increased taunting, pushing, shoving and crying. The fight got progressively worse until it appeared that the camera was destroyed.

The third-graders who had previously watched a violent TV programme took longer to seek adult help than the children who saw the non-violent film. TV violence leads children (and possibly adults too) to feel indifferent to real-life violence.

Small children are not able to make distinctions between

fantasy and real violence and respond equally aggressively to both fictional and real-life violence. The mothers who talked to us had often noticed this and commented that even programmes especially for children – cartoons like *Tom and Jerry* for instance – taught their children to be violent. The mother of a 2-year-old complained that her son has picked up bad behaviour from cartoons like this, including hitting, kicking, shouting and stamping his feet in anger.

Children may react to scenes of violence in other ways too. A woman with a 3-year-old says her child is confused and bewildered by violence on television. She has not become violent herself, but has disturbing dreams about it. Other mothers say:

I object to violence generally being shown on television as a solution to injustice.

I dislike violence being portrayed as the answer to any situation in children's TV programmes screened before 6 p.m. It is always the biggest and strongest who wins e.g. *Popeye*, *A-Team*, *Knight Rider*, *Dungeons and Dragons*.

I dislike TV violence so I turn off the set and explain my opinions.

I do not approve of telly. All the news is bad – violence, murders, sexual abuse, etc. I'm afraid she will think life is always like that.

Even if you are only 5 or 6 today you see violence everywhere – even in the films for children. That does worry me ...

One way in which they try to defuse the situation is to discuss the programmes with their children.

We talk about television, about when an animal is nasty to another animal, for example, and how that animal is hurt, and then I might say that he was nasty to his younger brother, and how that hurt him, too. I try and get him to reflect on his behaviour and use television in that way.

One mother is glad that her two boys do not watch TV at all:

> A lot of people say to me: 'You're over-protective.' My children have never seen American violence on television. They don't watch television. We've let them watch suitable programmes, but they don't ask. They've got better things to do.

Since it is very unlikely that any parents can effectively ban television from their children's lives – and even if they do not see it at home they will see it, and perhaps video nasties too, at friends' houses – it is important to have practical strategies for dealing with its effects on children's minds. It is possible to teach children – especially older ones – the cues to programmes which are likely to be violent. Sit down with them and flick through the different channels, seeing if you can find out from the background music, the setting, the actors' language and behaviour, and the intonations of their voices which ones will turn out to be violent and nasty. The child can then make the decision to switch off or switch over.

When children do watch TV, women believe it is helpful if parents can be present to comment on what they are witnessing and to explore the issues raised at whatever level the child wants to discuss them. News and documentary programmes showing violence should not be allowed just to wash over children. There is real danger that violence in such programmes gets viewed merely as exciting entertainment. These deaths take place as if in our homes. And what do we do? Go and make a cup of coffee, or switch channels.

Some of the women who talked to us want to make it clear to their children that news stories and documentaries are not fiction, but entail real human suffering. So they talk about the feelings of the people involved and the effect of violence on their lives. As one mother of a 10 and 12-year-old put it:

> If something is on the news their attitude is 'what is all the fuss about?' or 'why do people treat one another that way?' I explain why people feel like that and behave that way, especially when they are under pressure.

Another says:

> We always debate things. We discuss what is happening in this
> and other countries and always try and explain the reasons for
> violence in South Africa, why people are blowing themselves
> up in Northern Ireland, and so on. We want them to under-
> stand why people are violent in some causes. I draw a
> distinction between political violence – in pursuance of a cause
> – and gratuitous violence, like stabbing someone to rob them
> of their handbag.

Her son, now aged 13, says he has always enjoyed these discussions
round the dinner table. Another woman says:

> I watch television with my children and explain things to
> them. We particularly talk about the bombings and why
> people in Northern Ireland kill each other. I always stress the
> difference between a newsreel and a film (fiction).

A mother who watched the film *Cry Freedom* with her thirteen year
old says: 'Afterwards we asked him, "Would you like to live in
South Africa?" and "Could you be like the character in the film?"
and we had a discussion about it.'

Maire Messenger Davies[42] believes that children can learn important social messages from television and are able to discriminate far
earlier than we usually give them credit for. She points out that
nearly all the research on TV and violence has been done in the
USA and that TV programmes in Britain are much less violent. 'We
don't have to stand between children and television all the time
here,' she told us. 'By the time children are about 8, the more
they can use their own judgement and think for themselves the
better. We shan't always agree with them, but that is the way they
learn.' She goes on to say that often a distressed response of
children to disturbing items in TV news and documentaries is an
entirely appropriate one. Instead of shielding children from it we
should recognise that this response is good. 'It's sad, but we're
all crying together and talking about what it would be like if it

happened in our family.' She believes that there is a difference between that and the kind of distress when you realise a child is being psychologically harmed. 'Then it is common sense not to let them see it, and switch off and say they are not old enough.'[43]

Though mothers often see TV as triggering violence, adults have always been concerned about childhood aggression and in different historical periods have attributed it to various causes – the Devil, poverty and gin, or the innate characteristics of an inferior social class, race or culture. The chances are that even if TV were banned entirely from next week, many children would continue to be aggressive.

GAMES AND GUNS

In the eighteenth and nineteenth centuries there was a theory that nasty fairy tales caused aggression in children. Peter Parley warned American parents of the harm done by stories like Little Red Riding Hood, Jack the Giant Killer and Bluebeard, which he considered written 'for the express purpose of reconciling them (the children) to vice and crime'.[44]

Today firms compete to produce reading material and playthings and pastimes for children in which violence provides the excitement. Perhaps comics and space games are today's equivalent of the fairy tales spiced with murder and mayhem. Even in the golden oldies like *Beano* and *Dandy* the characters are always getting 'smacked' but survive unharmed. From one point of view it is, in a psychotherapist's words, a healthy 'outlet', and children 'learn that their angry, violent *wishes* and *feelings* don't damage and are a normal part of themselves'.[45] From another point of view this trivialises violence. Some children's comics – *Scream*, for example – are crammed with cartoon strips of vampires, executions, live burials and monster cats that devour human beings. Even bubble-gum cards depict children being tortured and multilated and include nasty characters like 'Decapitated Hedy' and 'Max Axe'.

Beside the soft toys, chess sets, musical boxes and stilts, toy shops are packed with playthings in which violence is a central ingredient. There are displays of swords, guns, armed vehicles and other weapons, and games like Lazertag in which one child pretends to shoot another who wears a 'star sensor' that registers a direct hit with an electronic bleep. The manufacturers claim that it is 'a good vehicle for bringing children together'.[46] For boys who prefer dolls there are macho Action Man, Rambo, and Nomad the Arab terrorist, his enemy.

A few years back an American manufacturer introduced a series of torture kits called Monster Scenes. A semi-naked female figure could be assembled and stuck to a platform with a guillotine at her throat. For variety, she could be imprisoned in a 'hanging cage' or 'pain parlour' with 'spikes or hot coals'. Eight hundred thousand of these kits were sold before being discontinued. Playthings like this 'reinforce the belief that manhood is achieved through power over others, and conditions boys to accept as normal a sadomasochistic relationship between men and women'.[47]

Women say there are often conflicts with other parents, their children's friends, and their own parents and parents-in-law about playthings in which violence is the main feature.

I had a battle with my mother who kept arriving with jumble sale bargains. One day we went to visit her and among an assortment of books she'd got at summer fêtes she had found for fifty pence a two foot plastic machine gun. To her it was a thrill. I refused to take it home with us on principle. My son hadn't seen it. But I was faced with getting in the car knowing that my mother was shedding tears in the bedroom and my father was getting shirty with me. This is *after* saying from the beginning, 'We don't want war-type toys.' She said, 'Well, it's only a toy!'

Guns symbolise power for the child. People with guns are people with power. Children are powerless and want power. The theory that if children are offered safe outlets for aggression it can be controlled often lies behind fathers' enthusiasm to teach their sons boxing and schools' encouragement of fiercely competitive games. Life is tough, violence is all around, and children – or at least boys – have to learn to handle it and need a vent for their inner aggression.

It is 'acting out' which will stop boys becoming real-life hooligans. Some parents approve of play with toy guns and knives for this reason, reckoning that if aggression can be 'released' in play it becomes harmless.

A male childcare worker, who admits that he dislikes seeing children playing violent games, believes that if he had come to terms with violence in his own life he would be able to accept them 'acting out their violent themes':

> The reason I can feel bad about myself around guns and violence is because I haven't worked through all the times I have been hurt myself and seen other people be hurt and killed in wars and other acts of violence. I was not offered the chance to work through and free myself of these hurts. It is because I have done it to some extent as an adult that I can at times allow children the space to deal with their hurts . . . The future lies in adults healing themselves and working to eliminate atomic weapons, wars and people acting out their violent feelings in destructive ways as part of building a better world for our children – not by pretending to children that these things do not exist.[48]

There are some flaws in this argument. First – play can readily turn into real-life violence. In the United States a youth was killed by a police officer who thought a Lazertag gun was real, and a man used a toy gun to take reporter David Horowitz hostage on live TV.[49] The childcare expert Benjamin Spock, who used to say gunplay was harmless, changed his mind after learning that some schoolchildren cheered the assassination of President Kennedy.[50] Celia remembers having one day just sat down for dinner at home with my partner when we heard a loud bang, and shards of broken glass from the shattered bay window exploded across the room and across our food. As we got up to see what was happening a second shot rang out and a pellet whistled past our ears. Realising that we were being shot at, we crouched under the dinner table as a third shot resounded. The police were sympathetic but not surprised when they inspected the damage, saying: 'Kids with air guns do this sort of thing all the time.' They made enquiries up and down the street and a few days later a tearful 10-year-old was dragged in by his parents to apologise to us for having used his 13-year-old brother's air gun without permission.

The 'outlet' or 'catharsis' theory does not really hold water. It is equally likely that gun play stimulates further aggression. Psychological research suggests that when children are irritated by or angry with another child aggressive activity (shooting at targets in this particular research) does not lower aggression any more than if they engage in an intellectual task (doing arithmetic).[51] When, however, the behaviour of the child towards whom they are hostile is explained and interpreted (e.g. 'he was sleepy and upset') aggression is reduced.

It is true that children have to learn to cope with death (see ch.9), and that we all live in a violent world, but violent play is not the only, or the best, way of enabling them to cope. Another childcare worker disagrees with the catharsis theory and says:

> There are many other more creative ways of dealing with the issue of death and dying with young children. For instance, by real-life human examples – relations, neighbours, people in the news, including people in countries at war who die as a result of the use of guns . . .

In answer to the question, 'Aren't you imposing your values on the children?' she agrees she is, but

> . . . for very good reasons. Those liberals who ask that question impose values on their children all the time, so why not over the issue of death and destruction of people . . . and to break the chain of power men and boys have over women and girls in sexist play.[52]

When parents refuse to buy toy guns they may find their sons adapting anything they can find to turn into imaginary weapons. A 6-year-old boy persuaded his mother to buy him a hairdressing set: 'Ignoring the brush and rollers, he immediately took out the hairdryer and pretended to shoot me with it.'[53]

Tina, one of the mothers who talked to us, who does not want her son to be violent, to 'follow the crowd' and 'be one of the lads', says that she has a friend who thinks the same way with a 4-year-old who goes to playgroup: 'She doesn't want him to have weapons so she won't give him any. But he's been beating up the other little boys so he can have their swords and guns. You can't win, can you?'

WHEN CHILDREN ARE VIOLENT

Angela says her son, who is now 13, was until recently 'horrendously obnoxious'. When he was born:

> I thought he would mould into whatever I expected. The most important values for me were that I wanted him to be a neutral person – not with any of this macho stuff, (but) non-violent and liberal. In fact, he is a rough and tumble tomboy. He always had a tendency to grab back a toy, to dominate.
>
> It started as soon as he went off to playgroup every morning. I noticed a change in the way he was talking, his mannerisms, and his attitude to toys. He became interested in guns. I had never bought guns, but he built gun shapes out of lego and bent sticks to make guns.

In boys, it seems, Cain and Abel will out, and some mothers wash their hands of it feeling it entails too much energy to struggle against. Even if you avoid the guns, military hardware is sold in other forms. You can buy hand-grenade bubble-bath for little boys, and for grown men aftershave lotion packaged in a nineteenth-century replica pistol. Boys will continue to be fascinated by violence and war as long as it is heavily marketed at them and seen as a macho part of male identity. In 1982 the European Parliament passed a resolution asking member states to cease the advertising of war toys, phase out their production and give help to manufacturers to convert to other production. Mike William, British Home Stores merchandising controller, said, 'There appears to be an arms race among certain sections of the toy industry for who can produce the next more horrific concept. Our children may love it, but it has gone beyond all reasonable levels.' In 1987 BHS introduced a new range of toys built on a non-violent theme which is intended to be highly stimulating while diverting children from violence and destruction.[54]

After a spate of armed robberies on Co-op stores in the South East of England in 1988, fourteen shops withdrew their supplies of He-Man, Action Man and toy guns. A spokesman said:

> Robberies are a growing problem and are an example of urban violence that the staff have to face. The decision to ban certain toys was partly made in this climate. We had a strong feeling that parents shopping for toys with their children did not want to see rows of guns and we are fulfilling our role in the community by taking this line. Comments have been favourable, and most people feel the decision is the right one.[55]

At one American school – in San Antonio – pupils dropped war toys into a hole to be buried and were given teddy bears instead: 'It's to be a peacemaker,' said Matthew, aged 5. 'They're for shooting and war. We're saying "yes" to peace.'[56]

Mothers sometimes express great uncertainty about how to treat their children's violence. Some told us that they never reacted to violent behaviour with violence because that taught the child approval of it. Others feel that the only way to teach a small child that what they are doing is wrong is to slap and that the punishment should fit the crime. One mother, for example, whose 18-month-old was biting, says she bites her back, but admits that 'she doesn't take much notice'.

A woman who says she has never used physical violence towards her son remembers one exceptional incident in which her husband caned the boy who was 8 at the time:

> A gang of small boys, a crowd of very loud, extrovert youngsters, went up to the downs and things got a bit rough. They were tormenting young partridges – with their wings clipped – chasing them – and some of these little creatures died of heart failure. The farmer drove to our house with an opened

boot and there were three young dead partridges inside. I thought, 'What kind of creature have I produced?' James admitted he had a hand in it. We had a plastic fish slice and my husband caned him with it. Because we had never done this before the children were absolutely stunned by it. It pulled him up sharply.

In Western culture, as in many other societies, the issue of aggression comes to a head with the rearing of boys. It used to be claimed that male aggression was hormone-based, and that because of their high level of androgen men were innately more combative than women. Research findings in neuroendocrinology in the 1960s and 1970s question this. Androgens and oestrogens are present in both sexes and are 'erotic' hormones. Androgens are not 'aggressive' hormones. Males *learn* to be more aggressive.[57]

Some of the women who talked to us were especially on the lookout for aggression in their sons – even when still babies – because they do not want them to grow up aggressive. In a letter to a friend, Rosie describes how she first took her little boy Tom, aged 2, to playgroup. It was in a church hall and she didn't know any of the other mothers, though they all seemed to know each other. She bought a cup of tea and started talking to a woman with a baby of about 8 months sitting on the floor in front of her. Tom found a toy garage and was playing happily:

I'd just started to relax when Tom wandered over. 'Baba!' he said, with a beatific smile on his face, and crouched down, as I thought, to kiss this little mite. He bit her on the forehead so hard that when I eventually prised him off you could see every toothmark. Jen, I nearly died. I picked him up by one arm and slapped his leg so hard you could still see the finger marks an hour later.

She and Tom never returned to the playgroup. What worries Rosie is not only her son's violent tendencies but her own response: 'I still can't believe I hit him – I always swore I'd never use physical violence against my children – but something snapped.'

171

There is another side to this story. When Tom had stopped crying after his mother lashed out at him 'he sat on my lap and wiped my tears away so gently you'd never have believed he could have harmed a living thing'.[58]

In a tender, caring relationship with his mother, Tom had learned from her what it is to give and receive love. At the age of two he knew already what boys are under pressure later to learn – how to nurture.

Growing up to be men, boys are forced to cut the emotional link with their mothers and to deny the tenderness, compassion and sensitivity that flows from it. They have to pretend to be tough, even when they do not feel it. They are told that they must be brave, never cry, never show any but the crudest emotions of hatred or triumph in public, and that, above all, they must not be 'tied to their mothers' apron strings'. For little boys this is an emotional castration. They suffer from it, and women suffer from it, for at the same time boys learn that women are inferior and are there to be used – as cooks, cleaners, child-rearers, as well as sexually – and generally to provide service so that men can wield power. To become men boys learn 'the first violence – the severing of intimacy'. They also come to recognise their mothers 'as socially inferior beings.'[59]

Parents who want to bring up their sons in a non-sexist way are often anxious that if they are not aggressive they may also be non-assertive and turn into 'cissies' or 'mummies' boys'. One woman describes how she and her husband discussed their hopes for their newborn baby:

I want him to be *nice* to people. To be concerned for them. He won't be sexist, racist or ageist. It's very important that he's sensitive to other people. But Tony is worried that if we bring him up like this he'll turn out to be a wimp and other boys will take advantage of him. I think this will not happen if I teach him to be gentle to those who are gentle to him and tough with those who are tough.

The only solution she can see is to train her son to have a dual standard of behaviour.

Sometimes there is conflict between parents and their own parents about this. Georgie has three boys and describes the middle one, aged 3, as 'a bit of a wimp'. 'My mother says, "he'll turn into a gay."' She told her, 'I really wouldn't mind if they were gay.'

One striking element that emerges from discussions with mothers who teach their sons non-violence and to be gentle and caring is that their accounts usually stress their sons' 'masculinity'. In describing their sons' sensitivity and sympathetic nature they add that they are also 'rough and tumble', 'boisterous', that they 'talk tough', are strong, shoulder responsibility, identify with their fathers – and so make it clear that they can take on the accepted male role in society. Claudia, for example, says that she teaches her children, two boys of 16 and 12 and a daughter of 13, 'to respect and care for people, to see things from their point of view', and after talking about her sons for some time adds: 'My kids are normal. They are out with their leather jackets on bikes around the town – but I hope with that other dimension – awareness of other people.' Ruth, who is happy that she has taught her children a similar awareness and sensitivity, says that her son, aged 10, who is 'very tender with little children' and 'incredibly compassionate' also 'has the whole armour of the macho male' and is as 'tough as old boots at home'.

We were surprised that mothers who talked to us did not discuss aggression by daughters. This may have been because in the questionnaire we coupled 'violence' with 'terrorism' under the heading 'society' and in interviews we talked about 'violence', but not 'aggression'.

Sheila has a vivid memory of a little girl of about 2 years old who appeared on a TV programme in which Sheila was supposed to be solving children's behavioural problems in six minutes flat. The format was that child and mother sat on a couch beside her, the mother described the problem, the child looked adorable for the camera, and Sheila asked a few questions and then gave advice.

This particular 2-year-old was a pretty little girl with saucer-blue eyes and curly ringlets. She was dressed in pink and white frills and ribbons from top to toe. Her mother said she bit. She bit everybody. In fact, she warned me that at any moment she might move forward and bite *me*. I asked the mother if she would feel the same if her daughter had been a boy. She looked at me in amazement and said, 'Of course not. Boys behave like that. You expect that of boys.'

Mothers of daughters can usually think of many examples of girls' aggression, though it may be expressed in a different way from that of boys. A mother of seven comments: 'The boys always came straight out when they had done something naughty and said, "I did it." The girls managed to avoid that. They had ways of getting round it.' The implication is that girls get what they want with covert rather than overt aggression. Their aggression is canalised in behaviour which is socially acceptable for females.

Yet girls are often overtly aggressive with their dolls, and mothers are anxious that other people, witnessing this most peculiar 'mothering' behaviour in playground or nursery class, which consists of ordering and pushing the doll about, scrubbing its face clean, forcing it to sit on its potty, threatening, punishing and smacking or shaking, will think that they mother in the same way – for surely the child must have learned it from her mother?

A mother of two sons felt embarrassed about her boys' aggression and 'rumbustiousness'. One day she sat watching two little girls of about two and four in Kate Greenaway dresses with pinafores, a picture of sweetness, playing around a park bench. The younger child climbed onto it, and the older one, after a sideways glance to check that no one was looking, gave her a shove and toppled her to the ground. She had a momentary shock of pleasure that little girls could be like that, too.

Girls are often drawn into boys' violent playing as victims and property. They are sometimes used as a decoy or a quick 'front' for violence. The weekly newspaper of a small market town in England reported that a woman was robbed of £1,000 by a child gang. The children, all aged between ten and twelve years old, arranged for one child, described as 'a fair-haired little girl in a pink dress' to knock at the front door and ask for a drink of water while the others sneaked round the back and searched the house for valuables.[60]

Overt aggression does not pay off in the same way for girls as for boys. There are no social rewards in the form of power or progress up the ladder of career success. Their aggression is more likely to be expressed in words, a quicker, more precise command of language, and a sharper tongue.

DEALING WITH AGGRESSION

One way of dealing with children's anger and aggression is to help them acknowledge their feelings. Children's *feelings* of anger and jealousy, and even hate, are normal parts of life and we should acknowledge and validate them. We can suggest ways of dealing with these feelings that do not involve aggressive acts of violence.

Victorian child-raising manuals emphasised control of the emotions: the mother was enjoined to be calm at all times, communicating by her own behaviour to her children that only gentle unruffled feelings were permissible. The home was supposed to be a place of safety untroubled by the chaos and strife of the outside world. The same is true of Japan today. Japanese mothers aim to be always calm, controlled, pleasant and smiling, and to discipline their children in a quiet, orderly way, without coercion. Western psychologists, however, are more likely to suggest nowadays that we express our anger to children honestly and without aggression, as a way of modelling for children how they can deal with their own feelings.

The poet Audre Lorde strives to offer her son an alternative to violence by relating the child's experiences at the hands of aggressive boys to similar experiences in her own childhood. She believes the first step that boys must take if they are not to conform to the macho image is to acknowledge their vulnerable feelings. She describes how she reacted when her 8-year-old son Jonathan came home crying after being bullied at school:

My fury at my own long-ago impotence, and my present pain at his suffering, made me start to forget all that I knew about violence and fear, and blaming the victim. I started to hiss at the weeping child, 'The next time you come in here crying . . .' and I suddenly caught myself in horror. This is the way we allow the destruction of our sons to begin, in the name of protection and to ease our own pain. *My son get beaten up?* I was about to demand that he buy that first lesson in the corruption of power, that might makes right. I could hear myself beginning to perpetuate the age-old distortions about what strength and bravery really are.

And no, Jonathan didn't have to fight if he didn't want to, but somehow he did have to feel better about not fighting. An old horror ran over me of being the fat kid who ran away, terrified of getting her glasses broken . . .

I sat down on the hallway step and took Jonathan on my lap and wiped his tears. 'Did I ever tell you about how I used to be afraid when I was your age?'

I will never forget the look on that little boy's face as I told him the tale of my glasses and my after-school fights. It was a look of relief and total disbelief, all rolled into one.[61]

Small children believe their parents are omnipotent. It is tempting to play along with this so that they can feel secure in a dangerous world and also because it makes child 'management' easier. But we owe it to them to help them learn that parents can feel themselves powerless too, that might is not right, that we have our own fears and humiliations and that we strive to overcome problems, to cope with failure, and can be strong and firm in our convictions even though we do not always win. It is easy enough for children to handle success. What they need to learn from the adults they love is how to handle failure – and how to confront fear and humiliation.

In family life children are often aggressive because of fierce competition and jealousy between siblings. A woman in her forties describes how she felt when her mother had another baby:

I hated my sister's guts when she was born. When I say I was jealous, that's an understatement. I was 6. I was staying with my grandfather, and they phoned to say that my mother had had a baby girl. Grandma said 'Aren't you lucky?' I said, 'Tell them to send it back.' And she smacked my legs for it. 'God gave you a baby sister', but I hated her. I tipped her out of her pram and when we had a bath together, I gave her soap to eat. It's a wonder she survived.[62]

Thomas, aged 4, was extremely jealous of his brother Benjamin, 18 months younger. The family were living in Hong Kong at the time and Thomas, meeting a man on the beach who was attracted by the little one's blonde hair – which symbolised good luck – swapped him for something he had always wanted – a puppy. Police searched for the child for two days before finding him, very well looked after, in a Chinese gambling den.

Comparing children – 'Why can't you be more like your sister. She has beautiful table manners' – exacerbates competitiveness and jealousy. Acknowledging children's feelings is sometimes all that is necessary to prevent a violent outburst. One mother told us about a time when her 3-year-old was on the verge of throwing a tantrum: 'You are really angry,' she said to him, and grabbing a piece of paper drew heavy red lines all over it.

Is this how angry you are? He had been about to scream. Closed his mouth and took the pen from my hand. 'I'm this angry,' he said, adding more red lines. 'That really *is* angry,' I agreed. He seemed content at that. End of outburst!

It is especially important for girls to know how to become assertive and to express anger. Anger can be a good, healthy emotion. Anger about oppression and injustice can generate creative energy to right wrongs.

Those who profess to favor freedom yet deprecate agitation are men who want crops without plowing up the ground; they want rain without thunder and lightning. They want the ocean without the awful roar of its many waters ... *Power concedes nothing without demand.* It never did and it never will. Find out just what any people will quietly submit to and you have found out the exact measure of injustice and wrong which will be imposed upon them, and these will continue till they are resisted with either words, or blows, or with both. *The limits to tyrants are prescribed by the endurance of those whom they oppress.*[63]

Aggression between parents and children can be dealt with by expressing anger and by making it possible to be angry without the other person feeling the whole relationship is threatened, or out of control, or damaging. This may be especially important when children are in the 'terrible twos' and in the process of differentiating themselves, expressing their differences and asserting their wills. The temper tantrum is an assertion of self, an attempt to protect and insist on a still fragile and developing separate identity. It is an indication of growth towards individuality and independence. The mother's role then can be to acknowledge the child's anger, accept in a matter-of-fact, calm way that she and the child have incompatible needs, offer simple choices, negotiate gently and make compromise possible.

Sometimes books can help. Catherine Storr writes stories that could be described as psychofantasy in which the problems of children and young people are worked out in fantasy form. In *Marianne Dreams*, Marianne, 10 and ill in bed, draws a house and dreams herself into it; dreams a sick boy called Mark into it too; then, in anger, scribbles over his face at the window, draws prison bars and walls around the house and changes boulders around it into malignant one-eyed creatures. The real-life Mark's illness gets worse. Marianne helps dream-Mark in a brave escape. Real-life Mark gets better. The atmosphere in the dream sequence is one of fear, and although in a sense Marianne is only acting out a childish fantasy of hating and harming and she resolves the situation by getting dream-Mark out of the danger she got him into, what comes across with tremendous force is an awareness that one person can actually do terrible things to another person.

We can also show children the harmful effects of their hostility and coach them in ways of solving conflict.[64] In an experiment to help children see their behaviour and its effects from the point of view of the victim, and so develop a different perspective, 11–13 year-old boys classified as 'delinquents' made video films and plays in which they acted different roles. To assess the effectiveness of this approach, in another group the boys made cartoons and documentaries which did not include role-taking. And in a third they did nothing special at all. It was discovered that playing different roles and learning to see themselves through the eyes of others significantly reduced aggression and enabled the boys to develop more mature moral reasoning. The behaviour of boys in the other two groups stayed the same.[65]

Even very young children can understand the negative consequences of aggression and be helped to think about alternative conflict solving strategies. Mildred Masheder's book[66] is full of suggestions for forestalling aggression in primary school age children through use of role-play and imaginative games. She runs workshops for children in which they are helped to think about competition, co-operation and aggression.

The problems which children enjoy acting through and solving are about everyday, familiar kinds of conflict. A child has lost her pen, for instance, and she sees one just like it on another boy's desk. She takes it and the boy threatens to hit her if she doesn't give it back. What happens now? Two children are building a big castle with bricks and their little brother wants to knock it down every time. What should they do? A bigger child wants to borrow another's bicycle, or two children each want to watch a different programme on television. The children explore ways of sorting things out, first brainstorming what might happen next – then taking on different roles and acting them out with an adult's help, sometimes using puppets.

Instead of having to step in, take sides, play judge and come up with a solution, parents can restate the problem and put it right back where it belongs – with the children. Children can create their own original solutions – which are much more satisfying than solutions imposed on them by parents. Carol Gilligan tells the story of a little girl who wanted to play at keeping home and the boy who insisted on pirates. The girl finally said, 'Okay, you can be the pirate who lives next door.'

We need to help children find self-confidence and self-esteem. When we do this they are less likely to explode into violence, and more likely to believe in their own abilities to arrive at peaceful solutions.

The strongest lesson I can teach my son is the same lesson I teach my daughter: how to be who he wishes to be for himself ... and the best way I can do this is to be who I am and hope that he will learn from this not how to be me, which is not possible, but how to be himself. And this means how to move to that voice from within himself, rather than to those thoughtless, persuasive, or threatening voices from outside, pressuring him to be what the world wants him to be.[67]

We need also to recognise that the biggest problem is not the violence that children commit, but the violence that is perpetrated against them by adults. Children suffer the violence of poor housing, inadequate food, prejudice and discrimination. They suffer the violence of war and famine. They are victims of violence just *because* they are children. It is these social and political forms of violence against children that we must address.

CHAPTER
9

DEATH

Children's questions about death are the hardest to answer. Women say they find talking about death more difficult than any other subject they discuss with their children – including sex, birth and contraception. Part of the difficulty in talking with children about death is that dying is a much less common experience in the West today than it used to be in the past. We don't *expect* death. We act as though it never happens except to the very old and ill. We certainly don't expect children and young people to die.

But death continues to be of deep concern for many children, and it is a topic which cannot be concealed from them. It is beamed into the home on the TV screen – the deaths of evil monsters in the cartoon programmes, victims of famine and war on the news. The lifeless bundle of feathers in the winter garden, the squashed hedgehog at the roadside, the dying and much loved pet cat or dog – all provide the child with early awareness of death. Many children also have to face the deaths of family members – often a grand-parent, sometimes their father or mother. Adults usually find talk-ing about these deaths very painful. Sometimes they avoid such discussions altogether. Ofra Ayalon, now a psychologist specialis-ing in childhood bereavement, remembers when she was seven and went with her mother to visit a friend whose husband had been killed. She was crying and Ofra asked why. Her mother did not reply. Years later, she explained that she did not want Ofra to know that such things happened: 'It breaks my heart,' she said, 'to see my child being sad.'[1] Another mother rushed out to buy an identical hamster when she found her child's pet dead in its cage one morning. 'I couldn't face telling her that it was dead,' she said. 'I didn't know how to explain it.' To pretend that death doesn't exist, to push it away from us, is to imply that this is the proper way of dealing with other unpleasant realities in our lives. We teach children that pain and suffering are best ignored.

In eighteenth- and nineteenth-century London, as many as three in every four children christened were dead before they were 5 years old[2] and high child mortality rates are still the norm in many parts of the world. A 1989 Unicef report says that 150,000 children die each year in Southern Africa from the effects of armed conflict.[3] In the squatter settlements of Jordan four in every five children die before the age of 3 years.[4] Under conditions of famine or political tension, the death of children is not only a tragedy but may also be a necessity for the survival of the community. Where infant mortality is high, parents' attitudes to death have to be more pragmatic. One worker in Bangladesh recalls entering a hovel at a time of famine and watching a woman rocking backwards and forwards, wailing, on the mud floor. Beneath a dirty covering at the other end of the hut, two skeletal children lay limp with starvation, and beside the mother were two fish. 'Why do you not give them the fish?' he asked. 'I am waiting for them to die, and then I will eat the fish myself,' came the reply. Without their mother, the children would die anyway. She was choosing the practical course of action, even as she grieved for what she was doing. In the same way, Jewish women in hiding in Nazi Germany sometimes smothered their own babies to death rather than allow their crying to betray the presence of the many adults with them.[5]

Where infant mortality is high, it is usual for boy babies to be favoured over girl babies because when they are older they will be able to support the family and customarily take their aged parents into their own homes. Boys tend to be breastfed longer, given more food and are more likely to be taken to hospital when they are sick; in parts of India, the mortality rate for girls is 30 per cent higher than for boys. In China, with the one child per family policy, girls are much more likely to be aborted, or killed at birth.

Death is, for most people in the world, a fact of life; the sight and smell of it is all around – it cannot be tucked away in old people's homes or antiseptic hospitals. Our embarrassment about death in Western society today, our uneasiness with the topic, reflects our own unfamiliarity with it. Many adults have never been with anyone as they died, never seen a dead person. Few of us find it possible to really believe that we will die ourselves. Few have any confidence about what happens after death. In place of an afterlife, or a cycle of birth and rebirth, there is a great void. Death has become a harsh, meaningless state of non-being, an obliteration of self.

Yet until quite recently, death was a common topic of conversation with small children. Death was everpresent, and the child was reminded of this not only by the death of brothers and sisters from diseases like measles, scarlet fever and tuberculosis but also by discussion of her own possible death in the near future. In a book called *Spiritual Counsel: A Father's Advice to his Children*, written when his eldest son was about 5 years old, John Norris, a seventeenth-century writer, counsels his children 'to be much in the Contemplation of the shortness and uncertainty of life ... Act over frequently in your Minds the Solemnity of your own Funerals, and entertain your Imaginations with all the lively scenes of Mortality.'[6] James Janeway, one of the leading Puritan writers for children in the seventeenth century, published a book entitled *A Token for Children, being an exact Account of the Conversion, Holy and Exemplary Lives and Joyful Deaths of Several Young Children*. It tells of saintly children who died young in a rapture of prayer and was popular for many years, with reprints continuing into the nineteenth century.[7] John Locke recommended that the schoolboy wear leaky shoes to keep his own mortality in constant memory,[8] and one Victorian children's song had a verse which ran:

> There is an hour when I must die
> Nor do I know how soon 'twill come:
> A thousand children, young as I
> Are called by death to hear their doom.[9]

Today, most people would consider it quite wrong – evidence of a morbid imagination – to talk to children about death like this. But it seems that we have not yet developed an alternative approach. Many women comment how difficult it is to deal with this subject. One Japanese woman, whose 5-year-old son was with her when she gave birth to her second baby, says: 'He understood about birth, and he knows how the baby got inside. I tell him everything about sex.' When this baby died seven months later she told him that the baby was dead and that it lives on in her body and in her spirit: 'But I don't think he understands. It is difficult to explain death.' Like most mothers, she found sex and birth far easier to explain than death. Death has replaced sex as the great taboo subject.

Some parents reassure themselves that there is no need for discussion because children are tough and resilient, and they may point to children's callousness about death. One child's reaction to the death of her dog was 'Oh good, now I don't have to keep taking it for walks'. Another woman remembers that her chief worry about the death of her grandfather, whom she had hardly known, was related to questions of social etiquette: 'My main feeling was that I didn't know how to behave. I thought, "What am I supposed to do? How am I supposed to react?".' Like adults, children may be relatively indifferent to some deaths, and we should not urge children to express unfelt feelings or insist that they react to a loss with the emotions *we* consider appropriate. With other deaths, children may defend themselves against intensely painful feelings by assumed indifference or by 'forgetting' about the death. This is a common reaction to death for adults too. We may block out the pain by refusing to believe what has happened, or by acting as though the dead person might walk into the room at any minute. Among seriously ill patients who learn that death is near, at least one in five have no memory, after a few days, of having received such news. Faced with intolerable anxiety, they have blocked out the information.[10] Adults may be misled by this kind of response to label children 'callous' or 'indifferent'. But, like adults, they may also feel intense grief when people important to them die. Then we may be able to help the child to understand and come to terms with this grief rather than trying to minimise or dismiss it.

'Children bounce back after experiences like this,' said one mother, whose 5-year-old was deeply upset at the death of his grandmother. 'I know he's unhappy about it now, but he'll be over it in a couple of weeks. Talking about it would just prolong the agony, and anyway, he's really too young to understand.' The television presenter, Frank Bough, concluded a discussion about the little boy who lost all his family in the Zeebrugge ferry disaster with the comment, 'Well, children soon get over these things.'[11] Psychologist Ofra Ayalon, whose working life is spent with Israeli children, many of whom know at first hand what it is to be held hostage, shot at, and see friends and family die, comments:

> The attitude that children 'get over' bereavement, abandonment, humiliation and cruelty is adopted by those adults who are too frightened and too unsure of themselves to face up to the hard facts of life and the even harder facts of death. They impose on children the silence which prevents children from expressing their own thoughts and feelings, and through such expression mastering their experience. 'Mastering experience' means coming to understand the experience, and structuring our memory of the experience in such a way that we are no longer overwhelmed by it. We may still feel sad but we can cope with living.[12]

Anguish, pain and grief cannot be avoided. They *can* be borne, understood, and used for growth.

ACKNOWLEDGING GRIEF

A vital element in coming to terms with the experience of death is talking about it – acknowledging the child's grief and giving it a name. Anne's mother died when she was 9. Now 27, she remembers how the grandmother she went to live with 'never let me speak about my mother which I was longing to do. I didn't want Mum put in a drawer and forgotten about. But despite my efforts she became a taboo subject.' A man in his 70s remembers when he was ten: 'My mother had just died and my sister and I were standing beside the casket bawling. When my father saw my tears, he grabbed me and said, "We're *men*; we're not going to cry. We're going to be strong".' Long after, he writes: 'I've swallowed my tears for sixty years and all I've got to show for it is a lifelong lump in my throat and mean memories of my father.'[13]

Several adults who talked with us remember how much they valued the opportunity to share their grief and to discuss the person who died, reviewing both the pleasant and the unpleasant memories. This sometimes caused conflict with other people:

> I talk with my 12-year-old about her father and we discuss things we did together, and share our memories of him. My husband's parents find this totally unacceptable – they want him to be treated like a sort of saint and referred to only with proper reverence, 'never speak ill of the dead' etc. Whereas I want to remember him as a human being who was lovable, goofy, funny, sensitive and sometimes very irritating, forgetful and careless. I have had to tell Sally that Grandpa and Grandma feel different about Daddy and she understands that they have a different perspective and doesn't talk about him when she visits them.

Parents who find it easiest to talk about death with their children are often those with firm religious convictions. 'I told him that Grandad had gone to heaven to be with Grandma and Auntie Sarah and that he was happy now and in no more pain. He seemed to accept that,' says the mother of a 3-year-old. Another woman, a Roman Catholic with children aged 5 and 8 told them 'what I believe myself, that although her body is dead, her soul is still alive and has gone to be with God in Heaven and is happy there, and that soul and body will be reunited one day'. Religious explanations of death can often lead to quite complicated theological discussions with small children who want to know all the details about heaven: 'Is there ice cream in heaven?', 'Do wasps go to heaven when they die?' and 'Do angels wear knickers?' One woman who had explained about heaven to her children said:

When their dog died they asked if he was now in heaven. I had to say what I believe – that only people have immortal souls and that dead animals are just dead. They cried about that because they had thought they would see him again in heaven.

Other children reject the God who takes people away from them as cruel and unloving. 'When my mother died I was 9,' says a young woman in her twenties who had a Roman Catholic upbringing.

I lost my faith overnight. She was very religious and taught me to believe in God, but when she died I decided that there couldn't be a God, or if there was he was so horrible that I wanted nothing to do with him.

This is an old problem. James Boswell, the famous biographer of Samuel Johnson, describes in his diary how he talked with his daughter Veronica, aged 4, about heaven:

I talked to her of the beauties and charms of Heaven, of gilded houses, trees with richest fruits, finest flowers and most delightful music. I filled her imagination with gay ideas of futurity instead of gloomy ones, and she seemed to lift her eyes upwards with complacency. Yet when I put it to her if she would not like to die and go to Heaven, the *natural* instinctive aversion to death, or perhaps the *acquired*, by hearing it mentioned dismally made her say, 'I hope I'll be spared to you.'

Two years later, Veronica, now aged 6, told her father that she no longer believed in God.

By talking calmly with Veronica, I discovered what had made her think there was not a God. She told me 'she did not like to die'. I suppose as she has been told that God takes us to himself when we die, she had fancied that if there were no God, there would be no death [. . .] I impressed upon her that we must die at any rate; and how terrible it would be if we had not a Father in Heaven to take care of us.

Boswell adds, with some concern, 'I looked into Cambray's *Education of a Daughter*, hoping to have found some simple argument for the being of God in that piece of instruction, but it is taken for granted.'[14]

The Russian novelist, Leo Tolstoy, remembers his childhood ideas about death:

Remembering all of a sudden that death awaited me at any hour, at any moment, I made up my mind . . . that man can be happy only by making use of the present, and not thinking of the future; and for three days, under the influence of this thought, I neglected my lessons, and did nothing but lie on the bed, and enjoy myself by reading a romance and eating gingerbread.[15]

Adults are often disappointed in their hopes that children will respond to information about death with renewed faith in God and by striving to make best use of the time alloted them on earth. Like Veronica, they may deny the existence of a God who allows death to happen, or like Leo Tolstoy, they may decide to live only for the present.

Even without religious convictions, many parents resort to religious explanations of death because they don't know of any other way to approach the subject. Melody says she told her children of 2 and 3 years old that 'Daddy had gone to heaven to live among the angels'. She says:

I don't know why I said it. I don't believe it. I think it was the wrong thing to say because since then I have been bombarded with questions about what heaven is like and how angels behave and I just have to keep saying I don't know. Also, they can't understand why I'm so unhappy if Daddy is having such a good time, and they want to know if we can go and visit him there.

Feeling that their own ideas about death are too stark, adults cling to conventional beliefs of which they are not themselves convinced. A mother tries to comfort children on the death of their father by telling them that he will live eternally, while she herself is mourning a husband irretrievably dead. Or she talks about a grandmother being 'happy in heaven', while hopeless finality fills her own heart. The child is confused by these double messages, tests the mother's belief with constant suspicious questioning, and panics not only because of the loss but also because of the mother's inexplicably agonised reaction.

When parents attempt to reassure children with falsehoods, saying that the dead person is on a long journey, or has 'gone to sleep', they may be imparting new fears to children who feel betrayed by the person who abandoned them, going away without saying goodbye, or who are then terrified of going to sleep in case they never wake up again, like Grandad.

CHILDREN'S IDEAS ABOUT DEATH

Children develop theories of their own about death. Before striving to reassure them, we would do well to listen to their own thoughts on the subject. One woman remembers how, when her goldfish died, her mother flushed it down the lavatory and 'for a week I couldn't sleep for worry about how I was going to get mummy down the loo when she died!' A mother explained death to her 4-year-old son by saying that the world was not big enough and that some people had to die to make room for new ones. The child later said that he hated his little sister, born three weeks after his grandfather's death, 'because Grandpa had to die to make room for her'. Some children believe that death is a punishment for being bad. On the television screen and in the fairy stories, wicked and evil people die and the good live 'happy ever after'. Since they know that they are often 'bad', children may expect to be killed.

Children also often believe that they have in some way *caused* the death. This is especially clear when a parent commits suicide – an event which often leads the child to feel tremendous guilt and to believe that this resulted from their own disobedience. In one study, coming home late from the playground, a bad report card, and fighting with the boy next door, were all given by children as reasons for the parent's suicide.[16] A child's sense of guilt about the death of a loved one may also relate to parents' rebukes ('You'll be the death of me!') or prohibitions ('Over my dead body!'). Children in anger sometimes retort 'I hate you Mummy, I wish you were dead', and parents who feel hard done by may retort, 'You'll be sorry when I'm dead' – all figures of speech which trade on and reinforce guilt when a death does occur. One woman remembers the effect of this on her own childhood:

> Once my mother, hoping to improve my character and not knowing that her words would leave a lasting impression, told me that some day I would be sorry for my bad behaviour when I no longer had my parents. This thought remained with me for years. One day, it seemed, I would be pursued by implacable remorse and so, of necessity, barred from happiness.[17]

Children start to develop ideas about death when they are still babies. One psychologist has suggested that the alternation between sleeping and wakefulness may endow the baby with a 'pre-idea' of the difference between being and non-being. Appreciation of this distinction is enhanced at three months, when the child becomes fascinated with 'peek-a-boo' games in which a loved person disappears and is restored or 'resurrected'. The words 'peek-a-boo' stem from Old English words meaning 'alive or dead'.[18] When young children enjoy games of disappearance and return (throwing toys off the high chair and reacting with delight when they are returned) they may be experimenting with ideas about disappearance and 'not being', and these early experiments may form the foundation of later concepts of death. Yet it is a very difficult idea to accept. Small children typically deny the finality of death. They will accept that Grandpa is 'dead', but want to know when he is coming for supper. One 18-month-old boy wanted to replace a dead bird in the tree 'so that it will fly again'. And children are accustomed to 'dead' television characters who are drowned, crushed or dismembered, only to return an instant later without explanation.

Gradually a child comes to suspect that some things do *not* return, and may instead be 'all gone' – frequently one of the child's first and most often repeated phrases. Experiments with 'all gone' experiences – such as blowing out matches and flushing things down the toilet – prepare a child for accepting the irreversibility of death. And with this dawning understanding, comes fear and anxiety.

From a very young age, the child applies the concept of death to herself. After the Chernobyl disaster, 5-year-old Richard was worried about getting radioactive rainwater into his mouth. He said, 'I might die from cancer before I see Daddy's new car.'[19] Along with fear of one's own death, the child's fear of a parent's death is especially vivid. Willie, not yet 3, declared one morning without warning 'I don't want to die':

His mother was startled because he had never before indicated even an awareness of death. She reassured her son saying, 'You won't die for a long long time'. He began to whimper, 'I don't want to die. Hold me! Hold me, Mommy!' She sat down with him and he, still sobbing, began to recite the names of members of the family, adding vehemently in each case that he did not wish them dead. Although his mother tried to comfort him by repeating that he would not die for a long time, he seemed unconvinced, and for the rest of the day the child played 'dead' – pretended he was a bird flying and would strike the wall or some object quite deliberately and shout that he was dead and lie motionless on the floor. The next day he panicked at the thought that his father, who was at work, might be dead, and when he returned in the evening, demanded that he not leave the house again.[20]

The novelist, Allison Uttley, remembers her own first realisation that her father would die one day:

One golden morning of spring, I sat on a wall, level with my father's head. I noticed for the first time a few white hairs in his whiskers, and I asked about them.

'They're a sign of old age. I'm getting on,' said he, and he laughed softly, for he must have felt himself to be in the prime of life, strong as a horse, indomitable of will.

'Can't you stop them getting white?' I asked, and he shook his head with the slow movement I knew so well. 'Nay. It's Nature. It's the way we must all go,' said he, and he suddenly sighed.

I was desolated. Did it mean that when all his hair was white he would die? I wondered sadly, but couldn't say the words. A terror shot through me, wounding me to the heart, for this was my first realisation of the mortality of those whom I had thought to be immortal. I turned away and hid my apprehensions. In my new knowledge I felt older and wiser than my father.[21]

When a parent does die, children may feel angry at the parent for abandoning them and angry with other adults for not being the loved person they have lost – who is idealised as perfect and all-giving. They may also feel panic about future practicalities: 'Who will take care of me? Who will earn the money? How will I get to school in the morning?' Mary, who remembers praying to die in place of her father, recalls how she was told about his death when she was 11:

My mother came back from the hospital holding my little brother, who was 6 months old, in her arms, and she was crying. She told me to go out and tell my brother and sister to come into the drawing room and we sat there and she said, 'Daddy is dead'. And I remember running out of the house and the sky was impossibly blue and the sun was shining and it was unbelievable that everything could still be as it was. I felt cut off from it all as though I was in a glass bubble – it was all separate, apart. And I knew it was the end of my childhood. Childhood was over, for ever.

She is in her thirties now but still feels guilty about the last time she visited her father in hospital when he looked so strange and different that she was frightened and didn't want to be near him. She remembers, too, her anger with her mother:

You know how the early pioneers, when they were attacked by Indians, would put their waggons around in a circle and turn in upon themselves, that's what my family did. My mother's parents came to live with us, and my mother, who was a lawyer, gave up law (she'd had a joint practice with my father) and became a school teacher, and moved us thousands of miles away to a new home where there was no one she knew, to a place which she'd never visited with him, so everything changed. She wouldn't talk about him with us, and I was told by my grandmother not to ask her about my father, and I remember feeling angry that she kept him to herself. She acted as though he was *her's*, not our's, and became totally wrapped up in her own grief, which excluded us. I think she wanted to die when he did, and couldn't because she was left with these four children to look after. I think she felt stranded and angry with us because for us she had to go on living. I think she resented that.

Mary went on to talk about the long-term consequences of her father's death which, she says, have been different for each of the children:

My sister, who was 5 when he died, was terrified of falling in love with anyone. She only just got married now she's in her thirties. She thought that love meant loss and death. You fall in love and then he leaves you. My little brother never knew my father. There are pictures of my father with all the other children but not with my little brother who was six months old when he died. My parents, I guess, thought that taking that photograph would be too distressing, but my brother feels very bad about that, and has asked many questions about his father.

Mary herself has gone through many stages of coming to terms with her father's death, and is now facing a new challenge:

I am now 38, a year younger than my father was when he died, and I'm very conscious of that. It seems strange that I should go on living longer than my father did – that I should be older than him. So I suppose this is a time of reassessment for me, a time when I review my life and ask myself what I have done and what I want to do with the extra life that might be allotted to me – the life my father never had.

CEREMONY AND RITUAL

Like Mary, many children resent being excluded from mourning, and from the rituals and rites associated with death. In Western culture children are usually kept well away from deathbeds and funerals. One study found that 44 per cent of children were not even told of the death of someone close to them.[22] Death is a time of crisis, an important event which is marked by rites of transition. All cultures regard death, like birth, as a significant event. In no known culture is the individual left to face death completely uninitiated. People are always provided with beliefs about 'the dead' and about their own probable fate after death, and all cultures include norms governing the disposal of the corpse and the re-establishment of the tear made in the social fabric.

When someone dies, your relationship with the world is altered – you may move from being a wife to being a widow, from being a younger sister to being an only child. After a death, the people left behind find that their roles and obligations must change. The priest, the medicine man, the shaman – such people occupy roles a major function of which is, through ritualised actions and special ceremonies, to move both the dead and the living on to new positions in society.[23] In this culture, funeral services and the other rites associated with disposal of the body play an important part in reorienting people to their new roles. When children are barred from attending the funeral, they miss out on this important symbolic event. Instead of feeling that they have been shielded from something ugly and damaging, they often feel excluded from something significant. A funeral is a crucial occasion in the life of a family, and if a child is shut out, she is deprived of a sense of belonging; her security is shaken. Ann, whose mother died of leukaemia when she was 9, says:

I'm sure my relatives were trying to protect me, but being kept in the dark made it worse. I would dearly have liked to have seen my mother after she died, so that I could have said a final goodbye. I also wish I'd been able to go to her funeral, to pay the proper respects.

Joshua remembers, vividly, the death of his aunt when he was a young teenager. His mother and all her brothers and sisters got together to mourn her death, and he recalls standing outside in the darkness, looking up at the light shining out from the second-floor windows, and waiting for the screaming of keening women, grieving for a loss from which he was totally excluded.

Even when children are physically present at mourning and funeral services – they may still feel excluded unless they have a positive role to play. One of us (Sheila) remembers being taken, once a year, on a ritual visit to her grandmother's grave. All my five aunts stood there, clutching bunches of violets and weeping. I stood beside them, desperately wanting to be on my best behaviour, and to contribute to the solemnity of the occasion. Then I would start to giggle. This was a regular ordeal. I would giggle and giggle and giggle until tears poured down my face. It was a child's reaction to a highly emotionally charged situation in which the adults were totally absorbed in their own grief and the child had no role to play. When Sheila's mother died, Sheila involved Celia, then aged 11, in the service of thanksgiving for her life, and Celia remembers, with a sense of positive participation, reading Tagore in the Unitarian chapel. Gail Gugle's father died when she was seven, in a car accident, and she too was offered a positive role to play in the service. She says:

We buried Daddy in Iowa because that's where he was born. First there was a memorial service in a chapel and the next day we had a graveside service for only the family. We put seven red roses on top of the coffin, one for each member of the family: Mom, Greg, me, his parents, his grandfather, and his sisters. Red is supposed to be the colour of love and the rose is supposed to be the flower of love. We sat in some chairs and said a prayer and then we waved goodbye to Daddy.[24]

When children are denied the opportunity to participate (with a positive role of their own) in the rituals associated with grieving, they often find it hard to accept the reality and finality of the death. 'Because I never saw my mother dead,' says a teenager whose mother died in a car accident when she was ten, 'I've never really accepted her death. I still expect to walk into the house and see her – I keep hoping she'll be there.' A study of deaths in military action in World War II showed that the relatives of the soldiers killed had great difficulty in accepting the reality of the death of their kin for precisely this reason – because they had no opportunity to see the body or witness its disposal.[25]

In many cultures children play an important role in burial rituals. Amongst the Edo, in Nigeria, the funeral rituals on the death of a man last for six days. On the evening of the sixth day, a child may be chosen to represent the dead man himself. Attired in their finest robes, the other children and grandchildren come and kneel before him and the 'father' explains (through an 'interpreter' as he is not permitted to speak himself) that he will not cease looking after them and will still punish them if they do wrong. Then the 'father' goes outside to dance with his children for the last time. They sing: 'My father, you will come back soon, you will go and you will come back'.[26] On the other hand, the fear of danger emanating from the recent dead is quite common – especially the idea that in their loneliness they may attempt to draw their relatives after them. Among the Dagaba of West Africa, ashes are smeared on the children's faces to disguise them from the dead person so that their souls will not be abducted.[27]

One of the most important things that a child can learn from a death is the way in which the people around her cope with a crisis. Does everybody collapse with grief and become incapable of action?

Do people hide their feelings and pretend that nothing is wrong? Do people rally together and support one another? One adult recalls: 'I think there were certain times when I saw real struggles, strength of character, compassion ... I remember my father consoling my mother when Grandmother died.'[28] Writing about children present at births, one author comments:

> Children can gain a great deal from being part of a crisis. The most powerful gift of all may be an awareness of how totally we respond when a loved one is in distress or in danger. That awareness certainly builds greater security for the child ...[29]

Most children present during times of crisis – births and deaths for instance – learn that people care deeply for one another and understand how quickly and totally their parents and friends would respond if *they* were in need. By contrast, when a parent or especially a sibling dies, and the parent hides her grief and doesn't allow the child to attend the funeral, the child may think, 'If I should die it wouldn't make any difference to anyone – they wouldn't really care, they don't really love me.' Being present during times of crisis allows children to gain a sense of being worthwhile people who can contribute to the situation and whose participation is valued. This sense of having a useful contribution to make is what is missing from this account of her father's death by a woman interviewed thirty years later who still feels that her father's refusal to let her help him meant that she was never a real person for him:

> I remember when my father was dying. I was ten. He was in hospital, and I went with mother and sister to see him. Actually, I'd been in hospital myself, I'd had my tonsils out, and it wouldn't heal. I felt I knew how horrible it was, being in hospital. I was determined to let him know that I understood how he must be feeling. We walked down the ward and came to his bed. He took one look at me and said, 'Get that pasty-faced child out of here.' That was the last thing he ever said to me. I had to go and wait outside in a little waiting room.

I was angry that I hadn't been allowed to share with him the horror of being in hospital ... I always felt I was never a person for my father.[30]

Another woman is both angry and deeply unhappy that she and her three children were denied the right to attend the funeral of her lover, her children's co-mother:

Alice was like another mother to the children, especially the youngest, who had lived with her ever since she was five years old. Alice's parents had never accepted her lesbianism. When she died, they refused to have anything to do with me or the children. Eight years of living together were just obliterated and we were excluded from the funeral completely. I feel angry for me, and also for the children whose grief is totally unacknowledged and unrecognised – by their friends and teachers at school, by Alice's family.

Children who feel very strongly that they do not wish to visit a dying person, or to attend a funeral, or who, for whatever reason, are unable to attend, can often be involved in some other way in the crisis situation – answering the telephone while other members of the family are away, or caring for smaller children. If they later have regrets about their choice, they can then be reminded of the positive contribution they made, in their own way.

'DEATH EDUCATION'

In some North American schools, teachers have instituted 'death education', and the debate this has provoked is as ferocious as the debates around sex education when this was first introduced. There are horror stories about what goes on in these classes – tales of 6-year-olds being encouraged to make model coffins from shoe boxes, or taught the metric system by measuring themselves for caskets; rumours of 8-year-olds being asked to write their own wills as an essay project, or taken to visit funeral houses and crematoria as part of their social education. There's probably some truth in these stories – whatever is taught in school can be taught badly by insensitive teachers – but that's not an argument for not teaching such things at all.

Some children have clearly found such courses very disturbing. Tara Becker spent two weeks in a mental hospital diagnosed as suffering from severe depression after attending a 'death education' course at her high school. But others have more positive reactions. 'When my grandmother died last year,' says Wendy Dunn, 'I was able to help my mother to go through it. She told me to go away and leave her alone, but I was able to say, "I know how you feel".' Deborah Brodt felt that death education helped her to make sense of the grief and helplessness she felt after a sudden succession of deaths: 'My mom died, my boyfriend died, and a friend jumped off a bridge, all within a few months of each other. I can't say the course saved my life, but it did enable me to express my feelings.'[31]

By the age of 18, one in twenty American children has had to cope with the death of a parent. Many more have experienced the death of a grandparent, teacher, sibling or friend. Amongst one class of 15-year-olds in Washington, fourteen of the nineteen children had a friend or relation who had been killed: 'My cousin tried to stop an argument in the street,' said one girl, 'and they shot him. Twice in the neck and once in the heart.' Another girl describes how her 15-year-old friend met his death: 'There was somebody with a gun in Eastgate and he ran away but was shot and the hospital pronounced him dead.'[32] The death of school teacher Christie McAuliffe, in the satellite launch of which she was the first civilian member, was screened to the nation. Dozens of children watched as their teacher was killed in front of them on the TV screen. The need for counselling for those children was immediately recognised, and is part of the wider spectrum of 'death education' in the United States.

While this approach to 'death education' may have its excesses, the more usual British approach, which is total denial of death in school, is also problematic for many children. Cruse, the national organisation for the bereaved, found that bereaved children complained bitterly about the attitude of their teachers to their bereavement. Stephen, for instance, whose mother is dead, is facing the frustration of being given mail to take home addressed to 'Mr and Mrs'. Not only has he repeatedly complained, his teacher is now getting annoyed at his insistence. Other children have been hurt by the way teachers spread the news to their classmates without first consulting them. 'I didn't even know the teacher had told the class till a girl turned round and said "I knew your dad died before you did,"' said Anna. Teachers often seem impatient with grieving pupils, or seek to protect themselves with platitudes.[33] One primary school teacher recalls her colleague's surprise that a child whose mother had died was behaving untypically six weeks later because she felt 'She ought to be over it by now'.[34] Children are expected to have magical powers of recovery.

DISCUSSING DEATH

Like teachers, parents find it difficult to discuss death with children. The most difficult time, of course, is when someone close to you has died. Wrapped up in your own grief it can be hard to respond to a child's needs. One woman whose husband committed suicide when her son was 9 weeks old, said, 'Sometimes when he says Da da da (they all do around that age) I shout at him "Don't, you haven't got one".'[35] Another mother explained her father's death to her children in terms of ageing and fulfilment of purpose, describing how the new shoots bursting on the trees in spring become the withered dry leaves falling in autumn in the inexorable cycle of birth and death. Her children were aghast and incomprehending when their new baby sister died at 4 months, and the mother was so depressed that she was unable even to attempt an alternative explanation: 'The children were completely taken aback.' She says, 'Nothing had prepared them for this, and I couldn't cope at the time and neglected their feelings completely. I'm still coping with the fallout of that two years later.'

Others wrote of times when they felt they coped well, and when the grief was shared by children and adults in a way that brought those involved closer together. A woman whose father died of cancer, tells how he made a last 'goodbye' phonecall to his grandchildren, speaking to each of them in turn, telling them how much he loved them, and how important they had been to him. Susan, an atheist from a Christian background, found the Hindu concept of death the most useful in talking to her children:

> I told them that the human soul – the most essential part of us – is like air, temporarily trapped inside a jar (the body). At death the air is released and becomes part of the endless space. They seemed to understand that, and it avoided all those questions about heaven and angels.

Other adults use the imagery of a drop of water joining the sea. Julie told her children, on the death of their grandfather, that 'though people as you know them disappear, they reappear through different generations. It's a candle that's passed on from one generation to another.'

The story of the Little Prince by St Exuperé was useful for another woman. 'I cannot carry this body with me,' says the Little Prince. 'It is too heavy. But it will be like an old abandoned shell. There is nothing sad about old shells.'[36] For older children, the Christian allegory of C. S. Lewis's books has proved useful, and so too has *Charlotte's Web*,[37] describing the death of Charlotte, a spider, whose death is made bearable by the continuance of life through the offspring.

Most difficult of all situations, is the case when a child is dying. How can you talk to a child about her impending death? It is hard enough to cope with our *own* feelings about the death of a child – the sense of shock, of numbness or unreality, the anger that this could happen and impotence because we are powerless to do anything about it. Many parents feel guilty and, especially when the child is dying of an inherited abnormality, responsible for causing their child's suffering. Each partner may blame the other for 'causing' the disease, and both sets of grandparents may blame the other family for passing on faulty genetic material. One way in which parents may try to protect themselves is to cut themselves off emotionally and snuff out feelings that are too painful to endure.

Sometimes parents experience a loss of feeling for the dying child as they begin to separate themselves from her in anticipatory mourning. Healthy children in the same family may be overprotected lest they too be taken away. Or the very opposite may happen and they may be virtually abandoned as parents put all their time and energy into the dying child. The mother of a 9-year-old dying of a brain tumour describes her hostility to her other children: 'When I come back from the hospital I can't bear the other children near me. It seems such an insult to her to be cuddling them.'[38]

To live with the knowledge that a child is dying is a harrowing experience. Because it is so painful, adults may try to avoid open discussion with the dying child. Many people (parents, doctors and nurses) deny that young children can be aware of the implications of their illness and so avoid initiating any such discussion. One doctor has described some families in which children are dying of cystic fibrosis as locked in 'a web of silence'.[39] Parents find it hard to discuss their child's death either with each other or with the child. One father, struggling with the question of what to say to his dying 4-year old daughter, says:

We were told by the consultant that the child would not live beyond 5. There is a problem now in relation to what we should tell her. You can't just rush in and say, 'You're not going to live beyond this year,' and yet she is entitled to know. What would you tell her? There's no sense in only giving her half the truth. If you're going to say anything you've got to say the lot or she'll wonder what you're hiding . . .[40]

Even very young children often work out that they are dying before they are told so by their parents – perhaps as a result of overheard conversations, discussions in front of them by doctors who assume they are 'too young to understand', or from the media. One 5-year-old overheard a visitor remark that 'these children die before they become teenagers'. Her mother reports: 'She couldn't get it out of her mind. She kept saying: "I'm not going to die. He's not going to make me die. I'll die in my own time."' A 10-year-old with cystic fibrosis watched a television programme about his condition and realised from this that he was going to die.[41]

Many childhood illnesses like leukaemia and cystic fibrosis are genetically inherited, so that a child dying of them may well have had a brother or sister who died of the same disease. Children are quick to notice similarities between themselves and the one who died, and even if reassurances concerning their health are given, they treat them with cynicism. One 8-year-old, told that her illness was under control and that she was 'doing fine', protested 'That's what the doctor said about Mark [her brother] and he died'.[42] The youngest child in another family had already watched his older brother and sister die of degenerative brain disease, and when he too began to show symptoms he talked openly and accurately about how he believed the illness would develop in him and cause his eventual death.[43]

When adults refuse to talk about death with these children, they are condemning them to fear and loneliness; they come to believe that no one else knows what they are experiencing, or that the disease is too awful to be talked about. This is made worse in hospital wards where doctors are concentrating on the children who can be made well again. For some hospital staff the dying child is a symbol of medical failure, and may be avoided for this reason. Nurses are sometimes embarrassed and upset by the knowledge that the child is dying, and feel they have to protect themselves from becoming too attached. As a result, the child may feel totally abandoned. 'Nobody really talked to me,' says one child with leukaemia. 'It was like they were getting ready for me to die.'[44]

Describing their own experiences in telling dying children about their diagnosis, two doctors have written that 'every child who is lying in bed gravely ill is worrying about dying, and is eager to have someone to help him talk about it'.[45] According to another doctor[46] many children ask their doctor whether they are dying long before their parents consider telling them, and the child's first concern is, ironically, often to conceal this from her *parents*, 'so as not to worry them' and 'because I don't want to be a nuisance'. Many children express concern about the time and money spent on them, and feel guilty and ashamed about the grief they are causing their parents. They hope that by concealing the fact that they are dying from them they can spare them some grief. Other children feel very angry with their parents for 'allowing' them to become ill and die, or interpret medical procedures as unfair punishment. Only by asking children what they think, and openly discussing with them their illness and approaching death, can adults help them to understand what is happening and deal with their fears about dying. One mother discovered that her 8-year-old daughter's main fear about dying was of being put in a box in the ground. She told her this wouldn't happen, and the child became much calmer. Another child wanted, more than anything else, to be told that his parents were glad to have had him, that they didn't wish he'd never been born just because 'now I won't be able to support you in your old age'.

Like adults, children can become resigned to death, and ready for it. One 7-year-old said: 'I'm tired of being sick. I want to go to Heaven. I told God last night that I want to go to heaven as a little girl – not to grow up.'[47] Another child said, two weeks before she died, that she was 'ready to die' and 'wanted to stop fighting for life'. Parents who impose their own desperate wishes for life on to the child are not necessarily being helpful. We need to allow the dying child to lose the will to live, and to accept death when that becomes inevitable.

Children can be realistic about death – perhaps more realistic than we may be ourselves. They can also show great courage and sensitivity when someone they love dies, or when they are dying themselves. Adults can help by talking as simply and honestly as we can, and by being willing to discuss our own feelings and ideas about death as well as listening to the child's views. If we try to 'protect' children from knowledge of death and from the rites and rituals associated with it, we exclude them from significant social experiences. Given the opportunity actively to participate in times of crisis, children learn important values – about how much people love each other and about our readiness to respond to suffering and pain.

CHAPTER
10

RELIGION

When schools in the American deep south were first desegregated Ruby Bridges, a black child in New Orleans, walked past heckling mobs to and from school for months while they jeered, hurled insults and spat at her. She was 6 years old.

Ruby's family were sharecroppers who had just arrived in the big city in search of a better deal. For the best part of a school year Ruby attended classes by herself, while white families boycotted the school and kept their children at home.

A teacher watched Ruby from the window as she walked to the school one day, protected against the mob by federal marshalls, and described what she saw:

> The crowd was there, and shouting, as usual. A woman spat at Ruby but missed. Ruby smiled at her. A man shook his fist at her; Ruby smiled at him. Then she walked up the stairs and she stopped and turned and smiled one more time! You know what she told one of the marshalls? She told him she prays for those people, the ones in that mob, every night before she goes to sleep.[1]

When a psychoanalyst, called in to advise the teachers, interviewed Ruby, she told him:

> They keep coming and saying the bad words, but my momma says they'll get tired after a while and they'll stop coming.

They'll stay home ... The minister says if I forgive the people and smile at them and pray for them, God will keep a good eye on everything, and He'll be our protection. I'm sure God knows what's happening, and He can't help but notice. He may not rush to do anything, not right away. But there will come a day, like you hear in church.[2]

The values of Christianity – love your enemy, do good to those that harm you – gave Ruby courage to meet the challenge of that hostile mob of adults, day after day, week after week, month after month – an experience that might have crushed another child.

RELIGION AND MORALS

Many people see religion as central to morality. Historically, children have always been taught how to be 'good' within the context of religion. Until the end of the seventeenth century in the West children's leisure reading was limited to the Bible and religious tracts, and there were no books written specially for them. Even *Pilgrim's Progress*, published in 1688, was intended for adults. In fact, not until 1780 did professional authors turn their attention to writing for children in any other than the narrowest religious terms.

At the beginning of Elizabeth's reign, to ensure conformity to the new Church of England it was made compulsory to attend parish church on Sundays and Holy days. Anybody not there had to pay a fine of twelve pence. Laws were passed requiring all heads of families to teach their children the catechism and the principles of religion. Roman Catholics and members of other sects were forbidden to send their children to be educated on the Continent in the faith of the parents, and if children were discovered being smuggled out of the country, the Anti-Recusant Acts of 1585 and 1593 gave the Crown power to lodge them in the homes of staunch members of the Church of England. This was not always successful, as the experience of John Fitzherbert's two daughters illustrates. After a whole year in the household of William and Richard Sale, both Church of England rectors, they continued in their 'obstinacie' and could not 'be induced into conformitie from their superstitious and eronious opinions'.[3]

Calvinism taught that children were born sinful and were in the same danger of perdition as the most hardened adult sinners. Parents were haunted by the belief that 'children are not too little to die, they are not too little to go to hell'. Preachers advised parents to start giving religious instruction when babies were still in their cradles, or were being dandled on their knees. 'So soon as the children be able to speak plainly,' wrote Thomas Becon,

> let them even from their cradles be taught to utter not vain, foolish and wanton, but grave, sober and godly words; as God, Jesus, Christ, faith, hope, patience, goodness, peace, etc. And when they be able to pronounce whole sentences, let the parents teach their children such sentences as may kindle in them a love towards virtue and a hate against vice and sin.

He proposed as suitable aphorisms, 'God alone saveth me'. 'There is no damnation to them that are in Christ Jesus' and 'Learn to die'.[4]

Puritans wished their children to live in the consciousness of the hereafter. In *A Token for Children* James Janeway warned his young readers that 'Children who lye, play the truant and break the Sabbath will go into everlasting burning ... They which never pray, God will pour out his wrath upon them.'[5]

The conviction of sin and of everlasting punishment affected some children very deeply. John Bunyan wrote in later life of terrible visions of Hell derived from a sermon denouncing dancing and games that he heard preached when he was nine: 'These things did so distress my soul, that then in the midst of my merry sports and childish vanities, amidst my vain companions, I was often much cast down and afflicted in my mind therewith.'[6]

Books for the moral education of children first really came into being in the eighteenth century. John Newbury, a painter, saw a gap in the market and the commercial possibilities of publishing children's books. He wrote some himself, published many others and opened the first children's bookshop, in St Paul's Churchyard. One of his early books, written in 1743, was *A Little Pretty*

Pocket-Book, intended to 'make Tommy a good Boy and Polly a good Girl. To the Whole is prefixed a Letter of Education humbly addressed to all Parents, Guardians, Governesses, etc., wherein Rules are laid down for making their Children strong, healthy, virtuous, wise and happy.' With the book there was a ball (for boys) and a pincushion (for girls) coloured half red, half black. Pins were to be stuck in one side or the other to record the good or bad deeds of the child who owned it.[7]

This children's literature began a new era of moral and religious education in which the emphasis was put on amusing as well as instructing children. Mrs Barbauld, who wrote stories of moral instruction for children aged two to four, defined her task as being 'to impress devotional feelings as early as possible in the infant mind . . . by connecting religion with a variety of sensible objects, with all that he sees, and he hears, all that affects his young mind with wonder and delight; and thus by deep, strong and permanent associations to lay the best foundation for practical devotion in future life'.[8]

Many of these publications were specifically for boys or girls, it being taken for granted that a boy should 'turn out a brave, helpful, truth-telling Englishman, and a gentleman and a Christian'[9] and a girl a good wife and mother. There were titles like the *Boy's Week-day Book*, which 'reproved folly and vice (and) commended wisdom and virtue. It has endeavoured to amuse and instruct you and to excite in your heart the disposition to avoid all that is evil and to attain everything which is good.'[10] In 1879 *The Boy's Own Paper* was first published, its focus on adventure, the outdoor life and cold baths. This journal of muscular Christianity ran successfully for more than eighty years.

Though in most of this literature virtue is rewarded and vice punished (in a more or less appropriate fashion) children must often have observed a discrepancy between the lessons taught and their actual experience. Gwen Raverat, writing about her Victorian Christian upbringing, says:

From my earliest childhood I knew very well that Being Good did not pay. It was just a thing that you might – or might not –

like for it's own sake; and the verse about the wicked flourishing like the green bay tree, was one of the few texts that went home to me with a click.[11]

She goes on to say: 'Goodness never made me feel nicer; I must be abnormal, for the reputed afterglow of virtue simply did not occur. Goodness-against-the-grain simply made me feel mean, hypocritical and servile.'[12]

With the colonisation of newly discovered lands, children were taught to save their pennies to give to missionaries so that 'poor black children' could 'be taught to fear the great God and love Jesus Christ' and 'die happy'. They were told that 'you might as well pray to your whipping top or a stone in the wall' as to the idols worshipped by the heathens. The pilgrimages of other faiths were 'mass delusion'. On these pilgrimages:

Many of the men and women fall down and die on the road as they are going or coming back. If a poor man falls down on the road in England, the first that comes past will try to help him, but there they never do. He is left to die alone.[13]

Not only was Christianity prescribed as the only religion in which any social concern existed, but the issues of poverty, disease and starvation were wholly evaded in explaining the pilgrims' deaths as due to sun-stroke, 'Do all you can for missionaries,' children were told, 'that the people all over the world may burn their stupid wooden idols.' In England poverty and homelessness were caused by parents being 'either very silly people or very idle,' or by the father's drunkenness – never by a social system in which a whole section of the population was deprived and powerless.[14] Children were being taught ethnocentrism and uncritical acceptance of Victorian imperialism and capitalism, which was seen as the pinnacle of history and summit of all human achievement, along with a strong belief in human progress.

Even today some parents and educators are critical of children's literature which fails to provide religious instruction. In 1986 twenty-three children's books went on trial in a court in Tennessee because they were accused of violating fundamentalist Christian beliefs. One was the story of Goldilocks, who never got punished for breaking and entering the three bears' house and for eating their porridge and wrecking their furniture. Another was the Three Little Pigs, whose whooping it up at the demise of the Big Bad Wolf smacked of witchcraft. Other books told children about evolution instead of teaching them that God made the world in six days. 'Our children's imaginations have to be bounded,' said Vicki Frost, a member of a right-wing organisation called Concerned Women of America, criticising a reading exercise in which twelve year olds were asked to 'use the powerful and magical eye inside your head' in order to imagine themselves part of nature because 'the children of Christians cannot violate their religious beliefs by participating in an occult practice'.[15]

SEPARATING RELIGION AND MORALS

Other parents who are atheists or agnostics strongly object to the imposition of religious ideas on their children. 'My children are indoctrinated with Christianity at school,' one mother told us. 'I don't want them stuffed full of mumbo-jumbo about angels and devils and such. I believe in humanistic values of love and justice and want to share those with my children.'

A person can be highly moral, yet not at all religious. Equally, someone who is religious may have questionable morals. A study of almost 3,000 senior high school pupils in Lutheran schools revealed that 'religious activity and cognitive beliefs are quite unrelated to much or little involvement in questionable or immoral practices'.[16]

Ronald Goldman, an educator in the Church of England, believes that 'to use religion directly as a means of teaching moral values is to start the wrong way round':

There is no Christian moral specific about war, divorce, family planning or race relations, much though some of us would like such practical directives about these problems. Christians disagree among themselves on all these issues, and many more, *because they have to interpret the meaning of the law of love in each situation . . .* (our italics).

He sees this law of love as essential to Christian faith and agrees with St Augustine, 'Love God and do as you like', 'for if the implication of love is followed, then all that we do will be consistent with love'.[17]

The internalisation of morality through religious precepts is only one among a variety of approaches to moral education, and morality that is inculcated with fear of triggering God's vengeance is unlikely to stimulate spontaneous loving and caring for other people. Those who believe in a punitive God are convinced that they can never ultimately get away with doing wrong. In a sense, the guns are always pointed at them. You can't sneak past God, and He has all eternity to make you pay for your sins. Since He can read minds, even bad thoughts can be dangerous.

MEANINGS OF WORSHIP

Many women who talked to us saw religion as providing a systematic framework in which morality could be taught and justified. For some – 1 in 25 – the most important element in communicating values to their children was regular attendance at a place of worship: 'If my daughter goes to church regularly she will learn all the other values. We have set a good example ourselves, regularly attending worship and trying to be aware of our conduct and its effects.'

These mothers often criticise their parents who professed religious observance but were superficial about it and merely conformed to social custom which included a particular style of worship:

Mum took us to church at Christmas and Easter only and did not encourage us to go at other times. I take all three children to church every Sunday, and help them to understand and enjoy the service as much as possible, and we pray together and talk about Jesus as we go about our daily living.

My mother encouraged 'freedom of thought' and is basically Catholic. Her 'no action' left me wondering, wanting to find out more, but suspicious of religion and too afraid to go on my own. I'm giving my children a chance to find the Lord themselves.

Women who were sent off to church or Sunday School by their parents in order to get them out of the way are determined never to do this with their children. Janet says her parents 'never set foot in a church', but packed her off to Sunday School. She, on the other hand, takes her children regularly to church and is very happy with a church school she has selected for their general education as well.

These mothers sometimes start praying with their babies in the first year of life and begin to take them to a place of worship when they are still very young. Fiona's daughter is 2 years old. Fiona says: 'Being a Christian and all this entails is the top priority in our lives. We have taught her that God loves her and that Jesus died for her. She loves going to church.' Erica has a 2-year-old son. She says: 'The most important thing is to go to a place of worship, where they learn all the other values, plus love and fellowship. God can put a "light" into a child's life.'

The mothers most likely to take their children to church regularly before they are 2 years old are also those who are most critical of their own parents' lack of religious conviction. They say things like:

We have attended church since he was a baby ... Belief in Jesus Christ is paramount – His teaching leads to all the other values.

I am taking him regularly from an early age so that it becomes a natural part of his life – but not just a duty.

I feel everything stems from one's faith. My son attends Mass with us now.

They try to make it all fun for their children and emphasise that it is important to have a happy atmosphere and a church where children are welcome.

A Jewish book on religious education also emphasises the importance of creating a happy atmosphere:

> Properly observed, the Shabbat can quickly become the high point of the very young child's weekly experiences. The festively set dinner table, the lit candles, the dressing up of each other, the recitation of the Kiddush and the sip of wine that follows, the special *hallot* on the table, the singing of songs – all of this is an eagerly awaited occasion, sometimes mystifying and filled with wonder, always happy and gay for the child.[18]

Knowing how to make religious instruction pleasant for children is not a discovery of the twentieth century, though there are stereotyped views that in the past it consisted entirely of warnings of damnation and threats of Hell Fire. In fact, loving parents were often concerned, like the mothers who talked to us, to avoid forcing the pace of religious instruction and to engage their children's interest. It was not just a constant stream of indigestible sermonising. There is a long tradition – back as far as Puritanism – of trying to attract children to religion by things that please them.

Cotton Mather, a late seventeenth-century Puritan, recorded in his diary that he had introduced religion 'with delightful Stories' and presents a rather touching, if slightly inept, picture of how he dropped nuggets of religious wisdom: 'When the Children at any time accidentally come in my way, it is my custom to let fall some *sentence* or other, that may be monitory and profitable to them.' Some time between the ages of 9 and 11 he took each child alone into his study to pray and made this a special privilege – a symbol of growing up.[19]

A mother in the early nineteenth century wrote:

> I begin to have my children in the room at prayers, within the month after their birth; and they always contrive to be present,

unless they are sick, or are excluded the *privilege* as a punishment for having been very naughty. It is difficult, when they are quite young, to keep them perfectly still ... After they get to be two years, or more, old, and are able to understand the meaning of your conduct, if they play, or in any other way make a disturbance, they may be taken out (of the room).[20]

Another woman wrote that she showed her son pictures illustrating Scripture stories: 'Sunday is made very much of a treat: the cake, clean clothes, a large picture Bible, walks with poppa and momma in the garden.'[21]

For parents in many different countries attendance at a place of worship is an outward sign of resistance to a social system which they believe to be evil, tyrannous or just plain wrong. This is how it is for many black parents in South Africa, fundamentalist anti-evolutionists and 'pro-lifers' in the American South, and for those who oppose the dominant political system in Communist states. Their children's attendance at church services and church schools is intended to provide a bulwark against the power of the state and to counteract the teaching about values which children receive in the established school system. A Polish woman with two children told us:

The Catholic church represents opposition to the authoritarian state. We send children to church schools on Saturdays, and people attend church as a gesture of defiance and a symbol of freedom. I don't believe in God, but we are bringing our children up as Catholics because Catholicism in Poland is not just a religion. It's about being a particular type of person, someone who is *for* certain political values and against others. And we want to identify ourselves with those people.

Worship in common represents a shared culture, too. For British settlers in far-flung posts of the Empire family attendance at the Anglican church was a symbol of identity, even though they did not necessarily believe in the teachings of the church. Another Pole, one who is living in England, says he and his wife send their children to the Saturday school for this reason: 'It makes children feel secure,' he says, and reinforces this view by reference to what he sees as the church's historical function in Poland:

> The church has always protected the people against the system – since medieval times. It has a unifying function and provides a cultural focus. Much of our culture is associated with Catholicism, so this is an important element in my children's moral education.

Parents believe that the power of shared worship, knowing where you belong and with whom you belong in terms of faith and values, can give their children confidence to face a hostile and ugly world in the same way as it did for little Ruby Bridges. In store-front churches in the inner cities of North America, in red-brick chapels in England, in tin shacks in the Caribbean, Pentecostalist, Baptist, Rastafarian, and parents of many revivalist and millenarian faiths, hope their children will find their identity in God's family – even, in the case of the Rastafarians, as princes. Becoming differentiated from other people, they are the chosen, the elect of God.

In Jamaica preparation for church can take hours. Clothes are laundered, starched and ironed, shoes polished, the children bathed and scrubbed, hair washed, little girls' hair meticulously plaited and beribboned and food prepared for the long day ahead. Up in the hills all the women and children of a dispersed community may gather, along with some of the men, and the whole day, from sunrise to sunset, is spent at church. There are exultant hymns, spirit possession and ecstatic speaking with tongues, rousing sermons, fervent prayers and vigorous dancing. It is the big event of the week. Children who every other day live in the dust of poverty celebrate a shared faith and inherit the riches of the Kingdom.

Many of the mothers who talked to us and who believe strongly in regular attendance at a place of worship are certain that it helps children be more secure in their own identity – as Christians, Jews, Muslims, or whatever. As an Evangelical Christian expresses it, she hopes to provide 'a framework in which the child can flex itself a bit and know where the boundaries are. I'm sure this must make a child feel more secure and wanted.'

Sarah says she is determined to give her children awareness of their Jewish cultural heritage and a sense of identity. This is especially important because the family is rather isolated and most of the children's friends are not Jewish: 'Part of that identity is the strong family ties and gathering together as a large family on occasions like Passover. I try to mix with Jewish friends whom I've met through the Synagogue for the same reason.' Her son, aged 4½, realises that he is Jewish. When he was 3 he became very interested in churches because he thought they were 'forbidden fruit'. Now he 'covers his ears when Auntie Grace is watching Songs of Praise on TV and says, "I mustn't listen to this!"' It makes her wonder whether she has over-done her teaching about the Jewish faith being different and 'special'.

The fear that their children will not 'belong', that they will be deprived of their roots, makes some parents anxious that cultural diversity and learning about other people's faiths – at school, for instance – will be harmful. In some religious communities, where emphasis is put on traditional culture and unchanging beliefs, primary school age children are carefully and systematically shielded from as much knowledge of the outside world as possible. In one English school, the Talmud Torah Machzikei Haddass school in London, boys' education follows traditions which are 3,000 years old. Five-year-olds spend most of the day learning Hebrew, and reading passages from the Bible in Hebrew with Yiddish translations and from the Talmud. If it were discovered that a child was watching TV at home he would be dismissed. The headmaster says: 'The whole aim of the school is that there should not be conflict in a child's life ... This is why the community doesn't want outside influences brought to bear.'[22]

During the 1980s many schools in Britain organised their assemblies to meet the needs of pupils from different cultural and religious backgrounds, and the act of assembly was intended to gather all together in one community. In areas where there was an immigrant population, head teachers incorporated stories, hymns and acts of worship from many faiths. When the children met together it became an affirmation of the richness of cultural diversity and respect for each other's beliefs, and a way of growing to understand the spiritual values of holy books other than the Christian bible.

Some parents always felt very uncomfortable with this. It came to a head when two mothers in Manchester, one of whom admitted that she was not religious in any way, insisted that if their sons, aged 8 and 7, were going to learn about any religion, then it must be Christianity. When the primary school they attended, in which nearly 40 per cent of pupils are of Asian and other ethnic minorities, continued to celebrate Hindu and Jewish festivals, they kept their children out of school, and were supported in this by the right-wing Freedom Association. One woman said that her child was 'confused' by celebrations of Eid, a Hindu festival, the Jewish feast of Hannukah, and Divali, the Hindu festival of lights, and got all these muddled up with Christmas.[23] The Freedom Association paid for them to switch their children to a private Christian school.

A few months later the government proclaimed that schools must teach Christianity, the established religion. Children could opt out if their parents wished it and timetables must be arranged so that if there were large numbers of non-Christians they had their separate assembly. There is great concern amongst some parents and teachers that this is a retrogressive and divisive measure and, in cutting children off from each other, will lead to increased race prejudice and conflict.

One of the advantages of belonging to a traditional religious system, is that 'it provides ready laid-on answers to all the Big Questions: Why am I here? What is the meaning of life? Where was I before I was born and where will I go after I die?' Annette Hollander, writing about how parents can help their children have a spiritual life, quotes parents who are struggling to answer children's difficult questions:

Joshua often asks about God. I tell him that I'm not sure that there is a God, and don't believe in it; but many other people believe that there is God, or in different gods ... I find that hard sometimes – my answers are not as clear-cut and simple as if I did subscribe to some religion.

I told them about the Christian Heaven and Hell, the Buddhist reincarnation, and added, 'I really don't know.'[24]

Women who are Evangelical Christians say that they want their children to have Jesus for a friend. They stress that children who have faith are no longer alone because whatever they do, wherever they go, Jesus is beside them. This brings security, inner certainty about morality and happiness. They see themselves as facilitators of a process through which Christ enters their children's lives. They are not in charge. Jesus is in charge. There is an immediacy in Christ's presence which actually lifts from them the frightening total responsibility for turning a child into a good person.

June would like her son to read the Bible – 'the Maker's Handbook for people' which contains 'God's instructions'. She also hopes that he will come

to see Jesus as being a normal part of everyday life and someone whom he can get to know as a friend. Children can have a very real knowledge of Christ, even at the age of three or four, and can talk with him and see his answers to their prayers.

She describes one child, aged 5, who used to be scared of the dark but now has such a sense of the presence of Jesus that he is no longer frightened.[25]

On the other hand, all these women – whatever their sect or creed – stress that going to a place of worship is not enough. Their faith must be expressed in their lives. They are concerned to make the secular sacred: 'It is not an end in itself. As a committed Christian, I would like John to grow up "in the knowledge and love of the Lord".' And she says she wants his life to be 'guided by God's Holy Spirit'.

EFFECTS OF COMPULSORY WORSHIP

Women who have themselves had a strict religious upbringing with compulsory attendance at a place of worship are more likely to want their children to be free to explore and to find their own spiritual way. In talking with mothers in Japan Sheila found that this is as much the case for women who have grown up in a Buddhist tradition as it is for children of Christian homes in Britain. They do not want to impose their religion on children and often think that insistence on church-going is harmful:

> My mother and father made us go to church. I'd like my son (5 years old) to go because he wants to go. Although I do go every week, and want to, my mum *forced* me to go and at one point I hated it.

A woman whose parents made her attend church says that she takes her daughter, who is nearly 7, when either of them feels they want to go – 'not because we *have* to go.' Another says: 'I will try and teach my children that the place of worship is the world around us – everything that God gave us – and not a building where people go once a week.'

Compulsory church-going led to many conflicts with parents when these women reached their teens. A woman who says it was 'inflicted upon us at an early age' rejected religion as a teenager but in her late twenties discovered that she enjoyed going to church: 'I have no intention of making any of my children go through what I went through, and hope that eventually they will decide for themselves.'

This concern – to avoid their children 'going through what I went through' – is a recurrent theme for women who had to attend a place of worship when they were children, and is the reason why many – more than one in ten – want their children to be free to come to their own decisions. They feel that religion was 'forced' on them – that word occurs frequently – and some describe childhood rebellions. Charity says:

> My parents are very religious and we had to go to church every Sunday. When I was 14 we staged a protest by locking ourselves in our bedrooms. After that, we had a choice. I only go now at Christmas, Easter, Harvest Festival, and Jason (who is three) loves it when we go.

Ann, who has a son of two and a bit, says: 'Ours was a narrow and bigoted experience. We were forced to conform, without discussion or debate. My son will not be taught spiritual values in this way.' She has become a Buddhist, but says: 'He is not expected to believe what I believe. I can only point him in a sane direction – and hope.' Paradoxically it seems that if you want your children to be committed to a religious faith when adult, there is something to be said for being casual about religion. If, on the other hand, you would prefer them to become agnostic, give them a strict religious upbringing!

The women who talked to us who had children already in their teens have often come to realise this. Lucy says her Catholicism is important to her and she has brought up her three children as Catholics, two now in their teens and a third aged 10. The oldest 'has dropped out completely', the second is 'lapsing': 'I don't think I can do anything about it, but I wouldn't ever have wanted them to have an atheistic upbringing.' This presents a quandary for women who are themselves committed to a faith. As one Christian mother said:

> I believe it's important for Christian parents to bring up their children with Christian values and that Muslims bring up their children with their own cultural and religious values. But I realise that Alec may rebel when he is a teenager. *I* rebelled when I was teen-age. I didn't appreciate religion as a personal thing until I was seventeen.

Then the stimulus came from outside rather than within the home: 'A friend's life was so absolutely changed that I thought "there must be something in this"!'

It works the other way, too. For it is typically children of easy-going, tolerant, agnostic parents who in adolescence become Moonies or born-again Christians and, as one mother says of her son, 'as convinced as any bigoted elder of bygone days that every word within the Bible is absolutely true'. This woman's son is now training at a Bible college. He has obviously struck his parents where it hurts most. She described their horror at his rebellion:

If we had discovered that he was a drug addict, sniffing glue or drinking himself into oblivion; if he was obsessed by gambling or almost any sexual deviation, we would have worried but been able to understand what attracted him. The zombie-like unquestioning elements in his favoured brand of religion seem to us a harsh rejection of everything we've tried to do.

For these parents drugs and sex are not taboo areas. The important thing is to reach out and grasp experience, to try everything, to explore. What they cannot tolerate is that a child of theirs should choose a rigid, narrow framework and shut himself off from all the possibilities of an abundant life. This drives some parents to hire kidnappers to trace and smuggle their children home and to engage psychologists, counsellors and hypnotists to brainwash them back into their ways of thought.

What many women see as 'religious bigotry' or 'hypocrisy' in their own childhood is behind rejection of organised religion. Teresa says:

My mother forced me to attend (Catholic) mass every Sunday until I moved out at 19. While I do not want to force my son to stay away from church, I will certainly not encourage him to go because I'm still angry with my Mother and her narrow Catholic hypocrisy.

She goes on to say that she resents her mother's attempts to teach religious practice to her child:

My mother took the first opportunity of babysitting to pray with my son when he was 3 months old – probably to make up for the fact that he had not been baptised. I do not want to make an issue out of it, 'cos it would only lead to pointless quarrels ... and might spur curiosity in my son later (what is this that Mum is withholding from me?).

A Jewish mother, deeply concerned to bring her child up to be a good Jew, is intensely irritated by her mother-in-law who asks questions in front of the children like: 'What would you do if David married out?'

Some women who are agnostic express as much concern to teach their children to question everything as other women to teach religious faith – like the woman who states: 'Established religion is a bulwark of oppression.'

Others hope to communicate spiritual awareness and affirmation of life without formal religion, like the Japanese woman who says that she wants her seven-year old son to 'appreciate natural things, things like sunshine and rain. I don't like religion. I want to teach them about life and birth and death.'

Besides talking about conflicts with their own families on the subject of religion, women sometimes describe conflicts with their partner's family. Jessica, who has now divorced her husband, says:

> There was always a very submerged conflict about values – unspoken and obvious differences. His family are all rather excessively religious. My children have reacted against that. A godless bunch at the moment! . . . But I believe they are still growing spiritually.

Conflicts like these are, of course, not only inter-generational, but tend to take place whenever there is moral confrontation in cultures marked by heterogeneity of values, where the faithful feel bound to defend their beliefs in the face of a rising tide of agnosticism or of other religious faiths which hold different values. Sometimes the solution is sought in the formation of an exclusive community of believers, a kind of walled Holy City.

RELIGIOUS COMMUNITIES

In communities which are grounded and framed in religion like this, every aspect of a child's life is regulated by obedience to the faith. In his study of the interaction between Christianity and the world, Ernst Troeltsch distinguishes between the church – which conforms and adapts to come to terms with secular society – and sects, voluntary societies of strict believers who set themselves apart from the world.[26] Some sects like the Amish and the Hutterites dwell in territorial isolation. Others, like Jehovah's Witnesses and

Seventh Day Adventists, live inside modern society but differentiate themselves. Many established churches and socio-political groups – early Christianity, Quakerism, Mahayana Buddhism and Hassidic Judaism, for example – once had or still have the characteristics of sects.

Sect members form a religious elite and are willing to suffer persecution to uphold their faith. They may mark themselves off from the rest of society by wearing different clothes from other people, by not consuming certain kinds of food and drink, by their manners and style of speaking, by refusing to obey certain laws, by conscientious objection to military service, and – most important – by endogamy, marriage only to other believers. Strict penalties are imposed on members who offend against principles. Among eighteenth-century Quakers in Pennsylvania, for example, the misdemeanour of a child could result in excommunication of the whole family.

Today in communities like those of the old order, fundamentalist Mormons in Utah, who conform to 'the Principle' and still practise polygyny, a powerful male patriarchy coupled with strong sister-hood among the wives orders the whole of life, making clear distinction between 'inside' and 'outside', training children in strict obedience as well as in 'gentleness and respect for light', and aiming to produce children so perfect that they are 'scoured clean'.[27]

At birth babies are firmly bound, with a tight binder round the umbilical cord stump, their feet tucked under, and the sleeves of their nightgowns closed. The whole emphasis in child-rearing is on gentle restraint and control. The little girls wear their hair braided like their mothers and every movement they make must be closely controlled. All the sister-wives are responsible for disciplining the children of the family, and each is addressed as 'Mother' followed by her first name. Discipline begins when a child is old enough to reach for food from the table. Then someone will take the child's hand, hold it firmly and say 'no'. Until that time children are fed whenever they ask and there are always arms eager to hold the baby. One who is noisy and uncontrolled is held close and the woman whispers 'Hush, be quiet,' maintaining the grasp until the child becomes peaceful.

Punishment always consists of restriction on movement, and the child who has been naughty may be told by the father to sit still on a chair for one hour. It is the mother's duty to obey her husband and to see that this is done. Children are very rarely smacked and adult voices are never raised. All the women's activities and children's play take place in the inner courtyard or basement where sister-wives share childcare and may breastfeed each other's babies.

But for boys there comes a big change when they are about 11 years old. They are prepared for the Aramaic Priesthood and, if worthy, they enter it at the age of 12 and progress through various stages of Priesthood, each with its own responsibilities and rewards, developing their powers of leadership. It is their task to communicate with God and to do His work in the world. Girls, on the other hand, are prepared for marriage, which usually takes place at about the age of 15, and to be always subservient to men, on whose power they are dependent.

Thus every aspect of daily life is regulated by religion and everything that happens in the world outside is interpreted and explained in terms of religion.

PUNISHMENT AND PRAYER

Within a closed community, islanded in faith, explaining life exclusively in religious terms may not be so difficult to do. For those who live in the world outside such a community, however, this is fraught with difficulty. Religious symbolism, religious meaning, can illuminate significant life events and give them ceremonial significance, poetry and drama. But they may rule out other explanations, too, and distance us from reality. Religion can also impose definitions of reality which are not suited to our place and time but are bound, for example, to a pastoral society, a culture of warrior tribes or of desert nomads.

Describing his boyhood, Hart, a spastic, writes:

For me, the 'Five Books of Moses' had slowly become the most living and terrible of all penal codes, I an unpardonable offender against all its precepts: and it had been with despair that I had read, in the sixteenth, seventeenth and eighteenth verses of the twenty-first chapter of Leviticus: 'And the Lord spake unto Moses, saying Speak unto Aaron, saying Whosoever he be of thy seed in their generations that hath any blemish, let him not approach to offer the bread of his God. For whatsoever man he be that hath a blemish, he shall not approach: a blind man, or a lame, or he that hath a flat nose, or anything superfluous . . .' If, I thought, God felt that about a lame man who was a descendant of Aaron, what must He not feel about a lame boy with spastic muscles, who wasn't even a priest or anything like one?[28]

Children often want to test the religion they are being taught, and they do so by checking whether prayer works. In Somerset Maugham's autobiographical novel, *Of Human Bondage*,[29] the boy Philip read in the Bible that if you have faith you can move mountains and he 'prayed to God with all his might that he would make his club-foot whole. It was a very small thing beside the moving of mountains.' The next morning he awoke and

remembered at once that this was the morning for the miracle. His heart was filled with joy and gratitude. His first instinct was to put down his hand and feel the foot which was whole now, but to do this seemed to doubt the goodness of God. He knew that his foot was well.

Finding that it wasn't, he accepts his uncle's explanation that the failure of his 'miracle' means that he doesn't have enough faith.

One mother, remembering her own disappointment as a child when God failed to respond to her prayers for a puppy, tells her children to end their prayers with the words 'If it be Thy will', explaining that God doesn't give people everything they want because it might not be good for them. Yet for some children the fact that God has *not* answered their prayers is evidence that He is incorruptible. Gwen Raverat describes the first religious experience she can remember as kneeling under the nursery table to pray that the dancing mistress might be dead before she got to the dancing class:

> I have sometimes wondered what would have been my reaction if the dancing mistress had fallen down dead as I came into the classroom. I suppose I should have felt rather guilty; but after all it would have been God's doing, not mine; and that He should have done such a thing at my request would have destroyed my respect for Him for once and for all.
>
> For the only virtue God had, to my mind, was that of impartiality; and so prayer itself seemed to me to be an immoral proceeding. It was as if you were trying to bribe the Judge. My idea of prayer was: 'Please God, if you will let there be Chocolate Pudding for lunch, I will be very good today'. I am now told that this is not the right idea of prayer, but it was mine then. Well, now: could it be right that God should suddenly put Chocolate Pudding into the head of the cook, when she had intended to make Marmalade Pudding, which I hated, but which other people liked? No, it would be exceedingly unjust. In fact, it would be a shabby thing for me to try and do a deal for myself in that way; and most unfair of God to agree to my terms. But, anyhow, He never did; God simply never did what I asked Him; so that on the whole I thought Him incorruptible, which was just as well.[30]

SACRED MYSTERIES

In all religions sacred symbols are complex and mysterious. The problem is that 'Every symbol opens up a level of reality for which nonsymbolic speaking is inadequate.'[31] In a child's mind a concept like 'Heaven', becomes a garden above the clouds, 'God' a white-haired old man, the 'Holy Ghost' a shrouded spectre, whereas 'goodness' all too readily becomes mere obedience, and naughtiness 'sin'. Formal prayer turns into garbled mumbo-jumbo: 'Our father Richard in heaven' . . . 'Harold be Thy name' . . . 'Give us this day our jelly bread' . . . 'Deliver us some evil,' and the colourful drama of religious ceremony is debased into mere spectacle.

A Victorian mother, earnestly trying to inculcate religion in her 4-year-old daughter Frances, wrote:

> She asked me yesterday whether when chimney-sweeps die they become 'black angels'! She also asked 'If God has not got a great many pieces of people ready to make up into whole people'! How difficult it is to make a young child understand anything clearly of the attributes of the Almighty; the omnipresence of the Deity puzzles her very much; on hearing a story of two men who were drowned she said, 'Well, Mama, God cannot catch their souls, for they are at the bottom of the sea'![32]

It may not matter that children don't understand these concepts and that a parody of religion is produced. But there is a problem in that some of it, at least, must be unlearned. There comes a time when children realise they were mistaken and feel they have been deceived, and in putting away childish things they reject the faith of which they were part.

SPIRITUAL DEVELOPMENT

As children develop, too, they become critical of their parents, seeing discrepancies between what they believe and how they live, between the faith they profess and the quality of their lives. Children are often treated as if they only know what we have taught them. Parents approach the responsibility of child-rearing as if the whole burden of forming a child's character is on their shoulders.

Yet in each child there is an inner dynamism, a pattern of growth, which will find expression if we can create the right environment for its unfolding. Until about the age of 7, according to Rudolf Steiner, what we tell a child, that which we deliberately teach, 'does not yet make any impression, except in so far as he imitates what you say in his own speech'. Steiner expresses what many of the mothers who talked to us believed:

> But it is what you *are* that matters; if you are good this goodness will appear in your gestures, and if you are evil or

bad-tempered this will also appear in your gestures – in short, everything that you do yourself passes over into the child and pursues its way into him. The child is wholly sense-organ, and reacts to all the impressions aroused in him by the people around him.[33]

Children learn spiritual awareness and sensitivity from being part of a loving community. Many of the Japanese mothers who talked to Sheila emphasised this within a non-religious approach to life and stressed loving relationships between human beings in place of traditional Japanese forms of religion. A woman who has a daughter and son of 5 and 7 crystallises the attitude of these Japanese mothers when she says: 'The most important thing is that they relate to people with humility and sincerity – in heart-to-heart communication with other human beings.' When asked about whether she wanted them to become Buddhists she replied: 'They must have their unique individuality and their own beliefs.' And she adds:

> But just *telling* these things in words is not at all effective. The only way a mother can communicate to her children is by having her own values, so that they are taught through how my husband and I relate to one another.

Adults often act as if children are empty vessels into which religion must be poured. Yet children are capable of their own religious experiences though these may bear little relation to any formal religious system. There is in the inner life of the child a capacity for wonder, intense sensory experience and creativity. Thomas Traherne described this state of being when he wrote: 'With much ado I was corrupted, and made to learn the dirty devices of this world, which now I unlearn, and become, as it were, a little child again that I may enter into the Kingdom of God.'[34]

Adults recollecting mystical experiences often describe occasions of heightened spiritual awareness during childhood: 'Several times – at ages 3, 4, 5 – I would feel such a oneness with everything around me that it was awesome and wonder-filled. I talked to God out loud.'[35] A man remembers that when he was eight he was at camp, watching the sunset from his bunk:

> I can still see the circle of barbed wire lying on the rock, each point silhouetted. Suddenly something went BOING – words fail me here – everything was exquisitely beautiful and I was very happy. For a while, everything was perfect, and I knew all about it. I returned to that rock many times that summer. Even now, a certain quality of light at sunset can trigger something reminiscent of that feeling.[36]

Another remembers 'incredible mystical experiences as an altar boy singing from 4–5 until 13–14':

> I remember most vividly when I was 10 I figured everybody was having it – it was only later when I shared it that I found out it was okay to listen to talk about Jesus, but not to be talked to by Jesus.[37]

Ideas of God that grow out of personal experience are likely to be very different from that of the white-haired old man leaning out over the sill of Heaven. Sheila was told by her mother that the first time she spontaneously talked about God was at about the age of three on a day at the seaside when the waves were running wild. She was bathing with her mother and, excited by the power of the enormous waves, exclaimed, 'Oh, isn't God *wonderful*!'

Annette Hollander asked her two daughters what God was. Eve, aged 5, said:

> God is like the wind, the rain, the snow and the moon and the sun ... and all of those things are all put up in the sky and all of those things create a mixture, and all of those things are God. Well, God's all living things – like God made everything and everybody, from the first dinosaur to the last – God made everything we use, and us.[38]

Amelia, aged 3, said:

> God protects you from the scary dark ... and you can't feel a
> god and you can't hear it and you can't touch it, and you can't
> smell him but he's still there ... and he watches over the big
> girls and the mommies too, and the poppies, and he watches
> over babies so they wouldn't get scared and cry.[39]

In helping children to find a spiritual dimension to life, it may be
better to draw on and to trust their own deeply felt experiences than
to superimpose our adult ideas. The second-hand religion we offer
is unlikely to hold deep meaning for them. What we teach them
may later be rejected. But their own experiences will always have
validity.

It is when parental teaching rings true for and illuminates
children's own experiences that they can, like Ruby Bridges, hold
fast to religious convictions in a hostile world and live out in
everyday life the moral values central to their faith.

CHAPTER
11

POLITICS AND PREJUDICE

Children shouldn't be expected to know anything about politics or race prejudice or discrimination. Let them enjoy their childhood. They're only young once. Why worry them about all the terrible things that human beings do to each other? A parent's job is to protect them from these things.

Or is it?

One of the most difficult questions any parent faces is that of how far a child must be protected. We know we must give children as safe an environment as possible at home, protecting them from electric wires, boiling kettles, dangerous falls; and we are all anxious about how to shield children from other people's brutality and violence while at the same time bringing them up to be friendly and outgoing. We don't want our children to live in fear. But we can't help being afraid ourselves. We can't open a newspaper or switch on the TV without being aware of cruelty, exploitation and evil.

Children – even very young children – are not cocooned from this. When children have been asked about stories they remember from newspapers and on TV, they don't describe comic cartoons, special children's programmes or articles about pop stars. Instead they talk about major disasters in foreign countries – earthquakes in Armenia and floods in Bangladesh; about wars and terrorist attacks; the Arab/Israeli conflict or the bombing of aeroplanes – and they discuss issues which have been presented on the TV news, all of which bring to startling life, and often in horrendous detail, the disastrous effects on human beings of social and political problems all over the world.[1]

Most mothers who talked to us are appalled by this and do not know how to deal with it. Disasters like earthquakes, famine and war, the AIDS crisis, the extinction of animal species and the effects of large-scale pollution on our human environment, and the right social and political response to these, seem far too complicated and too painful to explain to small children.

Some women say that they want to shield their children from harsh political realities and so deliberately avoid discussing these subjects. One mother of a 6-year-old, for example, says:

> There's plenty of time for him to worry about nuclear weapons and famine in the third world and all that sort of thing when he's grown up. I want to protect him from all that now, give him security and happiness while he's young. Childhood is too precious to be squandered worrying about adult problems.

When her son asks questions about current affairs programmes he sees on television she tells him 'not to worry about it, that there are lots of clever grownup men working hard to solve all those sorts of problems, and that it's too complicated for him to understand anyway'.

But is this the best way? Whatever we do, children cannot inhabit a sheltered and separate world. They share with us a world of injustice and inequality and – depending on the social class or ethnicity they inherit from their parents – they are the losers or beneficiaries of this inequality. Racism, sexism, heterosexism and class bias are part of all children's everyday lives. For children in many parts of the world, violence, famine and war are part of everyday life too.

Though for more fortunate children the suffering of war or famine is not directly experienced, it is beamed into their homes on the television screen, photographed in the newspapers lying on the breakfast table, discussed (often over their heads) by adults. And it triggers some of the most difficult questions parents have to try to deal with, raising issues which we find it hard to understand or face up to ourselves. For this human suffering touches our own raw exposed nerves. We feel baffled, frustrated and overwhelmed by its scale. It challenges us to take action when we feel there is nothing we can do to lessen the horror with which we are confronted.

It is clear that as children get into their teens older parents are more likely to confront these issues. A father of five, whose children are now in their twenties, says: 'I wanted to teach them that they ought to achieve something, put something into the world, make the world a better place and life a worthier thing.' Many women are determined to be as honest as they can about political issues, even with very young children. They do not just wait for their children to ask questions but talk with them about things in the news because they believe it is an important part of their social development. 'The world is so full of injustice and oppression,' says the mother of a 10 and 12-year-old, 'I want the children to see the possibility of social and political change because it's our only hope of survival.' Another woman, with children still under 10, adds that 'it's the way to make things better for our children and for our children's children'. In fact, for a small number of women who answered our questionnaire, 'working towards change in the world' is the single most important quality they want their children to develop. They are concerned about the materialism of the world today, the oppression of Afro-Caribbean and Asian people, anti-semitism and sexism, the increasing prejudice towards lesbians and gay men, and they worry about nuclear weapons, war, poverty, famine, the Third World and the destruction of the natural environment.

Women describe how they watch the news with their children and discuss it afterwards. Instead of leaving them exposed to whatever the TV offers, they use news and documentary programmes to explore values. They encourage their children's participation in a range of social and political activities – and this even before they start school. Caroline's two sons are both under 5:

Sponsoring a deprived child in a third world country brings home an understanding of the importance of bringing about change in the world. This is how we plan to teach our children. We already sponsor a small boy in Togo and will encourage them to take on a second.

Jo says she makes a 'positive effort' to introduce her three year old to children from different social classes and ethnic groups. She takes her to work with her occasionally – her job is with disabled children. She offers her daughter 'a broad range of books' that they can talk about together and says, 'We watch the news and discuss and pray together over world issues.' Other women say they have talked about famine in the Third World with their children

so that they can appreciate the things that a lot of us take for granted, so that they can understand how lucky we are in the West, and to counteract some of the materialism which is encouraged by TV all the time.

A woman with a 5-year-old puts it succinctly when she says: 'My son has "Run the World" – and knows why; has been on CND demonstrations – and knows why; isn't allowed to drop litter – and knows why; is encouraged to be helpful to all – and knows why.'

Almost every woman says that her own approach to social and political issues is different from her mother's. Claudia, for instance, comments that her mother 'thought that children ought to be "allowed to be children" with very little political input or knowledge of the adult world'. 'My mum gave us a very enclosed environment,' Jo remembers. 'We only mixed with the "right" type – I didn't know any other sorts of people existed.' Another says that 'my parents never mentioned the idea of changing the status quo as far as I can remember,' and one whose own mother believed that 'individuals can change nothing, so it isn't worth trying,' says, 'I believe we *must* try.'

There are other women, however, who gratefully recall open discussions of social and political issues around the kitchen table when they were children. In *Growing Up Free*, Letty Pogrebin remembers sharing in such discussions with adults: 'If we had something to offer, they swept us into their discourse and at that

235

moment each of us became a thinker – a *person*, not a child'. She goes on:

> At 5 years old, I heard about the bombings, the concentration camps and the departure of my uncles to fight the Nazis. I'm not sure if my parents talked openly about Major Events because they thought I didn't understand, or because they wanted me to understand. I choose to believe the latter.[2]

One of us (Celia) also enjoyed debating moral and political issues with sisters and parents: comparative religion, the ethics of vegetarianism, questions of war and pacifism, women's rights and the effects of racism. At the age of 8 while at school in Jamaica for a year, Sheila, who was doing field work there, took me into the hills to the peasants' homes. The shock of seeing people living in shacks made of corrugated iron sheeting and packing cases, chickens scratching on the dirt floor, the potent smell of poverty, saltfish, cannabis and kerosene left a deep impact and formed the basis for later discussions about class, race and social structure.

Exposure to these realities, confronting these issues as a challenge and seeing the need for social change, enlarge children's sense of the world. It gives them confidence in their own ability to explore and develop ideas based on first-hand experience instead of being merely passive recipients of whatever the media has to offer and going with the crowd because that seems the safest, or the only, way to respond.

FAMINE AND POVERTY IN THE THIRD WORLD

The first political questions that children ask are often about famine, and they ask them when they are very young. 'Laura, aged three, was puzzled by the pictures of starving Ethiopian children she saw on the TV screen,' writes her mother. 'When I said their mummies had no money for food, she wanted to know why they didn't go to the bank. I found it very hard to explain.' Another woman said that 5-year-old Stephanie 'cried and cried about the starving babies in Ethiopia – she was inconsolable for a while, until

I thought to suggest helping by sending her pocket money, and she has done this for some weeks now'. Wanting to help by giving toys or money is a common response even in these very young children. In families where there is a religious commitment helping may sometimes include prayer or meditation. 'I practise Buddhism which involves meditation – clearing heart and mind for a better world,' says the mother of a two year old. Another woman told us:

Daniel is still very young (not yet 3) but I pointed out to him how thin the children were on the TV news. We talked about food and what he likes to eat, also about it not raining and nothing growing in the fields. We agreed that we were very lucky to have so much. Daniel finished the conversation by saying God would give them their tea. We prayed for them in church the following Sunday.

As children grow older they can understand how governments in the West, the multinational companies and financial institutions are part of the cause of Third World poverty. Alison explained to her nine year old that 'people in the wealthy countries like England and America do not do enough to help and even make things worse', and Kate told us about a discussion with her three children, aged between seven and twelve, when a Sunday newspaper colour supplement showed photographs of poor women and children in Third World countries working in a factory making components for computers sold in the West. 'I said that we are responsible for some of the poverty in those countries,' she said, 'and they understood that Western greed leads to exploitation in the Third World.'

Kate's oldest daughter decided to do a project on Western exploitation of the Third World, and found a great deal of information from the local library and the alternative bookstores. All the children became very concerned about this and decided they didn't want to buy exploitative products. They boycott South African products, and have discovered organisations (like Traidcraft) which buy goods at fair prices from co-operatives set up with local support and encourage community development. (She recommends honey which comes from Third World co-operatives and is called

'Sweet Justice'.) The children have also discovered the strengths and capabilities of Third World countries and no longer see them solely as the passive, needy and helpless recipients of Western charity.

With small children, the desire to give immediate help is so strong that suggesting gifts of money and toys seems most appropriate. As they grow older, they can begin to understand, in Martin Luther King's words, that 'true compassion is more than flinging a coin to a beggar; it understands that an edifice which produces beggars needs restructuring'.[3]

WAR AND NUCLEAR WEAPONS

'It's hard to help a child understand something you don't even understand yourself,' one woman pointed out. 'I have just told her that nuclear weapons and war are wasteful and pointless and would be unnecessary if we could all live and let live.' Many women said something like this.

Over the last twenty years there have been seventy-two wars in various parts of the world, and for many children war is part of their everyday experience – on the streets of Belfast, in the occupied Gaza strip, in the Nicaraguan slums. One thing this means is that there are few safe places to play. In Nicaragua, fields and forests that beckon young explorers can explode into violence without warning. Ten-year-old Alfredo Lopez and his 5-year-old brother Bayardo were playing near their home in a remote village when they uncovered a buried landmine, apparently placed by retreating 'contras' in order to prevent Sandinista soldiers from pursuing them. They survived the explosion deeply scarred and burned, and may never see again. Josefa Gutierrez, 11 years old, says she realises that the loss of her leg in a landmine planted by the Sandinistas means that she will never walk again but the journalist who interviewed her comments that 'as her parents sat beside her wheelchair, she seemed not resigned, nor enraged, but disoriented and overwhelmed'.[4]

Children in these countries miss out on education too. Instead they learn survival skills, along with hatred of the enemy. Schools in the occupied Gaza strip are closed and shuttered, and the last thing many Palestinian children remember learning is that toilet paper soaked in perfume can be used against tear-gas. Nine-year-old Suheir says: 'In the day I'm not scared. My worst moments are at night. I dream badly, of Israeli soldiers kicking me and beating me.' Ashraf, aged twelve, says: 'I don't know their names, but I hate those Israeli soldiers I see on our streets. I would be proud to die for my country fighting the Israelis' – but he adds wistfully, 'sometimes I wish I could have a normal childhood'.[5] In any war, wherever it takes place, families are destroyed and relationships permanently mutilated. For all those children whose fathers were maimed or killed in the Falklands war, or in Northern Ireland, war has a direct, personal meaning. Suddenly a father or older brother or uncle disappears forever, or is away for a long time and comes back, but looks and behaves in a different way.

In many countries children are directly involved in the fighting 'Shabab' means 'young ones' in Arabic and it is what the Palestinians call the young people who throw the stones and petrol bombs at Israeli soldiers, fly Palestine's horizontal tricolour from the telephone wires, light the tyre barricades and taunt the Israelis with portraits of Yasser Arafat. As in Northern Ireland, many of the stone-throwers are not youths but children. One journalist[6] describes how a suspected petrol-bomber, aged 10, was shot dead in the doorway of a mosque in Gaza, and tells the story of a 6-year-old stone-thrower, captured by the Israelis, who is forced to admit that his brother put him up to it. The soldiers then accompanied him to his home so that they could confront the instigator of the crime. When they got there, the boy pointed to a 4-year-old sibling peeping out from behind his mother's skirts: 'There he is – that's my brother.' Parents' feelings about children's involvement are ambivalent. Of course they admire their courage, and feel a certain guilt at their sacrifice, but they are also worried that their children are out of control and adult authority is on the wane. What do you say to a child who comes home late after rioting for Palestine?

In Iran, too, young children are enlisted and sent off to the front

Drawings made by Kurdish children from Iraq who have escaped to refugee camps in Turkey

A 9 year old draws planes dropping canisters from which a mixture of mustard and nerve gas bursts. 'All the birds fall out of the sky. All the leaves turn black and fall off the trees. The donkeys die. The people die.' Note that buildings remain undamaged.

Children distinguish carefully between gas canisters and rockets. A boy of 9 draws a rocket-launcher firing at a village. There is a soldier with a machine-gun and one with a bazooka. Dismembered and headless corpses lie on the ground with blood flowing from them. On the right, a mother is running away with her baby who is covered in blood.

A 6-year-old girl draws planes dropping gas canisters on a village. In the middle is the smoke. Mothers with babies on their backs are running away. Birds fall out of the sky and leaves drop from the trees. 'It was the day when all those who smiled died, when everything is dead: the chickens, the birds, my mother, my father – all of them dead.'

A 12-year-old boy illustrates what happened in his village when missiles from planes destroyed houses, gas exploded from cannisters dropped by the plane on the left and a rocket attack was launched at the same time. The gas 'smells of rotting fruit and hot asphalt.' With burning skin and eyes people run to the river to try and wash it off, while others lie dead on the ground.

as 'martyrs'. Religious leaders go from door to door explaining to parents the need to send their children to war, warning them that this may be the only way to prevent the enemies of Islam from destroying everyone. If they agree to send their children they receive 400 tomans (about £40) and sometimes a 'Martyrs Card' which confers privileges on them and their families in shops and jobs. Interviews with small children on the battlefield are shown on prime time television to urge others to enlist. One 4-year-old was asked 'Who are you?'. 'A pious servant of Islam', he replied. 'What do you want to become?' 'A martyr.'[7]

A British advertisement which has appeared in young people's magazines reads: 'Yes, you can be a soldier at 16. You'll be working with some of the Army's most sophisticated weaponry. And at 16 years of age you'll have a head start in life.'

Even those children who are not themselves enlisted in the army or beaten up and tortured by soldiers learn violence and enact it in their games. Though they may not be physically harmed, war imprints itself on their minds. One psychotherapist has described the stress reactions of children in Northern Ireland. A boy experienced his first asthma attack when he heard gunfire, and later got asthma when he heard similar noises – a car backfiring or a door slamming. A girl who hyperventilated when the house next door was set on fire had later attacks when she heard the school bell, and when someone spoke about a bonfire. There is a children's book, *Two Dogs and Freedom*, written by black pupils (aged 8 to 10 years) in Soweto. They describe their own experiences in the ghetto township, their hopes for peace and freedom, and their stories are illustrated by other children whose drawings show everyday events in their lives – including children fleeing from rubber bullets and the batons of the police. The South African government has banned the book.[8]

As we have seen, other children learn about violence, war, terrorism and nuclear weapons from their TV screens. One study estimated that the average American child between the ages of 5 and 15 watches the violent destruction of more than 13,400 people on television. Unlike famine in the Third World in response to which mothers find it possible to provide their children with positive action (such as sponsoring a child or sending clothes to Oxfam), the problems of war seem insoluble and inexplicable. 'I find the unmitigated horror of nuclear weapons too much to take,' wrote one woman, asking, 'What can I say to comfort my children?' After watching a terrorist attack on the news, a 6-year-old asked: 'Why do they do that?' Her mother said 'because they are nasty, unkind people,' but adds, 'I don't really know why. I find the issues and grievances too deep and the results too horrifying to explain.' Many women said that they didn't know how to explain war and violence to their children because it was beyond their own comprehension. They feel completely helpless:

> I have found it extremely hard to talk about terrorism and violence with my 6-year-old. How do you explain to a child about extremists, bombs, kidnapping and murder? I don't understand how people can do these things to each other and I find it very hard to answer the questions he asks.

> My son has always been very interested in guns and soldiers and a conversation developed into war and why people shoot each other. I found it very hard to explain and felt at the end of the conversation that my son hadn't really understood. Probably because I don't really understand it either.

Some women hoped that their husbands might be better able to understand and explain subjects like war and mob violence. One woman whose 6-year-old asked 'why the ladies at Greenham Common were making a fuss,' says, 'I'm very much afraid I said "ask Dad".' Another woman just commented sadly that 'my husband knows much more about society and politics than I do, so I would tell the children to ask him'.

Children's questions about war raise fears in our own minds, fears that we often want to push away and deny. Many people react with a sense of numbness to the stockpiling of nuclear weapons and talk of nuclear deterrence; rather than face the awfulness of the mass destruction of the human race, we blank it all out. Teachers avoid the issue too – most British children in one study (63 per cent) said they had learned nothing in school about nuclear war, although the vast majority (75 per cent) would like school lessons on the subject. As the researcher comments, 'These results indicate a need among children for more discussion and information which is not being met.'[9]

Children, though, develop their own theories. Many children see war as caused by one country's greed and another's need. When 8 to 10-year-olds in Australia were asked how to avoid wars, they emphasised the importance of share and share alike:

The way to get peace is if you have enough materials, share them with other countries so they won't have to fight you to get them. We've got some things here that other countries don't have ... we'll tell them they can have some of them.

I don't see why everybody can't have bits of all the other countries; we could share it around by taking it in planes.[10]

Younger children can understand Third World poverty if it is linked with their own experience of 'being greedy' and 'grabbing'. One mother told her 2-year-old that 'some greedy people grab all the food so that other people have nothing to eat. We mustn't be greedy like that.' Some wars can be explained in these terms too, 'greedy' countries wanting more than their fair share. Older children can be given simple but accurate information about Western affluence and Third World poverty. A textbook of social education puts it this way:

If the world were a global village of 100 people 70 of them would be unable to read, and only 1 would have a college education. Over 50 would be suffering from malnutrition, and over 80 would live in what, by North American standards, is substandard housing. Of the 100 people, six would be Americans, and these six would have half of the village's entire income and the other 94 would exist on the other half. How would the wealthy six live 'in peace' with their neighbours? Surely they would be driven to arm themselves against the other 94 ... perhaps even to spend, as we in the West do, more per person on military defense than the total per person income of others.[11]

Organisations like Oxfam, UNICEF, and the Peace Pledge Union offer education packs, books and videos for parents and children. Some children have started a letter-writing exchange with children in the Soviet Union to form friendships and promote international understanding. Others take part, with their parents, in political action – participating in demonstrations and writing letters to political representatives. Many children went with their mothers to the Greenham Common Peace Camp and saw the power of women's united protest. Two of Sheila's earliest memories are of being on a Peace Pledge Union demonstration with her mother, a life-long pacifist, and of being allowed to stay up for supper when pacifists, who were by then members of parliament and well-known public figures, dined together and swapped tales about their experiences of prison as conscientious objectors. These were obviously people her mother admired and trusted. They wanted to make a better world, and suffered ridicule, deprivation and even imprisonment to try to do this. They became my heroes too. It was the beginning of social concern and I am very grateful to my mother for this. The example provided by the adults in a child's world is what makes the most impact: their commitment, beliefs and actions carry more conviction than words.

Parents sometimes respond to a child's questions by saying that they don't know the answer but that there are ways of finding out. One woman told us how, when her 4-year-old son asked about famine, she went to the library with him and helped him to find books on the subject, and how they visited their local branch of Oxfam for further information. Deirdre Rhys-Thomas describes how her 12-year-old son, Theo, asked her about nuclear war.

Perhaps it was something he had seen on the news: something which had caught and held his attention in a way which touched his deepest fears. Theo spoke in that deceptively quiet way that children do when they're frozen with terror and can't get their feelings out. 'Do you think there's going to be a nuclear war, Mum?'

For an odd, still moment I couldn't think or speak. I sat down on the bed again, took his hands, tried not to let him see how upset I was, tried to reassure and comfort him so that he could go to sleep ... And yet afterwards I stood outside his door, immobilised by a strange mixture of anger and panic. I had had to lie to Theo to comfort him, and in so doing I felt that I had betrayed his trust in me ... This trust had enabled him finally to drift off to sleep soothed by my empty promises into a false sense of security.

She wrote to MPs, military experts, the police, the Pope, and the US President asking for information, and shared the letters she received with her children.[12] After reading all this correspondence, together with the Government information about nuclear war, her son has a less positive view of governmental authorities than do most of his age mates: 'It was disheartening,' she comments, 'to find that he could be so cynical ... Theo was totally cynical about all these bureaucratic letters, and even about the forthcoming arms talks.' But perhaps it would have been more disheartening had he believed the official line.

In many countries children apparently take it for granted that public officials, such as police and MPs, are benevolent, honest, decent people. From the age of 2 or 3 they realise that there are people with powers superior to the authority of their parents. Through observation of police cars, traffic signs, parking meters they learn that the police are instruments of political power and represent governmental authority to which parents and children alike are subordinate.[13] One of the most dramatic and consistent findings of research on political socialisation is that children have a very positive image of political figures whatever their culture: 'The president gives us freedom'; 'The mayor helps everyone to have nice homes and jobs'. An American study found that 60 per cent of 8-year-olds agreed with the statement that the president of the USA is 'the best person in the world'.[14] This marked tendency for a majority of children to idealise political leaders has been observed in Australia, Britain, France, Germany, Italy, Japan, the Netherlands and the USA.[15] Compared with adults, children are far more positive about party politics: 66 per cent (compared with only 20 per cent of adults) say that it makes a great deal of difference to the country who wins an election. In part this is due to the sugar-coated explanations of political life they are given by adults – even otherwise sceptical adults – who present children with an oversimplified and benevolent version of government and political affairs.

Children pick up the political values of their culture without understanding the meanings of the value-laden words they hear. One white, middle-class North American ten year old, Judith, is typical in her response when asked what is meant by the word 'democracy':'It's what the people should have, they should have democracy, like be a good citizen, or something like that – I can't explain it, but it's something good at any rate.' Asked about the meaning of 'communism', she replies, 'To me it's *bad*. I can't explain it, just like democracy – it's sort of the opposite.'[16] When children 'know' that communism is wrong without being able to say what it means, or why democracy is better, they may grow up to become adults who, like 41 per cent of Americans, say they would rather die in a nuclear war than live under communism.[17]

ECOLOGY

The planet is under threat not only by nuclear destruction but also from pollution and devastation of its natural resources – the hole in the ozone layer, acid rain destroying the forests, species of flowers and animals that were once abundant now becoming extinct, and the dumping of chemicals at sea which poison marine life. Sonia, aged 5, 'cried and cried when the television news showed the dead seals being washed up on the Norfolk coast', says one mother, and a nine year old who enjoys birdwatching with his father was 'terribly distressed' by news stories about seagulls covered in oil. A 10-year-old who watched a documentary about the destruction of the ozone layer

went to the bathroom cabinet and threw away my aerosol deodorant. When I argued with her – I *need* deodorant! – she came into town with me and went round the shops asking for alternatives, and she discovered 'ozone-friendly' sprays which is what I now use.

Even small children can be encouraged to help in protecting the environment in ways which are creative and fun. They can join tree-planting schemes, can sprout beans, recycle bottles, foil and newspaper, or 'adopt' an endangered species. The City Farm Movement and Friends of the Earth are two British organisations which provide nature education, and there are several excellent books for adults about sharing nature with children.[18] The Wood-craft Folk is a co-educational alternative to the Guides and Scouts (with a membership of about 17,000) which speaks to children of a world transformed by peace, equality, co-operation and care for the environment. They have a national outdoor pursuits centre where children can experience communal living, learn about the planet and enjoy bracing walks across the moors. 'In their project work the children look at issues like pollution or apartheid,' says John Keyworth, one of the adult leaders in the organisation. 'They learn citizenship through understanding things like local government. All the children can be involved in how the group runs – the smallest child learns that he or she has a right to be heard.'[19]

Children, who after all are likely to be on this planet longer than the rest of us, can take the lead in ecological issues. Children in a Norwegian primary school went round their neighbourhood asking people whether they used a detergent laced with phosphates. When the answers came back – typically 'don't know' and 'what does it matter anyway?' – the junior researchers patiently explained that the purpose of the chemical additive was purely cosmetic and that when the suds were rinsed away, they helped to promote the multiplication of potentially harmful organisms in the community's water. The result: a significant change in the shopping habits of one Oslo suburb. But the children did not leave it at that. They went on to approach detergent firms and successfully persuaded one to start manufacturing phosphate-free washing powders.

Another spectacular example of children's involvement in ecology comes from Frankfurt where pupils living in the heart of the concrete jungle, where nothing green has flourished for years, dug up part of the asphalt playground, planted perennials and creepers, created a 'green classroom' in the open air, built from logs begged from the state forestry department and started a shop selling natural foods.[20]

Children can become actively and passionately concerned about political issues when they understand what is at stake – in this case, their own future and that of all life on this planet. They sometimes express doubts about the values of adults who have allowed the earth to be poisoned for their own short-term gains: 'I don't want adults telling me what to do,' said one teenager. 'It's the morals of adults that bother me – the way they're destroying the environment and wrecking the world they'll leave me when they're dead. Why don't they worry about that?'[21]

POVERTY AND SOCIAL CLASS

Disasters in far away countries are in some ways easier for children to respond to than the dull grey permanence of poverty in their own country. Poverty at home lacks the sense of crisis, the drama of emergency aid, the tales of heroism and endurance, the feeling that by pulling together we can make a difference. It is harder to explain to children about poverty in the midst of affluence – about the man sleeping rough, wrapped in newspapers on the park bench, or the gaunt and dishevelled woman who stops you in the street asking for a coin. It is harder to explain to your working-class child why she cannot have the toys and games displayed in High Street shops, or to a middle-class child why she can have ballet and riding lessons and holidays abroad while the children on the local council estate make do with the local youth club and less exotic holidays. In one of her novels, Margaret Drabble describes a middle-class girl's learning about poverty:

Alix had been told about poverty, in Leeds, at school and at home ... She had knitted woollen squares to raise money to sink wells in India ... She had donated pittances of pocket money to buy tractors for India. She had attended slide-illustrated talks on the agricultural problems of vast and distant continents. Poverty nearer home had been less vividly presented to her, and indeed it had been less colourful, less extreme. It was grey, shabby, and somehow infectious; to be avoided. It was also rough and noisy and unmannerly. It lived in back streets of terrace houses and on sprawling housing estates. It wasted what money it had on drinking and it spoke with rough accents. It was feckless, unthrifty, sluttish, violent, loud mouthed, and materialistic. Its children taunted nice little middle-class children in school uniform who strayed into its terrain. It did not need wells dug or tractors purchased. [Nor were they] poor, in terms of the poverty displayed in the colourful slides, where black children with hunger-distended bellies stared at the camera, where lepers crouched by begging bowls.[22]

It is hard to say just how people in Britain 'know' what class someone is, or what class means to us as adults. For most it is partly to do with education, money and what people choose to buy with it, and occupation. By the age of about 5 or 6, most children can recognise broad class differences on the basis of cues such as clothes, cars and the kind of houses people live in. Class tends to be seen in terms of dramatic contrasts of the sort that fairy stories portray – the extremes of abject poverty and immense wealth, the prince and the pauper, the princess and the swineherd. Television programmes like Dallas and Dynasty reinforce the image of wealth and power which in Britain have traditionally been associated with being upper-class, while others like East Enders and Coronation Street depict versions of working-class life. Many studies show that between the ages of about 8 and 12, British children construct a rough class system by inserting an intermediate group between the two contrasting extremes, and are able to describe social differences in their own neighbourhood. During the teenage years (twelve to sixteen) they add to this some kind of political theory to explain class differences.

It seems, though, that there are big differences in children's views about class depending on their own class background. In one study working-class girls, whose parents included canteen workers, shop assistants and van drivers, found it hard to say what class they were from and could not name the classes in British society. The researcher, Elizabeth Frazer, says:

> Traditionally we have worried about talking to teenage girls about sex. Now they talk frankly about sex but, for lower class girls, class is a dirty word. They found it excruciatingly embarrassing ... They had extremely vague and ill-defined notions of what class meant. Discussion about social divisions tended to dwell on matters like the Royal Family, friends with more pocket money and a few friends at private schools.[23]

None of these working-class girls talked about overt class conflict or hostility.

Middle-class girls in the same study, who were being educated at private schools and whose fathers were barristers, landowners, army officers and stockbrokers, had a very different view of social class. Unlike the working-class girls, they talked about class a great deal (even when asked to discuss other issues), and had a clear view of the class structure – with themselves somewhere near the top. They were particularly worried about conflict between themselves and the lower classes, and talked about being spat at and tripped up when they went into town, teased about their accents, or having stones thrown at them by children in the village. They saw working-class people as threatening and dangerous, although their fear of uncouthness, violence and stupidity was tempered with awareness of injustice.

Other researchers, too, have found that middle- and upper-class children have a much clearer understanding about social class. Children from about 10 years old usually have a rough idea of the relative salaries attached to different jobs. Given a list of occupations (doctor, architect, teacher, electrician, bricklayer, bus driver, roadsweeper) they can put them in order from the one who gets paid most to the one who gets paid least. Middle-class children are much better at this than working-class children. Children from all classes find it very hard to explain *why* some people get paid more than others but middle-class children are likely to say that the highly paid have worked harder, made more effort, and gained more qualifications. They see poverty as the result of wasting money.[24] While younger children are upset by unfairness and inequality in the class structure and want to change things, as they grow older they become more fatalistic, accepting class as 'given'. During the teenage years, those who earlier wanted to change things begin to say 'You can't change people. This is the way the world is. Some people are poor and some are rich, and that's the way people are – you can't change it.'[25] Compared with middle-class children – more aware of social inequalities and often prepared to admit to some unease about their privileged position – working-class children are less likely to perceive inequalities, more likely to believe that people get what they deserve in this world, and that 'anyone can make it if they try'.

Historically this is the explanation of class structure that children have been encouraged to accept. When compulsory schooling was first introduced in Britain at the turn of the century it was seen as a way of keeping working-class children 'in that station of life wherein Providence hath placed them.'[26] Victorian middle-class children were told that the poor are 'either very silly people, or very idle':

Poverty is almost always because of one thing – and that is drunkenness. The father spends his money in beer or ale, which he ought to bring home for his wife to spend in buying bread and milk, and meat, to feed the children, and with which she could get some furniture and other things which she wants to make the house comfortable. But sometimes, which is worse than all, the mother is a drunkard too, and loves gin; and if she does, there is sure to be no good; for she will go to the pawn shop till she has sold every bit of furniture in the house, and even the very clothes off her back, but she will have that nasty gin.

This is the way that poor, ragged, dirty, half-starved children are made. Oh how would you like to have such a home as theirs? See, then, what a good thing it is to have a good home. You can never be too thankful to God, and too thankful to your parents for such a home.[27]

Victorian children were exhorted to know their place, to behave as became their status in society, which was fixed and ordained by God. One verse of 'All things bright and beautiful' (now omitted from most hymnbooks) expresses this idea: 'The rich man in his castle,/The poor man at his gate,/God made them high and lowly,/ And ordered their estate.' Accepting their social status as given, children were expected to treat their social superiors with respect and their subordinates with compassion. There was a clear distinction between the 'deserving poor' – the honest working man and his family – and feckless spendthrifts and idle layabouts, like 'Sarah' in one Victorian children's rhyme:

> Old Sarah everybody knows
> Nor is she pitied as she goes –
> A melancholy sight.
> For people do not like to give
> Relief to those who idle live
> And work not when they might.[28]

This concept of poverty has been revived in Margaret Thatcher's Britain with the moral distinction between the entrepreneurial working man who saves to buy his own council house and starts a small business in the back garden, and the 'scroungers' who live off state income support.

Some women are very unhappy with stereotypes like these and are trying to teach children differently. A Scandinavian woman, now married to a British man and living in England, is appalled by what she describes as 'class violence' and 'apartheid' in Britain. She is a drama teacher and encourages children to explore the class structure through acting out the roles of people from different classes and backgrounds. The mother of a 3-year-old says: 'I've explained to her there are people in this country who can't afford nice things, but she doesn't really know what it's like for Mummy not to be able to treat her occasionally.'

Politically active adults often trace the beginnings of political awareness to their own experience of inequality in childhood. At

253

first, the way of life of their parents and companions appears both natural and inevitable but as they grow older and gain some knowledge of other life-styles, so they come to perceive deprivation and inequality. Samuel Bamford, who lived in the last century, was particularly aware of the way in which as a young child he had been receiving lessons about what was right and wrong in his society. One crucial memory was of the day his mother paid a visit to her sister who had married a woollen draper and was living in some comfort in Manchester. His aunt was so proud of her new-found status that his mother, who had married a struggling handloom weaver, was admitted no further than the servants' quarters, and walked back through the rain hurt and angry:

> Many of the earliest of my impressions were calculated to make me feel, and think, and reflect; and thus I became, imperceptibly as it were, and amidst all the exuberant lightsomeness of childhood, impressible and observant. The notice I took of my mother's anguish and her tears ... whilst it made me hateful of all wrong – hateful so far as my young heart could be so – disposed me, at the same time, to be pitiful towards all suffering. It was the means of calling into action two of the strongest and most durable impulses of my heart – justice and mercy.[29]

Experiences like these can form basic social and political values. Samuel Bamford became a radical politician and traced to this event the seeds of 'an unmitigatable contempt for mere money pride, much of it though there be in the world; and as thoroughgoing a contempt ... for the unfeelingness which Mammonish superiority too often produces'.[30] The miners' leader Edward Rymer located the origin of his commitment to trade unionism in the hardships suffered by his family during the 1849 Durham miners' strike when he was nine: 'What I heard and saw sunk deep into my soul, and left the principle and impression stamped in my nature that "union is strength and knowledge is power".' For some working-class children, then, the experience of injustice leads them to question the distribution of power and privilege in their society.

Low-income mothers often find themselves forced to explain to their children that other children can have playthings, clothes and outings that they cannot because there is simply not enough money and a friend's daddy or mummy earns more. Shirley has a 3-year-old and writes:

> I am trying to make her understand that she cannot have everything – especially as we are not very well off. It is hard because the other children at playschool all have expensive clothes and toys; their parents both work, I am a single mother in a low-paid job.

Holly says she has tried to be 'realistic' about money:

> My mother protected me from the fact that having money, and therefore having to work for that money, was so necessary to survive. I have to explain to Oliver that he can't have everything he wants because I haven't enough money.

'I often talk about how we are poor,' says the mother of a 5-year-old:

> I explain what this means, how it is nothing to be ashamed of, the differences between rich and poor, that loving someone is irrelevant to how many toys you buy them (!!), how we are rich compared to some people in other countries, to enjoy treats but not to expect them, that we work to improve our material life, but don't let it take over the meaning in our lives.

Darren, aged 10, was upset because his classmates were going on the school skiing trip to Austria and his parents could not afford to send him:

> I explained that there are lots of things we all want – his father would like a new car, and I would like a new washing machine, and Suzy, his sister, would like new shoes, and none of us are going to get any of those things, because Pete is out of work. I agreed with him that it was unfair. I said I often feel angry too,

when there are things I want and can't have. And I said the people to be angry with were not us but the government. The hardest thing is to get him to realise that it is not Pete's fault, and he shouldn't be ashamed of his dad. But I don't think he's let his schoolfriends know.

While working-class children confront the experience of their own relative deprivation, the children of middle- and upper-class parents sometimes become aware of social inequalities through realising their own privilege. Consuelo Vanderbilt, daughter of one of the wealthiest old families in the USA, remembers this:

There were times when ... I reflected with some discomfort on the affluence that surrounded me, wondering whether I was entitled to so many of the good things of life. This feeling was sharply accentuated by a visit I paid to the sick child of one of our Bohemian workmen, whose duty it was to cut the grass lawns that surrounded the house. One morning when wishing him good day I noticed how sadly he answered. 'Is anything the matter?' I inquired. Then he told me of his little girl, aged ten – 'just my age', I commented – a cripple condemned for life to her bed. The sudden shock of so terrible a lot overwhelmed me; and when the next day I drove with my governess to see her, the pony cart filled with gifts, and found her in a miserable little room on a small unlovely cot. I realized the inequalities of human destinies with a vividness that never left me.[31]

Many young activists of the 1960s came from affluent backgrounds and described their shock on realising that their own good fortune was not shared by everyone. Discussing the poverty of Mexican children, one student said:

I was the one that lived in a place where there were fans and no flies, and they lived with the flies. And I was clearly destined for something, and they were destined for nothing ... Well, I sort of made a pact with these people that when I got to be powerful I might change some things.[32]

Because children live in a society divided on class lines they inevitably confront issues of class prejudice and privilege. Class is difficult for adults to talk about – it is considered 'rude' by many – and many hope that conversation with children about these issues is unnecessary. What seems to happen is that children discover the class system for themselves and then, lacking any coherent explanation of it, develop theories of their own. Many, as we have seen, see it as a permanent and fixed part of human society. If we want to live in a more equal society, in which the gap between the 'haves' and the 'have-nots' is not so great, in which everyone has a fairer share of the nation's wealth, it is in our interests to encourage children to believe that a fairer society is possible – and that they can help to bring it about.

RACISM

Many of the (predominantly white) parents in our study were concerned about racism. They took care not to express racist ideas themselves and were taken aback when their children made racist comments. 'The black people are taking all the jobs and that's why Daddy hasn't got one,' commented one 6-year-old whose mother says,

> I don't know where he got this idea from – certainly not from me or my partner. I suppose from television or school. How is it that someone else has influenced my child to this extent without my even knowing?

Sara was shocked when she took her 5-year-old out for a meal and the boy refused to eat his pizza because it was served by a black woman:

> He hadn't met black people before – we were in the UK for a visit but normally live in an all-white community near the Austrian border. I have tried to be anti-racist with him since then, but as there are no black people here, it's rather academic.

Caroline, aged 4, came back from her grandparents using words like 'nig nog' and 'Paki', and 9-year-old Steve comes home from school with an endless supply of anti-black and anti-Irish jokes. Another mother told her 4-year-old that 'some unkind people are horrible to people with different coloured skins' but adds: 'The problem is she says she doesn't like people with "purple faces" and she copies school friends in calling them names.' Regardless of their mothers' best intentions, white children in a racist society learn racist attitudes.

Racial or ethnic self-identification and ethnic preferences are found in children as young as 3 or 4. Racial awareness increases with age, and in general there is a sharp rise in hostility to other ethnic groups at about age 6 or 7.[33] Almost a quarter of infant teachers in one study[34] said they had heard children expressing extreme racial stereotypes such as 'Pakis stink' or 'Darkies live in mud huts'. Of 133 7-year-olds interviewed in another study, two in every three children agreed that children were teased because of their colour and that black children bear the brunt of this. 'Gollywog', 'Nigger', 'Chocolate head', and 'black bitch' were among the names children used. 'Most of the white children took teasing black children very much for granted,' the researchers report, quoting one child who cheerfully told them, 'I call them monkeys that escaped from the zoo last year.'[35]

Racist attitudes come not just from other children but also from teachers – often manifested in terms of lower expectations for black children and inadequate careers advice. This form of practice is so severe that members of London's Muslim and Chinese communities have united to call for an end to 'multicultural' or 'anti-racist' education (which focuses on a celebration of cultural differences) because they see it as distracting from the most important form of discrimination against Black and ethnic minority children. 'We are sick and tired of all this anti-racism,' said the Chinese community leader, Mr David Tan, demanding instead equal treatment for all children to help them 'get the qualifications to go to college or university or to get a good job'.[36] 'Patties and steel-bands may have lent the school Open Day a multi-cultural atmosphere,' says another group of black critics, 'but they presented no serious challenge to the numbers of Black pupils relegated to non-exam classes in the fourth year.'[37] As one Black 15-year-old told us:

'The white kids are the ones who need anti-racist education, not us.
We get it just living here. They could do multiculturalism while we
study Maths.'

Other black and ethnic minority children say that they are
constantly questioned about their backgrounds – what they eat,
what language they speak at home, what clothes they wear: 'Are
you going to have an arranged marriage?' 'Don't you get sick of
curries?', 'Why don't you eat pork?', 'How do you wash your hair?'
'You begin to feel so different, you feel uncomfortable, and because
you are so young you don't know how to deal with it,' wrote one
woman, remembering her school days. She decided in the interests
of self-preservation that she wasn't going to fight it, but just give in
to whatever they said:

> Every day at school, we had to write a diary of what we did at
> home. I wrote that in Jamaica we lived in trees and ran around
> with whatever they told us we wore, and I even drew pictures.
> I think it got to the stage where I wasn't sure what was true
> any more, the pictures they were showing me or the memories
> I had in my head.[38]

Racist language is used thoughtlessly by teachers and pupils
alike: it was a 'black' day, or someone had 'blackened' the good
name of the school. One young black woman tells how a teacher
who had to pick a team started chanting, 'Eenie, meenie, miney,
mo, catch a nigger by his toe, if he screams then let him go, eenie,
meenie, miney mo'. 'I looked at him in disgust and vowed never to
speak to him again.'[39]

Schools still incorporate a white Western version of the world
and minority children in white racist Britain may deny their colour,
their families, their languages and their cultural foods. While many
parents try to give children a sense of pride in their cultural, ethnic
or religious identity, many children seek assimilation. They want to
be the same as other children – to look the same, to wear the same
kinds of clothes, speak the same language, crack the same jokes, get
up to the same exploits, share the same codes. A Pole who was
born and brought up in England sends his 8-year-old daughter

and 5-year-old son to the Polish Saturday community school in Nottingham, but admits

it is difficult to sustain their interest in Polish culture. When I was young I resented having to go too. It meant I missed all school games and never got to go to the pictures with my friends. It made me different, and I didn't want to be different.

A young Muslim woman says: 'I would prefer to wear traditional dress at school, but I know that I would be treated so badly that I wear jeans and jumper like everyone else.' One mother told us that her daughter refused to allow her to plait her hair – she wanted it in a pony-tail like all the other children. A black mother describes how, when her youngest was at primary school, the only black child in his class, he 'would scrub at his skin in the bath, desperate to rub the black off so he would look white like all the other children'. Parental efforts to encourage cultural pride are eroded by overwhelming outside forces.

Anti-semitism is part of life for Jewish parents and their children. In Germany, illegally produced floppy discs with anti-semitic Nazi and racist contents are marketed by the neo-Nazi underground and aimed at children from about 12 years old with home computers. Players of 'Clean up Germany' are asked to kill beggars, homosexuals, Greens and Communists, to the tune of 'Deutschland über Alles' and the screen display 'Proud to be German'. Another game, 'The Aryan Test' greets the player with 'Hello, Nazi' and is presented by 'Adolf Hitler Software Ltd'. The choice is between emerging as an 'Aryan' or a 'wretched Jew'. In the process of the game, the player's qualification is questioned if her or his name contains 'suspect Jewish' syllables such as 'berg' or 'stein'. The player who does well can advance to the rank of an SS officer. 'Jews are our misfortune', the screen says to the sound of the German national anthem, and demands 'Death for all Jews'.[40] At the same time, in British schools, Christian festivals are celebrated and Jewish religious festivals ignored, anti-semitic phrases used freely and without awareness, Jewish children told by their classmates that they 'killed Jesus' and Jewish boys taunted and beaten up for wearing the yarmulke. Rachel describes learning about racism as a very young child:

> When I was little, just learning to write, I didn't know many words but I was learning how to do the alphabet. I came home and found something written on our front door and I was very interested in this and took quite a long time copying down this writing. Eventually I showed it to my mum and her reaction was very, very shocking. She screamed and slapped me round the face. I discovered afterwards that what I had written down was 'filthy Jews go back to Israel'. When she explained it to me, I didn't understand. I didn't know what Israel was, we had never lived there so how could we go back there? But I think I understood that there were people who hated us.[41]

What can the parents of children subjected to racism do or say to their children? Many children do not tell teachers about racist attacks in school; a seventeen year old says this is because 'they are scared of being suspended, and of the white pupils beating them up outside school'.[42] When Fatima Salaria, then at primary school, could no longer bear the constant abuse ('Paki', 'Chocolate drop' and 'Shit-face' were yelled at her every day), she told her head-master 'who then lectured me on how proud I should be of my colour and "Just think, you don't have to have a sun-tan because you are already brown – ha-ha".' Like many other children, she didn't tell anyone at home what was happening.[43]. One study found that only one in five of Black parents knew that their child was subjected to racist teasing and bullying.[44] 'I didn't tell my Mum because what could she do?' said one woman, now in her twenties, who was subjected to racist taunts and threats at school. 'After all,' she added, 'My Mum's black too.' Another woman remembers that she felt 'ashamed and guilty' about racist attacks on her – 'as though I'd brought it on myself, as though it were my fault'. She never discussed racism with her parents and, looking back, sees this as a conspiracy of silence in which both parents and children pretended that it wasn't happening – 'because it was too humiliating to admit that it was'.

Parents, too, may 'pretend it isn't happening' and say that there are other reasons why their child is taunted and abused. One mother told her child it was because she was too 'sassy'; if she were quieter no one would notice her. Another said that the gang of white boys who beat up her son beat up everyone they could, regardless of colour, although the child saw the attack as directed specifically against him as a black boy. Seni Seneviratne remembers how her mother would tell her 'they're just jealous' when she came home from school in tears having been called 'nigger'. And she worries, 'when my own daughter comes home from school/Asking why they call her 'Paki'/Shall I say "just jealous"/Or try to explain/ the centuries of racism/That are heaped behind that word?/And will it make it more sense/Than what my mum said to me?[45]

The problem of making racism intelligible is one reason why parents hesitate when trying to explain the harassment their children experience. There are other reasons too. Parents sometimes told us that they were afraid to discuss racism in case their children started to hate white people and become 'racist' against whites:

My children see violence on TV and they ask 'Why is he doing that?' They see what is happening in South Africa and they want to know about it. I don't know what to say because I do not want to teach them racism. I don't want to put things into black/white terms because I don't want them to grow up prejudiced against white people. They go to multi-racial schools and I want them to have white friends and feel that white people are okay. I can imagine children growing up in the camps in Palestine who only learn prejudice and hatred – I don't want my children to grow up like that.

When children from cultural or ethnic minorities are not given information about racism they have no way of understanding the assaults to which they are subjected except as attacks directed against them personally. Children often feel that they must have provoked the attack in some way – that it is 'their fault'. Children who grow up knowing nothing about the oppression of the group to which they belong, the history of slavery or the civil rights movement, the centuries of anti-semitism and the Holocaust, are being denied important knowledge about their people's resistance, struggle and survival. It is knowledge which they need for their *own* survival.

A group of Asian women believe that denial of racism is a form of defence: 'Many of us may not wish to confront the fact that we may be the "victims" of violent racist attacks . . . A denial that these are racist attacks is a form of psychological protection against the hatred that prompts these attacks'.[46] They argue that

> the acknowledgement of the existence and effects of racism is an important first step in challenging it . . . Things will only change when we teach our children to assert themselves – to say NO every time they are insulted by a racist remark.

Parents need to teach their children what racism is and how to recognise it, as well as giving them the skills they need to protest about and to survive it.

Those who are victims of racism are struggling to be survivors and, as one black mother, the poet Audre Lorde, says, 'for survival, black children in america must be raised to be warriors. For survival, they must also be raised to recognise the enemy's many faces.'[47] Another black writer, Maya Angelou, describes a time when her son Guy was banned from riding on the school bus for 'using profanity' (he had explained the facts of life to some classmates). Confronting three white teachers she writes:

> How could I explain a young black boy to a grown man who had been born white? How could the two women understand a black mother who had nothing to give her son except a contrived arrogance? If I had an eternity and the poetry of old spirituals, I could not make them live with me the painful moments when I tried to prove to Guy that his color was not a cruel joke, but a healthful design. If they knew that I described God to my son as looking very much like John Henry, wouldn't they think me blasphemous? If he was headstrong, I

had made him so. If, in his adolescent opinion, he was the best representative of the human race, it was my doing and I had no apology to make. The radio and posters, newspapers and teachers, busdrivers and salespersons told him every day in thousands of ways that he had come from nothing and was going nowhere.[48]

Children who have this kind of support are able to organise in response to racism. When one East London boys' school, which had been all-white, began to implement a policy of racial integration, the intake changed as Asian pupils, mostly from the Bengali community, entered the lower forms. A series of horrific racist attacks occurred at the school and the Bengali children began to organise themselves. They formed protection gangs, but developed a political programme too. Abdul Hoque, of the Bangladeshi United Youth Group at Daneford School explained what they did:

We made a list of demands of things that were important to Bengali boys. We wrote our own leaflets. We decided to form groups in the school to defend ourselves and fight the racists back. We had to demonstrate at the County Hall to fight the racists and get Bengali lessons for all boys. After all our struggling things started to get better. The racists were frightened by our power.[49]

Although the priority for black and Asian people must be to challenge the institutionalised racism in white society, some are also concerned about racism within their own communities. There are Asians who consider themselves superior, more intelligent and cultured than 'Blacks' (people of Afro-Caribbean origin).[50] And while Asian children in Britain have the common bond of living in a racist culture and being of Asian descent, some Asian parents still tell their children to steer clear of others because 'Hindu Punjabi girls smoke and talk to boys' or 'I'd rather see you dead than married to a Sikh'. A youth worker remembers a thirteen-year old Hindu/Gujerati/Brahmin girl (born in Britain) who talked about white people racially harassing the Asian community but still called

Sikhs and Muslims names and even made disparaging remarks about her best friend who was from the same religion and region but of a lower caste.[51] As she comments, however, despite the conflicts within the Asian community, the struggle against attacks on Asians is the focal point for discussions of racism: 'To them we're all the same no matter what.'

Racism is hard to explain to white children too. Most white parents who spoke to us had adopted a 'colour blind' approach, telling their children that 'everyone is the same underneath, we're all just people, whatever our colour'. One mother told her 4-year-old 'how horrible it was to be nasty to people just because of the colour of their skin – that we are all the same really. She can understand that because she has a skin disorder – psoriasis – and sometimes is teased because of that.' Another explained that 'black children are just like you but they come from a very hot country so they got burnt by the sun, like you do in the summer when you get a suntan'. The problem with these descriptions is that they deny the very real differences between people of different cultural, religious and ethnic identities – differences which are a source of pride and strength – as well as the differences caused by living in a racist society.

A young black woman, Laura Fish, now in her twenties, describes her personal experience of what she calls 'the disease of white liberals who claim to be "colour blind"'. She was brought up as an adopted daughter in a white family: 'My parents believe that everyone is equal and that colour doesn't matter,' she writes. 'This was the rule at home but the moment I stepped outside the warmth of my family, colour seemed to matter terribly. In fact, to my great surprise, it was the first thing that everyone noticed about me.' She describes how she was continully the object of curiosity and interrogation, how people would pat her head, feel her hair and comment on how well she spoke English. 'As a child I accepted racism quite calmly, I had known it from day one and nobody explained what was happening or why it happened.' She says:

I refuse to condemn my parents, they always did what they believed was best. My father in his well-meaning way would say, 'I don't see people as black and white, I just see people.' But black was what I was and I sometimes wonder whether he *sees* me at all. The more I meet black people and realise that I can share something special with them and regain some sort of identity, the more I become aware of the racist traits in the people I was once so close to.[52]

Many white parents are forced to explain racism to their children because of the overtly racist attitudes of people close to them. One mother says her child's grandfather is 'appallingly racist to the extent that he will not allow my son to bring black friends to the house'. She challenges the racist comments he makes but 'this invariably leads to a family row, which does not give my 4-year-old son a very positive idea of being anti-racist'. Her son 'often says racist things after a visit to his grandfather's so that I have to challenge him at home'. Another woman says that her parents are 'very racist and rather right-wing generally. They are great with my daughter (aged 2) but make odd remarks about black people in her hearing which makes me angry.'

In place of individualistic explanations which scapegoat some people as 'bad' because they are racists, some mothers try to explain racism to their children in *social* terms. One woman whose husband's parents use words like 'nig-nog' and 'Paki' in front of her 3½-year-old daughter explained that racism is 'bad' even though the grandparents she loves are 'good' people. 'I told her that even good people sometimes do bad things. She can understand that, because she is a "good" girl who is sometimes naughty.' Suggesting that racism is a problem of individual attitudes is unhelpful to black children, as well as to white, if it means seeing it only in terms of prejudiced people, and not in social systems.

White skin brings privileges in a racist society, whatever the attitudes of the person to whom it belongs. Whoever we are, whatever we believe, if we benefit from racism in any way we are *not* 'innocent' and cannot talk as though racism were only an attitude problem of a few prejudiced people. A white woman explained to her 9-year-old:

Racism isn't just *inside* people, it's out in the world too. I said it was like the river he goes swimming in and there is a strong current. Some people swim downstream and some people swim upstream, like some people are racist and some people are anti-racist, but the current is in a racist direction and that's what's got to be changed. If we can change the world so that it's fair and just for black people, that would be like changing the direction of the current, and most people will go along with that – will swim downstream, because that's always the easiest thing to do.

She says that she wants to 'explain the importance of changing social and political structures, not just individual attitudes', and adds that her son understands this, 'and we discuss how people have done this in the past through voting, demonstrations, strikes and boycotts'.

We can encourage children to discuss issues of race and ethnicity, to recognise racism in themselves and in others and to find ways of combatting it. We can give all children the support and help they need to stand up and speak out against racism whenever they are aware of it, to work so that we can change the way that river flows – and be proud to do so.

SEXISM

Many women who talked to us are concerned about sexism and are making a special effort not to stereotype their children on the basis of gender. They often give examples from restrictions in their own upbringings, and aim to treat their children differently. One woman says it is very important that her daughter Kathy 'accepts that she is a woman and is proud of it'. In her own family

we were very masculine. If mum and dad had only had girls they would have been very sad because they liked to have boys and they think boys are in some ways superior to girls. I don't believe this is right. I want her to like being a woman and to accept that women are equal to men.

She intends to teach Kathy that 'it is good to be a girl', and that 'a woman has to be proud to be a woman, and be responsible for her own life – not be dependent on some man'. The mother of two sons and a daughter says she was brought up 'in a very "feminine" way – dressed in frilly pink dresses, never allowed to get dirty, expected to play with dolls'. She strives to be anti-sexist with her own children:

> I am trying to give my daughter the same opportunities as my sons to muck around and try things out, and my sons are allowed to be fearful, gentle, clinging, instead of being exhorted to be 'real men' all the time.

Gender stereotyping begins at birth. People react differently to the same behaviour depending on the baby's sex. In one study, thirty sets of parents were asked to 'describe your baby as you would to a close friend or relative'. Their babies were less than twenty-four hours old. Sons were described as firmer, larger featured, better co-ordinated, more alert, stronger and harder while daughters were described as softer, finer-featured, weaker and more delicate. Hospital records show that the fifteen boys and fifteen girls were virtually indistinguishable from one another in terms of weight, height, muscle tone, reflexes and general level of activity. In another research project, adults were asked to play with a six-month old child who was either dressed in blue trousers and introduced as 'Adam' or dressed in pink and called 'Beth'. 'Adam' was offered trains and building blocks and rough and tumble games. 'Beth' got cuddles and a doll.[53]

Children's learning about sex differences starts young. At three weeks, babies already react differently to each parent's voice. When the father is placed behind the child so he cannot be seen, and then speaks, the baby's face lights up with joy. It appears that the baby is ready to play. When the mother does the same, the baby's face is much more composed – it seems that the child is waiting to be fed, clothed or changed – and it is Mummy who does that. By 8 months, before they can walk or talk, babies know mother as the caregiver and comforter, and father as the exciting playmate.[54] By the age of 2½, children can make a reliable distinction between 'male' and 'female' occupations[55] and by the time they are 3 or 4, children can 'correctly' classify such items as lawn-mowers, purses, tools and irons as 'men's' or 'women's' things.[56] In one cross-cultural survey of 110 different societies, researchers found in general that social practices were designed to make boys self-reliant and to encourage male achievement, while girls are trained to be nurturant, responsible and obedient.[57] No wonder that some parents look at their children even before they start school, see their perfect conformity with gender stereotypes, and think 'It must be genetic after all!'

Many women are particularly concerned about the effects of sex role stereotyping on their sons. They say that they don't want their sons to be like 'most men'. 'Most men are not in touch with their feelings,' says Andrea who hopes her 8-year-old son will 'stay in touch with his emotions'. Others comment that 'the male stereotype is stiff upper lip, destructive and violent – I hope my son will be different' and 'unless men change their macho image it means the end of all life on this planet'.

But over and over again women told us that despite their best efforts at anti-sexist childraising their sons were learning undesirable 'masculine' attitudes and behaviours. For some mothers this is very upsetting and alienating. Barbara Green describes the 'anger, rejection, and paralysis which I feel daily towards my 7-year-old son' who, she says:

> gives us regular exhibitions of aggression, domination and boastfulness which are unstoppable . . . I reject this machismo, in men, in society – the assumption of superiority, the denigration of women, the ready assertiveness. Yet here they are all wrapped up in a 7-year-old – and sitting next to me at the breakfast table . . . I suspect that my attempts to cope with the immutable machismo of my son will produce only cosmetic results – your original macho man disguised as a first-rate table-setter.

'I suppose boys will be boys,' another woman remarks about her

6-year-old, 'but it's hard to see a gentle, kind child turning to guns and becoming a typical male monster'. Polly Toynbee describes her son: 'His first word was "tractor". Now, at 3 years old he spends all day being a knight with a sword, or Batman, or He-Man, galloping about shouting 'power' and 'fight'! Where did we go wrong?'[58] A woman with three sons aged 12, 14 and 16 says:

> When they were small they were just babies – open and soft and vulnerable. Now they have withdrawn from me, won't talk about their feelings, are acting rigid and tough the way society (and their Dad) tells them men should be. So now I have four John Waynes swaggering about the house ordering me about and expecting to be waited on hand and foot. I hate it. •

However determined the anti-sexist teaching of mothers, other people constantly undermine this from birth onwards. Colour-coding by gender is still going strong – and while a girl can sometimes wear blue, a boy in pink causes discomfort. One mother whose 7-month-old son often wears pink says that people she meets casually (in the supermarket, on the street) begin to coo over her baby 'girl', and when she tells them he's male 'they act as though I've deliberately deceived them, as though I'm perpetrating some kind of fraud – they seem almost angry with me'. Sexism from grandparents was often mentioned, and this too starts with colour-coding. 'Grandma was very upset when baby brother wore a pink baby gro,' says one woman, and another: 'He's very sexist, my dad. Blue for my son, says he!' As the child gets older, these differences of opinion between the generations become more severe – often causing bad feeling:

> My 4-year-old son's paternal grandparents think that 'you should never refuse a little boy anything' and that little boys should play with guns and they're shocked if he picks up a doll. I do not agree with boys being given such a macho upbringing.

A few women felt that their husbands or male partners encouraged sex-role stereotyping in their sons, too. Mary, whose son is 3 years old, says 'My partner mocks my son for certain "inappropriate" sex role behaviours. Not seriously, but enough to irritate me occasionally.' The mother of an 8-year-old complains that 'My partner encourages him in male aggressive games.' Harriette is separated from her husband, and has a 16-month-old son:

> I have very firm beliefs about bringing up my son to be a loving, caring and sensitive man. My husband and his parents are selfish people who are racist and also believe that boys should only play with cars etc and be big and strong and tough, and NEVER cry.

While women often say they don't want their sons to be like 'most men', they tend to find anti-sexist childraising with boys far more challenging than rearing girls. One woman who wants to encourage emotional openness and sensitivity in her sons says that 'It's difficult being open with the boys.' With her daughters she has 'terrific rapport. They go into the world, they're subjected to the usual treatment for women. Since they're the victims, they come home and tell me how they're victimized. But I get more resentment from the boys.'[59] Another wrote:

> Peter is not allowed to fight or play with guns. Ever since he was a baby I have stressed gentleness and non-violence. This was fine until he went to school and other boys teased him, called him sissy, and beat him up. I feel he has to be able to stand up for himself. Is there some way he can hold his own at school without resorting to physical violence?

Women are sometimes ambivalent about anti-sexist childraising for their sons – even when they are enthusiastic about it for their daughters. Living in a society where males have more status means that being born male entitles boys to power and privileges as adults which will be denied their sisters. In such a context, bringing up boys to be anti-sexist means disadvantaging them in certain ways. They may benefit from increased sensitivity, awareness and emotional openness but they lose out on the ready assertiveness and capacity to act 'like a man' in situations where this brings tangible rewards. As one woman said:

> Television shows boys and men being violent and aggressive. I want him to be kind and thoughtful towards others, but not to the extent that he gets pushed around. He'll have to be able to stand up for himself. I hope he'll achieve what he wants, but not at the expense of others.

Girls, on the other hand, stand to gain from more flexible sex roles in terms of power and increased opportunities, and have the support network of the feminist movement – they have every motivation to change.

Women who spoke to us seemed, on the whole, to be much happier about anti-sexist upbringing for their daughters – and they were more likely to feel it was successful:

> My 7-year-old daughter now understands well, and tries to practice, despite outside influence, that sex is no reason for not doing what you think you can. She also dresses sensibly and according to the occasion, and not 'like a girl' all the time.

> Jackie's teacher asked for 'some strong boys to carry the chairs', and Jackie challenged her, and said girls were strong too. I think that was pretty good for a 6-year-old!

Nonetheless, girls are under considerable pressure to conform to traditional 'feminine' behaviour. Sexist attitudes are perpetuated in the nursery rhymes and fairy stories still told them today:

> Women exist in order to be recognised and chosen, like the right slipper for the right foot; or on the other hand to be punished ... Princesses are most admired in sleep – witness Snow White, Briar Rose and the soldier's bride in *The Tinderbox*. Mutes are next best: longing to reach her earthly

lover, the Little Mermaid has her tongue cut out. Failing silence or a useful coma, approval may be won by gratitude, self-denial and sexual acquiescence towards frogs and monsters . . .[60]

Grandparents and fathers insist on buying dolls and tea sets; some mothers counteract this by buying their daughters trains, cars and construction toys. 'My husband's parents still insist on giving her dolls as opposed to trucks and train-sets,' says one woman, 'but she prefers construction toys.' Another describes, with some exasperation, how, 'both sets of grandparents buy dolls for our daughters – which they don't like and don't play with. They can't understand this as girls "should" play with dolls.' Although the company that markets Barbie dolls claims that 69 per cent of girls aged between 3 and 10 in the UK own at least one Barbie doll,[61] perhaps the girls aren't playing with them!

The toy industry is selling much more than dolls and games; it is also reinforcing conventional gender stereotypes. In an advertisement for Zoids, dinosaur-robot models held by two small boys advance menacingly on each other. A deep male voice snarls, 'More power, tougher, more fighting features! They're meaner, nastier. The new zoids aren't on anyone's side – they're just looking for a fight.' In a Tiny Tear ad, a little girl hands her unwilling, protesting brother her doll to take care of. When it wets on him, he disgustedly thrusts it back, grumbling. 'Just like Daddy,' she whispers gleefully to the doll. Jane Ehrlich[62] watched scores of toy advertisements and says, 'The picture they paint of the two sexes is crude; boys are inarticulate, competitive brutes – always active – and girls are drippy, domestic, but much more sociable.'

'Femininity' is big business. Seven per cent of British girls aged between nine and ten years old purchase make-up, and American companies, already selling lipstick, eyeshadow, blusher and nail varnish to 6 year olds in the US are expanding into the UK market. One manufacturer, Tinkerbell, prepares 'tots, tweens, and teens for a lifetime of beauty' with such creations as lip pomades (for 3-year-olds) and brush-on, peel-off nail varnish for the sixes plus. The company advertises in comics like *Bunty* and *Judy*. Max

Factor woos little girls with a lipstick called Get Wicked and a temporary hair colouring (Hair Dare). An advertising campaign for their products featured a 14-year-old model and was entitled 'How far will you go?'. Competing products, aimed at ten to twelve year olds, are typified by Maybelline's flavoured lip glosses – Kissing Potions, Kissing Slicks and Kissing Koolers.[63] Acquiring the habit of make-up at such a young age insidiously implants into girls' minds the idea of being a sexual object – an essential component of 'femininity'.

Girls learn early that to be female means being looked at, assessed, packaged to be desirable. One woman says her parents 'have very stereotyped ideas about boys and girls' and she gives an example: 'Molly was watching her reflection in a glass door and my dad said to her, "You're looking in there because you are a girl and girls are vain"'. This sort of thing infuriates me. In her book – a diary charting the first three years of her daughter Anneli's life – Marianne Grabrucker tells of conversations she had with a friend (a lawyer like herself) when both their children were between 3 and 7 months old:

> Every time we meet, Karin admires Anneli, saying how pretty she is, how dainty and graceful her legs are, and what a good ballet dancer she'd make. She admires Anneli's long eyelashes and blue eyes and says that later on her flirtatious glance, her smile and delicate figure will turn men's heads and they'll run after her. 'Anneli will be able to twist men round her little finger,' she says.
>
> But neither his mother nor I say anything like this about her son. Neither of us paints a picture of a future geared to his appearance or of his market value with women.[64]

Even when people around a child do not reinforce this image of passive femininity, the advertising hoardings tell the same story – women as decoration, draped over cars or passive recipients of male heroism on their behalf. One of Anneli's first sentences is 'woman nothing on' – she says it after looking into a travel agent's window, with pictures of women in bikinis, while waiting for a bus near a newspaper stand with the usual display of magazines with cover illustrations of naked and half naked women, and after seeing the advertising hoardings. Women are passive, men are active. Women are looked at, men achieve. Women's achievements are overlooked or ignored. 'My partner tends to joke about my impracticality ("silly mommy can't mend cars/fix shelves" etc),' says one woman, adding, 'This is true of me as an individual, but I don't want her to get the idea that it's because I'm a woman that I can't do these things. I hope she doesn't apply these ideas to herself.'

For many parents who want to give their sons and daughters an anti-sexist upbringing, school is a major problem. While the tabloids sometimes present schools as hotbeds of feminism, the mothers who talked to us are deeply concerned that schools are continually reinforcing gender stereotypes. 'In his primary school, boys who like girls' toys are already called "pooftas"', one woman complains. 'At playschool the girls still tend to be expected to be "nice" and "quiet",' says another, who has encouraged her daughter to be 'brave and outgoing'.

At school the young headmaster has very traditional views about what is 'male' and 'female', about what constitutes a family, and about working women. Other boys at school are very rough and aggressive. Nicolas (aged 7) is small, 'feminine' and bookish – he gets pushed about a lot of the time. He feels he has to push and shove and shout to be heard and get his own back.

School seems to encourage sex-role stereotyping and racial stereotyping. My son (7 years old) once brought a card home for Mothers Day describing a mother who cooks, cleans, washes, bakes. I was then a mature student on a degree course with a part-time job at the time, and many other mums also work (including his teacher). I pointed out that his teacher had missed out most of the things I do regularly.

Other women who talked to us were critical of girls and boys being made to stand in different queues, their names read in two different lists from the register, boys hanging their coats one side of the classrooms and girls the other, the use of sexist books and dressing-up boxes divided into a boys' box and a girls' box – with cowboys for boys, and brides and nurses for girls.

Even when teachers are keen to avoid gender stereotyping at school, other children exert a strong influence. Boys monopolise the playground and the more popular toys, using intimidation and aggression to get their own way. In one school boys spent an average of twenty-two minutes at the sand tray and girls only four minutes. Although, perhaps surprisingly, the shop and house corner were used equally by both sexes, girls cooked meals, ironed clothes and put dolls to bed while boys turned sink taps and irons into guns, pans into helmets, knocked model furniture around as though it were a set of military targets and used the playhouse as a climbing frame.[65]

One mother, describing her 6-year-old son, says 'other children tell him it's good to be tough and that he should learn karate. He has a gentle nature, like his Daddy, and I would like him to stay that way.' Martha and her husband have 'always tried to bring our children up to believe the sexes are equal, but as soon as he got to school he would come home saying that so and so said "boys don't do . . ." whatever it was.' She is pleased that 'he is quite prepared to argue it out with them, and doesn't at the moment mind being in the minority'. But many boys find it very hard to take the minority position. Judith Arcana describes how her son, Daniel, talked about playtime at school:

'All the boys do is run around the playground, swooping their arms and yelling like monsters, chasing the girls. And the girls run away and scream, but the teachers don't do anything.' Hearing again in memory that hysterical shriek, I asked, 'What happens if the boys catch the girls?' 'They knock 'em down or push 'em around and say they're gonna look at their underpants.'

'So the boys run after the girls and yell, and the girls run away and scream. What do *you* do, Daniel?' 'I run with the boys. I know it's wrong; I don't even like it. I *hate* it, Mom.

But if I don't run with them, they do it to *me* – and call me GIRL! They yell GIRL, GIRL, GIRL, and chase *me*!' These last words echo the playground hysteria, wailing into tears and hiccups.[66]

Journalist Suzanne Lowry says that for her son too, the label 'girl' is an insult: 'To be mistaken for a girl even on the telephone is the most insulting thing that can happen to him. "It's all right if you are a girl," he bleats. "Terrible, yuk, if you're not."'[67] For a boy to be described as 'feminine', 'girlish', or 'mother's boy' is a terrible insult – far worse than 'tomboy' for a girl. This is because a boy belongs to the dominant ('superior') sex; to risk losing that is a real threat, whereas a girl who behaves 'like a boy' is accorded grudging admiration. The 'wimpish' or 'effeminate' boy is mocked as less than a real man, a 'pansy', or 'poofta'. The fear of homosexuality is used to keep even primary school age children in line.

Some mothers are anxious that an anti-sexist upbringing will turn their children into homosexuals, and this sometimes lies behind their ambivalence about anti-sexist upbringing for boys especially. Even if they don't see homosexuality as a perversion, they still describe it as a 'difficulty' and would be upset or disappointed if their sons chose this path: 'It would make life so much harder for him,' says one mother, 'and besides, I would like to have grandchildren.' It is easy to play on this fear of homosexuality in order to argue against non-sexist or anti-sexist childraising. The implicit message is, 'Do that, and your child will turn out to be queer.' In her book on 'the limits of non-sexist childrearing' Sara Stein devotes a whole chapter to gender confusions, and comments that 'the path along which effeminate boys and masculine girls have come is often a bruising one. Their futures may well be homosexuality'.[68]

Media publicity about 'gay education' in Britain has given some people the impression that schools are in the business of promoting lesbian and gay male sexuality, and give 5-year-olds detailed descriptions of homosexual sex. Not only has this never been true, but since 1988, when Section 28 became law, teachers are forbidden to present a positive view of homosexuality in the classroom, nor may they suggest that gay relationships are on a par with heterosexual ones.

While a very few of the parents who talked to us supported this view, many others were concerned about it. One mother said:

I want him to take people as they are and I don't think that sexual orientation is the most important thing about them. We have friends who are gay and I think it's the quality of the relationship that matters, not whether it's heterosexual or homosexual.

Children use words like 'poofter' and 'fag' against boys who don't conform to the macho stereotype while 'lesby friends' is hurled at girls who spend time together and enjoy each other's company. Hearing words like these, both teachers and parents sometimes intervene, although the legal implications for British teachers in this context are now unclear. In her book, Judith Arcana describes how her 10-year-old used the word 'fag' as an insult: 'I came down real heavy this time, because he's too old to let that go by ... The general use of that label for male homosexuals is the same as "dyke" or "kike" or "nigger" and I wanted him to see that. So I told him that it was an insult, and one that specifically affected men we knew, naming them.'[69]

Jo was concerned about the sort of sex education her children would be offered at school:

A letter came from school saying that they were going to have fairly explicit sex education. I went to see the Head and asked how they were going to approach the subject of being gay. I said that if there was any gay bashing I didn't want the children to attend the lesson. She assured me that there was going to be no mocking of homosexuals. We have brought them up to believe loving relationships are the issue.

Jennifer, aged 12, is the daughter of a lesbian and says that

school is a problem for children with lesbian mothers. They get teased and chased home. Other children can't go to their houses because their parents don't approve ... Lots of children feel they have to deny it to protect themselves from harassment.'[70]

Anti-lesbian and anti-gay attitudes are used to reinforce traditional gender stereotypes. Children who are terrified of being labelled 'queer' or 'lezzi' stick to the clothes, toys and behaviours prescribed for their sex. Parents who are worried that their children might turn into homosexuals do not deviate too far from traditional sexist childrearing patterns. Children cannot be protected from sexism or from heterosexism. They live in a sexist and heterosexist society – it is all around them. Though we may avoid these biases in the home, they pick them up from school or from television. If we want a less sexist world, a world in which women and men are truly equal, then part of that means creating a world in which there is no stigma attached to being lesbian or gay. We must be prepared to say, and to believe, that being lesbian or gay *is* good.

Some parents hope to protect their children from sexism by never pointing out the inequalities in society. They tell their daughters, 'You too can be a lawyer, a bricklayer, or a plumber, just as easily as a man can.' The problem with this assurance is that it isn't true – and girls only have to look around them at the jobs women do to see this. We need to be honest about sexism with children, helping them to perceive it instead of covering it up, giving them the name for it and suggesting ways in which they can challenge it. 6-year-old Judy watches the television advertisements with her mother and they discuss sexism together; Judy has felt so strongly about some of the advertisements that her mother has helped her to write to the toy manufacturers complaining. Another mother says she has

encouraged Natasha (now 7) to be on the look out for sexism and racism both in daily life – eg school – and in the media, eg books, television. She is becoming very good at this, mentioning instances and making critical comments. Vanessa (aged 4½) is starting to do this too.

For girls, learning about sexism brings the painful awareness that they are cast in the role of subordinate sex. Understanding this, they can struggle against it, particularly if they are offered social and political analysis rather than suggesting that through individual effort they can overcome, singlehandedly, the oppression of women. For boys, learning about sexism brings the different, but also sometimes painful, awareness, that they are cast in the role of oppressor. It is difficult for a child to accept that he is part of a powerful oppressor group, that this is wrong and that he should cast off that power, especially when, as a child, he feels he has very little power in an adult world. In her searingly honest account of bringing up her child with an understanding of the wrongs perpetrated against women under male supremacy, Judith Arcana remembers how her son once turned to her saying:

'You hate men. You hate me. I'm a boy, and I'll be a man when I grow up. You hate what I'm going to be when I grow up'. Shocked into silence, I recovered and began to talk. I explained why I 'hated' most men – as briefly and simply as I could lay out male supremacy to a 5-year-old, using examples from our lives that he already understood, like men who cruise by and call out to women on the street.

He seemed to be understanding, but what he wanted was reassurance, not politics. I told him that there were some good men, and that *he* was good. We hugged and kissed.[71]

Children need political understanding. They also desperately need a sense of their own self worth. They need to be aware of the political processes at work in gender stereotyping. But they need also the reassurance that they can be different, that they can struggle to step outside the limiting confines of macho masculinity or fragile, seductive femininity.

This is what parents involved in 'non-sexist childrearing' hope to achieve. In her study of such parents, June Stratham[72] says:

Parents concerned about 'non-sexist' child raising see it as opening up options for their children. They are not trying to reverse roles, or make boys more like girls, or girls more like boys, but rather encouraging children of both sexes to develop characteristics that the parents valued but which have traditionally been seen as 'masculine' or 'feminine'.

These parents saw their children as active participants in the sex role learning process – not lumps of clay to be moulded but rather people whose autonomy and critical awareness should be stimulated.

They made their own views about sexism explicit, but encouraged children to question and criticise these views for themselves. They were concerned less to produce a particular package of non-sexist behaviours, as to produce a particular kind of personality in their children, someone who could be open and tolerant, questioning and aware.

They also wanted their children to grow up to fight for political changes necessary for women's rights in society.

Non-sexist childrearing in a sexist society is, as we have seen, fraught with problems. Power and oppression are embedded in the way that society is structured. While individuals can try to provide for their children a safe haven from its worst excesses, the changes needed are large-scale and political. These political issues can be discussed with children and we can help them confront them, both in their own lives and in the wider society.

The world into which children are born is marked by gross injustice, deprivation and oppression. Each child is part of this political framework, gaining privileges because others are suffering, enduring hardships because others have power. We cannot protect children from racism or sexism in any part of the world. We may not be able to save them from famine or poverty, from war or violence. What we can do is help them to understand what is happening, and why, and give them hope for the future.

Many adults feel baffled, frustrated and overwhelmed by the scale of human suffering. We may feel powerless to change anything. When we communicate that sense of helplessness and futility to children they become frightened and bewildered. Most children want to *do* something – they want to send money, help the victims, and alleviate suffering. They want to complain or protest, they want to ensure that injustice is not perpetuated. Instead of communicating apathy and helplessness, we can nurture children's developing understanding and their critical consciousness about political issues. We can encourage a sense that what they do *matters* – that they can make a difference. The most valuable message we can offer children is that they too can be active participants in the struggle to create a better world.

AFTERWORD

The way we respond to children's first questions is a rehearsal for all the other questions that come later, and through encouraging children to question we prepare the ground for discussion and for sharing ideas about values and human behaviour. Right from the start we can either offer ready-made answers because that is easiest and seems safest, or we can enable their questions to stimulate our own thinking and challenge our behaviour. In that way we grow and learn *with* our children.

In trying to present ourselves as children's protectors the temptation is to masquerade as omnipotent. Far from protecting children, this may leave them overwhelmed by adult power and feeling that the expectations we have for them can never be realised. Moral education – or at any rate the kind that lasts – is not something that can simply be imposed on children. They are not empty vessels into which we can pour our own values. It has to be an interactive process, part of a living relationship in which we learn from each other. It is important to understand the ideas of right and wrong that children themselves construct and to listen to their explanations of their own values and beliefs, and help them to articulate them.

When we talk with children about things that matter we are also dealing with our *own* childhood. We look back to injustices we experienced – the times when we told the truth and it wasn't believed, the times we were blamed and were not responsible, the many occasions on which we were humiliated – and resolved never to inflict this upon anyone else. We remember the positive experiences, too – being free to explore in the countryside or play hopscotch and ball games in the street, for example, belonging to a close-knit extended family and celebrating family festivals with aunts, uncles and grandparents – and may feel sad that we can offer these to our children only as our own treasured memories. We sift through the values we learned, or those we felt were inflicted upon us, as children – reinterpreting them in terms of our adult priorities and a changing world.

The speed of change – new technology, new diseases, new threats and new opportunities – must make us reflect carefully on everything we are trying to teach our children. For one thing is sure: they will not inhabit a society identical to that into which we were born, and by the time they are into their twenties or thirties it may have changed beyond recognition. They will need the flexibility, courage and the strong personal values both to see and to adapt to new challenges and to strive with others to find solutions to environmental and human problems which may appear overwhelming.

The strong theme that has run through all the pages of this book is that children do not inhabit a separate world from adults and cannot be sheltered from reality. One of the most important ways we can prepare them for life is to help them face and deal with reality. There is no paradisical garden in which children can be nurtured like flowers. There is no cocoon in which they can be wrapped to protect them from outside influences.

It is bound to be painful for us to present children with the world as it is. Of course, there are all the good things: sun, sea and sand, trees, the sparkle of light and shadow, music, rhymes and stories, the first fall of snow, delicious tastes and smells, the delights of water, the wind on the hills – and above all our own love and caring. But there is also the inescapable fact of human self-destruction: violence and brutality, drug abuse, war, the sexual abuse of women and children, the ugly monuments to greed we can see in any of the world's cities, polluted beaches, rivers and lakes, and dangerously contaminated water, food and even the air we breathe. At a more personal level there is our own inadequacy, too: emotions we would rather not acknowledge, conflicts in our own lives, and our awareness that we fail children constantly and feel guilty about failing them.

All this we offer our children. And we choose either to stand beside them, being as open and honest as we can about it, or we lie and dissimulate and say 'not in front of the children', trying to hide from them the mistakes we have made, our own failures and vulnerabilities.

This book has not provided answers. It raises questions which only you can answer. There are clues that can be followed; suggestions about how we can talk with children. We believe that this approach can make the exploration of human values an exhilarating and rewarding journey of discovery about our children and ourselves.

NOTES

PREFACE

1   Cosby, Bill (1986) *Fatherhood*, Doubleday & Co. Inc.: New York.

CHAPTER 1   EXPECTATIONS

1   Lightburn, Angela (1989) Letter in the *Sunday Times*, 12 February.
2   Quoted in Boulton, Mary G. (1983) *On Being a Mother*, London: Tavistock.
3   Quoted in Boulton, op. cit.
4   Quoted in Boulton, op. cit.
5   Quoted in Wodak, Ruth and Muriel Schulz (1986) *The Language of Love and Guilt*, Amsterdam: John Benjamins Publishing Co.
6   Hoffman, Lois Wladis (1987) 'The Value of Children to Parents and Childrearing Patterns', *Social Behaviour*, 2: 123–41.
7   Kitzinger, Sheila (1989) *The Crying Baby*, Harmondsworth: Viking.
8   Houlbrooke, Ralph A. (1984) *The English Family: 1450–1700*, London: Longman.
9   Pinchbeck, I. and M. Hewitt (1973) *Children in English Society* (Vol. II), London: Routledge & Kegan Paul.
10   Quoted in Pinchbeck, I. and M. Hewitt (1969) *Children in English Society* (Vol. I), London: Routledge & Kegan Paul.
11   Whiting, Beatrice and John Whiting (1975) *Children of Six Cultures: A Psychocultural Analysis*, Cambridge, Mass.: Harvard University Press.
12   Reported in the *Sunday Times*, 13 November 1988.
13   Quoted in Roberts, Glenys (1988) 'When Running the House can be Child's Play', *Sunday Express*, 31 January.
14   Fitzsimons, Carmel (1988) 'The Captive Child', *Observer*, 7 February.

15 Hoffman, op. cit.
16 Caplan, Paula J. (1986) 'Take the Blame Off Mother', *Psychology Today*, October: 70–71.
17 Watson, J. B. (1928) *Psychological Care of Infant and Child*, New York: Norton & Co. Inc.
18 Stuart, Alex (1986) 'Lying on the Electronic Couch', *Guardian*, 25 September.
19 Whitfield, Richard (1988) 'The Needs of Children Revisited', in Digby Anderson (ed.) *Full Circle? Bringing up Children in the Post-Permissive Society*, London: The Social Affairs Unit.
20 Bettelheim, Bruno (1987) 'In Praise of the Imperfect Parent', *Guardian*, 2 September.
21 Coelho, George V. and Eli A. Rubinstein (1972) (eds) *Social Change and Human Behaviour*, Rochville, Maryland: National Institute of Mental Health.

CHAPTER 2   LEARNING TO BE 'GOOD'

1   Hoffman, Lois Wladis (1987) 'The Value of Children to Parents and Childrearing Patterns', *Social Behaviour*, 2: 123–41.
2   Dennis, Geoffrey (1957) *Till Seven*, London: Eyre & Spottiswoode.
3   Raverat, Gwen (1952) *Period Piece*, London: Faber & Faber.
4   Quoted in Powell, Douglas H. (1986) *Teenagers: When to Worry and What to Do*, Garden City, New York: Doubleday & Co., Inc.
5   Houlbrooke, Ralph A. (1988) *The English Family: 1470–1700*, London: Longman.
6   Baker, Donald (1975) *Understanding the Underfives*, London: Evans Bros Ltd.
7   Whitehorn, Katherine (1986) 'No Beanz Meanz Bedlam', *Observer*, 16 November.
8   Lloyd, Davina (1989) *Practical Parenting*, Jan/Feb.
9   Morreal, John (1983) *Taking Laughter Seriously*, Albany: University of New York Press.
10 Nicolson, Harold (1955) *Good Behaviour: Being a Study of Certain Types of Civility*, London: Constable & Co.
11 Morreal, op. cit.
12 Turiel, Elliot (1980) 'The Development of Social, Conventional and Moral Concepts', in M. Windmiller, N. Lambert and E. Turiel (eds) *Moral Development and Socialisation*, Boston: Allyn & Bacon.
13 Turiel, op. cit.
14 Pennebaker, Ruth (1986) *Parents: A Toddler's Guide*, New York: Clarkson Potter, Inc.
15 Quoted in Seabrook, Jeremy (1982) *Working Class Childhood*, London: Victor Gollancz.

16 Yarrow and Walzer (1978) cited in E. Mavis Hetherington and Ross
    D. Parke (1979) *Child Psychology*, New York: McGraw Hill, 2nd edn.
17 Williams, Norman and Sheila Williams (1970) *The Moral Develop-*
    ment of Children, London: Macmillan.
18 Latané, Bibb and J. M. Darley (1970) *The Unresponsive Bystander:*
    Why Doesn't He Help? Englewood, New Jersey: Prentice-Hall.
19 Likona, Thomas (1976) *Moral Development and Behavior*, New York:
    Holt, Rinehart & Winston.
20 Raverat, op. cit.
21 Shulman, Michael and Eva Meckler (1985) *Bringing Up a Moral*
    Child, Reading, Mass.: Addison-Wesley.
22 Hoffman, M. (1976) 'Empathy, Role Taking, Guilt and the Develop-
    ment of Altruistic Motives', in T. Likona, op. cit.
23 Dreikurs, Rudolf, with Vicki Soltz (1964) *Happy Children: A Chal-*
    lenge to Parents, London: Collins/Fontana.
24 Raverat, op. cit.
25 Dennis, op. cit.
26 Dennis, op. cit.

CHAPTER 3   FOOD

1   Houlbrooke, Ralph A. (1988) *The English Family: 1470–1700*,
    London: Longman.
2   Vuog, Mobi (Fall, 1981) 'Vietnamese mothering', *Mothering*.
3   Wannenburgh, A., P. Johnson and A. Bannister (1979) *The Bushmen*,
    Cape Town: Struik.
4   Rivers, W. H. R. (1967) *The Todas*, The Netherlands: Netherlands
    Anthropological Publications.
5   Lullaby for a newborn girl quoted in Landor, Liliane (1988) 'From
    the Caribbean to the Arab World: The Odyssey of one Dolores
    Quintero', in S. Grewal, J. Kay, L. Landor, G. Lewis and P. Parmar
    (eds) *Charting the Journey: Writings by Black and Third World Women*,
    London: Sheba Press.
6   Oakley, Ann (1972) *Sex, Gender and Society*, London: Temple Smith.
7   Lems, Marian (1981/2) 'Perspectives d'Analyse de L'Ideologie de la
    Difference', quoted in B. Jo, 'If Looks Could Kill', *Lesbian Ethics*,
    3(1): 48–54.
8   Grabrucker, Mariane (1988) *There's a Good Girl – Gender Stereotyping*
    in the First Three Years of Life: A Diary, London: The Women's
    Press.
9   *Newsweek*, 27 July 1987.
10 Wolfenstein, Martha (1955) 'Some Variants in Moral Training of
    Children', in Margaret Mead and Martha Wolfenstein (eds) *Child-*
    hood in Contemporary Cultures, Chicago: University of Chicago Press.

11   Wolfenstein, op. cit.
12   *Telegraph 7 Days*, 19 March 1989.
13   Boscawan, Frances quoted in *Admiral's Wife*, George Low (ed.) (1908) London: Hodder & Stoughton.
14   Quoted in Pollock, Linda (1987) *A Lasting Relationship: Parents and Children Over Three Centuries*, London: Fourth Estate.
15   Grant, Elizabeth (1911) *Memoirs of a Highland Lady*, London: John Murray.
16   Spencer, Colin (1987) 'Food for thought' *Country Living*, November, 91–2.
17   Neville, Helen and Mona Halaby (1984) *No-Fault Parenting*, New York: Facts on File Publications.
18   Scheper-Hughes, Nancy (1982) 'Virgin Mothers: The Impact of Irish Jansenism on Childbearing and Infant Rearing in Western Ireland', in Margarita Kay (ed.) *Anthropology of Human Birth*, Philadelphia: Davis.
19   Scheper-Hughes, op. cit.
20   Jenkins, Tina (1988) 'As I am', *Trouble and Strife*, 13: 20–26.
21   Pickard, Barbara (1980) 'Children's Nutrition: Progress and Problems', in Digby Anderson (ed.) *Full Circle: Bringing up Children in the Post-Permissive Society*, London: Social Affairs Unit.
22   Schoenfielder, Lisa and Barb Wieser (1983) *Shadow on a Tightrope*, Iowa: Aunt Lute Book Co.
23   Landor, op. cit.

CHAPTER 4   OBEDIENCE AND AUTONOMY

1   The Koran, Sura 4.
2   Both quoted in Hoffman, Lois W. (1987) 'The Value of Children to Parents and Childrearing Patterns', *Social Behaviour*, 2: 123–41.
3   Naherny, Patricia K. and José Rosario (1975) 'Morality, Science, and the Use of the Child in History', in V. F. Haubrich and M. W. Apple (eds) *Schooling and the Rights of Children*, Berkeley, Calif.: McCutchan.
4   Humprey, H. (1840) 'Restraining and Governing Children's Appetites and Passions', *Mother's Magazine*, VIII(6): 124–30, quoted in M. Mead and M. Wolfenstein (eds) (1955) *Childhood in Contemporary Cultures*, Chicago: University of Chicago Press.
5   Robertson, Priscilla (1974) 'Home as Nest: Middle Class Childhood in Nineteenth Century Europe', in Lloyd DeMause (ed.) *The History of Childhood*, London: Souvenir Press.
6   Woods, Margaret (1815) quoted in Linda Pollock (1987) *A Lasting Relationship: Parents and Children Over Three Centuries*, London: Fourth Estate.

7   1880 story, reprinted in L. De Vries (1967) *Little Wide-Awake: An Anthology from Victorian Children's Books and Periodicals*, London: Arthur Baker Ltd.
8   Kilner, Dorothy (1828) quoted in Sylvia W. Patterson (1971) *Rousseau's Émile and Early Children's Literature*, Metuchen, New Jersey: The Scarecrow Press.
9   Illustrated by Cruickshank, George (1820?); trans. Robert Samber from the French of Perrault (1729?), The Bodleian Collection.
10 Anon (1912–13) *Baby: The Mother's Magazine*, 26: 273.
11 Russell, John (1872) quoted in Pollock, op. cit.
12 Uttley, Alison (1937) *Ambush of Young Days*, London: Faber & Faber.
13 Anon (1987) 'Little Horrors', *Baby*, Spring/Summer.
14 Pogrebin, Letty (1980) *Growing Up Free*, New York: McGraw Hill.
15 Quoted in Pollock, op. cit.
16 Quoted in Mead and Wolfenstein, op. cit.
17 Quoted in DeMause, Lloyd (1974) 'The Evolution of Childhood', in L. DeMause (ed.) *The History of Childhood*, London: Souvenir Press.
18 *Guardian*, 14 May 1987.
19 *New York Times*, 12 June 1982, quoted in Letty Pogrebin (1983) *Family Politics: Love and Power on an Intimate Frontier*, New York: McGraw Hill.
20 Quoted in Pogrebin, op. cit.
21 Reported in the *Guardian*, 17 June 1988.
22 Anderson, Digby (ed.) (1988) *Full Circle? Bringing Up Children in the Post-Permissive Society*, London: The Social Affairs Unit.
23 Quoted in Houlbrooke, Ralph A. (1988) *The English Family: 1450–1700*, London: Longman.
24 Quoted in the *Guardian*, 4 March 1989.
25 Piaget, Jean (1932, reprinted 1965) *The Moral Judgement of the Child*, New York: Free Press.
26 Quoted in the *Guardian*, 19 December 1985.
27 Quoted in the *Sunday Express*, 31 January 1988.
28 Milgram, Stanley (1965) 'Some Conditions of Obedience and Disobedience to Authority', *Human Relations*, 8: 57–76.
29 Milgram, op. cit.
30 Brunswik, Frendel (1955) in Mead and Wolfenstein, op. cit.
31 Bretherton, I. and M. Beeghly (1982) 'Talking about Internal States', *Development Psychology*, 18: 906–21; Hood, L. and L. Bloom (1979) 'What, When and How about Why: A Longitudinal Study of Early Expressions of Causality', *Monographs of the Society for Research in Child Development*, 4.
32 Bird, Isabella (1973, reprinted 1980) *Unbeaten Tracks in Japan*, New York: Putnams.
33 Hoffman, op. cit.

34 Whiting, Beatrice and John Whiting (1975) *Children of Six Cultures: A Psychocultural Analysis*, Cambridge, Mass.: Harvard University Press.
35 Fisher, D. C. (1964) *The Montessori Manual for Teachers and Parents*, Cambridge, Mass.: Bentley.
36 Benedict, Ruth (1955) in Mead and Wolfenstein, op. cit.
37 Pogrebin, op. cit.

CHAPTER 5   LIES AND SECRETS

1 Sandburg, Carl (1970) 'What Kind of a Liar are You?', in Geoffrey Summerfield (ed.) *Junior Voices*, Harmondsworth: Penguin.
2 *New York Times*, 22 July 1981.
3 Steedman, Caroline (1986) *Landscape for a Good Woman*, London: Virago.
4 Steedman, op. cit.
5 Burton, Roger V. (1976) 'Honesty and Dishonesty', in Thomas Lickona (ed.) *Moral Development and Behavior*, New York: Holt, Rinehart & Winston.
6 Burton, op. cit.
7 Dennis, Geoffrey (1957) *Till Seven*, London: Eyre & Spottiswoode.
8 Hetherington, E. Mavis and Ross D. Parke (1979) *Child Psychology*, New York: McGraw Hill, 2nd edn.
9 Hale, Nancy (1971) *Secrets*, New York: Coward, McCann & Geoghegan.
10 Lickona, Thomas (1976) *Raising Good Children: Helping Your Child Through the Stages of Moral Development*, New York: Bantam.
11 Kohlberg, Lawrence (1971) 'Stages of Moral Development as a Basis for Moral Education', in C. M. Beck, B. S. Crittenden and E. V. Sullivan (eds) *Moral Education: Interdisciplinary Approaches*, Toronto: University of Toronto Press.
12 Lickona, op. cit.
13 Ibid.
14 Ibid.
15 Adams, Gillian (1988) 'The Great Pretender', *Guardian*, 27 July.
16 Hale, op. cit.
17 Lanfer, Robert L. and Maxine Wolf (1976) 'Privacy as a Concept and a Social Issue', *Journal of Social Issues*, 33: 29.
18 Bok, Sissela (1984) *Secrecy*, Oxford: Oxford University Press.
19 Quoted in Bok, op. cit.
20 Quoted in Bok, op. cit.
21 Ibid.
22 Bonhoeffer, Dietrich (1965) 'What is meant by "telling the truth?"' in *Ethics*, Eberhard Bethge (ed.) New York: Macmillan.

23 Sweet, Phyllis E. (1981) *Something Happened To Me*, Racine, Wisconsin: Mother Courage Press.
24 Pinchbeck, Ivy and Margaret Hewitt (1973) *Children in English Society II: From the Eighteenth Century to the Children Act 1948*, London: Routledge & Kegan Paul.

CHAPTER 6 SEX AND BIRTH

1 Updale, Alicia (January 1989) 'Economical With the Truth? Or a Bare-faced Liar?' *Parents*: 15.
2 Scheper-Hughes, Nancy (1982) 'Virgin Mothers: The impact of Irish Jansenism on childbearing and infant tending in Western Ireland' in Margarita Artschwager Kay, *Anthropology of Human Birth*, Philadelphia: F. A. Davis Co.
3 Cole, Norma (1896) *Songs for Little People*, London: Constable & Co.
4 Mitford, Jessica (1961) *Hons and Rebels*, London: Victor Gollancz.
5 Arcana, Judith (1983) *Every Mother's Son*, London: The Women's Press.
6 Ellison, Jane (1989) 'When we were young', *Guardian*, 2 March.
7 Quoted in the *Guardian*, 10 October 1988.
8 Quoted in the *Guardian*, 12 May 1986.
9 Binchey, Maeve (1987) *A Portrait of the Artist as a Young Girl*, London: Methuen.
10 Harrison, Fraser (1989) *Trivial Disputes*, London: Collins.
11 Stewart, Nora Mae (1982) 'Do Storks Really Bring Babies?', *NAPSAC News*, 7: 4.
12 Goldman, R. and J. Goldman (1989) *Show Me Yours: What Children Think About Sex*, London: Penguin.
13 Kitzinger, Sheila (1986) *Being Born*, London: Dorling Kindersley.
14 Pogrebin, Letty Cottin (1983) *Family Politics: Love and Power on an Intimate Frontier*, New York: McGraw-Hill.
15 Moser, Mary Beck (1982) 'Seri: From Conception Through Infancy', in Margarita A. Kay (ed.) *Anthropology of Human Birth*, Philadelphia: F. A. Davis.
16 Sheila Kitzinger, from field-work interviews in South Africa.
17 Anderson, Sandra VanDam and Penny Simkin (1981) *Children at Birth*, Seattle: Pennypress.
18 Hazell, Lester, foreword to Anderson and Simkin, op. cit.
19 Ibid.
20 Metraux, Rhoda (1955) 'Parents and Children: An Analysis of Contemporary German Child-care and Youth-guidance Literature', in Margaret Mead and Martha Wolfenstein (eds) *Childhood in Contemporary Cultures*, Chicago: University of Chicago Press.
21 Quoted in Neville, Helen and Mona Halaby (1984) *No-Fault Parenting*, New York: Fact on File Publications.

22 Shuttleworth, Penelope and Peter Redgrove (1978) *The Wise Wound: Menstruation and Every Woman*, London: Penguin.
23 Lein, Allen (1979) *The Cycling Female: Her Menstrual Rhythm*, San Francisco: W. H. Freeman.
24 Drabble, Margaret (1988) *The Radiant Way*, Harmondsworth: Penguin.
25 Quoted in the *Observer*, 14 December 1986.

CHAPTER 7   FRIENDS: THEIRS AND YOURS

1 Silberman, Mel (1988) *Competent Parenting*, New York: Warner.
2 Singer, Jerome L. (1976) *Daydreaming and Fantasy*, London: Allen & Unwin.
3 Angelou, Maya (1976) *Singin' and Swingin' and Gettin' Merry Like Christmas*, New York: Random House.
4 Quoted in Glew, Jenny (April 1987) 'Just Good Friends?' *Parents*: 133.
5 Pasternack, Laura (November 1983) 'Scolding Other Children', *Parents*: 92.
6 Quoted in Dreikurs, Rudolf (1964) *Happy Children: A Challenge to Parents*, London: Collins/Fontana.
7 Quoted in the *Guardian*, 14 July 1986.
8 Bombeck, Erma (1974) *Motherhood: The Second Oldest Profession*, London: Macdonald & Co.
9 Houlbrooke, Ralph A. (1988) *The English Family: 1470–1700*, London: Longman.
10 Ibid.
11 Ibid.
12 Ibid.
13 Spock, Benjamin (1987) in Eileen Shiff (ed.) *Experts Advise Parents*, New York: Delacorte Press.
14 Morgan, Patricia (1987) op. cit. 'For the sake of the children?' in *Full Circle: Bringing up Children in the Post-Permissive Society*, ed. Digby Anderson, Social Affairs Unit, London.
15 Morgan, op. cit.
16 Grollman, Earl (1987) 'Explaining Death and Divorce', in Shiff, op. cit.
17 Quoted in Watts, Janet (1988) 'Stepchildren speak', *Observer*, 12 June.
18 Ibid.
19 Ibid.
20 Ibid.
21 McShea, Marie (1986) 'Smile for the Camera', in Perlie McNeill, Marie McShea and Pratibha Parmar, *Through the Break: Women in Personal Struggle*, London: Sheba Press.

22 Shiff. op. cit.
23 Fulton, J. A. (1979) 'Parental Reports of Children's Post-divorce Adjustment', *Journal of Social Issues*, 35. 4: 126–39.
24 Morgan, Mary, in Shiff, op. cit.
25 Heather in Krememtz, J. (1984) *How it Feels When Parents Divorce*, New York: Knopf.
26 Morgan, Mary, in Shiff, op. cit.
27 Spock, Benjamin, in Shiff, op. cit.
28 Ibid.
29 All quoted in Mills, Jane Cousin (24 August 1988) 'Learning to love the "wicked stepmother"', *Guardian*.
30 Watts, op. cit.
31 Watts, op. cit.
32 Watts, op. cit.
33 Watts, op. cit.
34 Goodman, Gere, George Lakey, Judy Lashof and Erika Thorne (1983) *No Turning Back: Lesbian and Gay Liberation for the 80's*, Philadelphia: New Society Publishing.
35 Rhodes, Ann and Conway-Rhodes (1987) 'Family Matters' in J. St Vaughan Pollock, *Politics of the Heart*, New York: Firebrand Books.
36 Quoted in Krememtz, op. cit.

CHAPTER 8   AGGRESSION AND VIOLENCE

1   Bailey, Rosemary (1989) 'Out of Nappies, Straight into the Fast Lane', the *Independent*, 16 March.
2   Ibid.
3   Reported in the *Guardian*, 30 September 1985.
4   Reported in *Today*, 23 May 1988.
5   Reported in the *Guardian*, 30 December 1987 and 23 February 1988.
6   Reported in the *Observer*, 30 October 1988.
7   Wilce, Hilary (1988) 'City Stress that Hits the Under Elevens', *Independent*, 10 November.
8   Wilce, Hilary (1988) 'Opting for the "Lesser Evil"', *Independent*, 10 November.
9   Roberts, Steve (1988) 'Small is Beautiful', *Guardian*, 24 January.
10 Quoted in the *Daily Telegraph*, 11 July 1986.
11 Pilbeam, David (1988) 'The Naked Ape', *Children and War*, 2: 14–22.
12 Malinowski, Bronislaw (1929) *The Sexual Life of Savages in North-Western Melanesia*, New York: Harcourt, Brace & World.
13 Kagan, Jerome (1977) 'The Child and the Family', *Daedalus*, 106, 2: 39.
14 Hetherington, E. Mavis and D. Ross Parke (1979) *Child Psychology*, New York: McGraw Hill, 2nd edn.

15 Quoted in Harvey, Pamela (1989) 'Not in Front of the Children?', *Practical Parenting*, January/February.
16 Ibid.
17 Ibid.
18 Hetherington and Parke, op. cit.
19 Dobash, R. Emerson and Russell P. Dobash (1979) *Violence Against Wives*, New York: Free Press.
20 Dobash, R. Emerson and Russell P. Dobash (1982) 'The Violent Event', in Whitelegg *et. al.* (eds) *The Changing Experience of Women*, Basil Blackwell: Oxford.
21 Dobash, R. Emerson and Russell P. Dobash (1982) 'The Antecedents and Nature of Violent Episodes', paper presented at annual meeting of American Sociological Association, San Francisco.
22 Newson J. and E. Newson (1966) *Infant Care in an Urban Community*, London: Allen & Unwin; (1968) *Four Year Olds in an Urban Community*, London: Allen & Unwin.
23 Quoted in the *Guardian*, 17 June 1988.
24 Report in *Parents and Children*, Australia, January 1989.
25 Charlton, D. (1985) 'Spoil the Rod and Spare the Child', *Report*: 10, December.
26 Roberts, op. cit.
27 Quoted in the *Guardian*, 21 November 1986.
28 Reported in the *Guardian*, 1 October 1985.
29 Reported in the *Telegraph*, 11 July 1986.
30 Quoted in the *Sunday Times*, 8 May 1988.
31 *USA Today*, 31 August 1988, international edn.
32 Patterson, G. R. (1976) 'The Aggressive Child: Victim and Architect of the Coercive System', in E. J. Marsh, L. A. Hamerlynck and I. C. Handy (eds) *Behavior Modification and Families*, New York: Brunner/Mazel.
33 Hetherington and Parke, op. cit.
34 Maurer, A. (1974) 'Corporal Punishment', *American Psychologist*, 29: 614–26; Helfer, Ray, John McKinney and Ruth Kempe (1976) 'Arresting or Freezing the Developmental Process', in Ray Helfer and C. Henry Kempe, *Child Abuse and Neglect: The Family and the Community*, Cambridge, Mass.: Ballinger.
35 Wright, Derek (1971) *The Psychology of Moral Behaviour*, London: Penguin.
36 Radecki, Thomas (1989) 'Television and Film Entertainment', *Mothering*, Winter.
37 Gerbner, George (1972) 'Violence in Television, Trends and Symbolic Functions', *Television and Social Behavior* 1, Media Content and Control, Washington DC: Government Printing Office.
38 Hooks, Jennifer (1989) 'What Harm Do They Do?', *Parents and Children*, Australia, January.

39 Liebert, Robert M. and Rita Wicks Poulos (1976) 'Television and the Moral Teacher', in Likona, Thomas (ed.) *Moral Development and Behavior*, New York: Holt, Rinehart & Winston.

40 Radecki, op. cit.

41 Dominick R. and B. S. Greenberg, 'Attitudes Toward Violence: The Interaction of Television Exposure, Family Attitudes, and Social Class', in G. A. Comstock and E. A. Rubinstein (eds) *Television and Social Behavior* III, Television and Adolescent Aggression, Washington DC: Government Printing Office.

42 Davies, Maire Messenger (1989) *Television is Good for Your Kids*, Hilary Shipman.

43 Davies, Maire Messenger, personal communication.

44 Garland, Madge (1963) *The Changing Face of Childhood*, London: Hutchinson.

45 Vas Dies, Susan (1987) in a letter to the *Observer*, 16 August.

46 Reported in the *Observer*, 14 December 1986.

47 Pogrebin, op. cit.

48 Goode, Steve (1987) 'Gun Play in Nurseries', *London Child Care Network Newsletter*: 12–13, Spring/Summer.

49 'Worldwide' (1988) *Children and War*: 6, 2 September, London: Peace Pledge Union.

50 Spock, B. (1974) *Bringing up Children in a Difficult Time*, London: The Bodley Head.

51 Baron, R. A. (1978) *Human Aggression*, New York: Plenum.

52 Gudgeon, Jennie (1987) 'Exploring Death and Power – Towards a Policy on Gun Play?', *London Child Care Network Newsletter*: 12, Spring/Summer.

53 Greenwell, Jayne (1988) 'Shooting Times', *Guardian*, 29 November.

54 'Toys' (1988) *Children and War*: 10, 9 April, London: Peace Pledge Union.

55 'Newspoint' (1988) *Children and War*: 3, 2 September, London: Peace Pledge Union.

56 'Worldwide' (1988) *Children and War*: 6, 2 September, London: Peace Pledge Union.

57 Rossie, Alice (1976) 'A Biosocial Perspective on Parenting', *Daedalus*, 106, 2: 10–11.

58 Letter from Rosie (1988) 'Help! I've got a bruiser!' *Parents*: 151, October.

59 Rutherford, Jonathan (1987) 'I want something, something that we men have no language to describe, to look after a baby at home, not like a mother, but as a man.' *Woman's Journal*.

60 Reported in *Ely Weekly News*, 12 June 1986.

61 Lord, Audre (1984) 'Man Child: A Black Lesbian Feminist Response', *Sister Outsider: Essays and Speeches*, New York: Crossing Press.

62 Seabrook, Jeremy (1982) *Working-Class Childhood*, London: Victor Gollancz.
63 Black American Frederick Douglass in his West India Emancipation Speech of 1857, quoted in Wren, Brian A. (1977) *Education for Justice*, London: SCM Press.
64 Zahari, S. and S. R. Ashar (1978) 'The Effect of Verbal Instruction on Preschool Children's Aggressive Behavior', *Journal of School Psychology*, 16: 146–53.
65 Chandler, M. J. (1973) 'Egocentrism and Antisocial Behavior: The Assessment and Training of Social Perspective Taking Skills', *Developmental Psychology*, 9: 326–32.
66 Masheder, Mildred (1989) *Let's Cooperate*, Peace Education Project, London: Peace Pledge Union.
67 Lorde, op. cit.

CHAPTER 9   DEATH

1   Rowe, Dorothy (1988) 'A Matter of Death and Life', *Guardian*, 19 July.
2   Pinchbeck, I. and M. Hewitt (1969) *Children in English Society* (Vol. I), London: Routledge & Kegan Paul.
3   *Independent*, 5 April 1989.
4   Tekce, B. and F. Shorter (1984) 'Determinants of Child Mortality: A Study of Squatter Settlements in Jordan', in W. H. Mosley and L. C. Chen (eds) *Child Survival: Strategies for Research*, Cambridge: Cambridge University Press.
5   Laska, V. (1983) *Women in the Resistance and in the Holocaust: The Voices of Eyewitnesses*, Westwood, Conn.: Greenwood Press.
6   Published in 1694 and quoted in Pinchbeck and Hewitt, op. cit.
7   Quoted in Townsend, John Rowe (1974) *Written for Children: An Outline of English-Language Children's Literature*, Harmondsworth: Penguin.
8   Lyons, J. O. (1978) *The Invention of the Self: The Hinge of Consciousness in the Eighteenth Century*, Carbondale and Edwardsville, Ill.: Southern Illinois University Press.
9   Quoted in Shipman, M. D. (1972) *Childhood: A Sociological Perspective*, Windsor, Berks: NFER Publishing Co. Ltd.
10 Bok, Sissela (1984) *Secrets*, Oxford: Oxford University Press.
11 Quoted in Rowe, op. cit.
12 Ibid.
13 Quoted in Pogrebin, Letty (1983) *Family Politics: Love and Power on an Intimate Frontier*, New York: McGraw Hill.
14 Quoted in Pollock, Linda (1987) *A Lasting Relationship*, London: Fourth Estate.

15 Tolstoy, Lev (1980) 'My Encounter with Philosophical Ideas', in Gareth B. Matthews (ed.), *Growing Up with Philosophy*, Philadelphia: Temple University Press.

16 Cain, A. C. and J. Fast (1966) 'Children's Disturbed Reactions to Parent Suicide', *American Journal of Orthopsychiatry*, 36: 873–80.

17 Hamilton, Elizabeth (1954) *A River Full of Stars*, London: Andre Deutsch.

18 Maurer, A. (1966) 'Maturation of Concepts of Death', *British Journal of Medicine and Psychology*, 39: 35–41.

19 Cockshott, Trix (1986) *Guardian*, 16 May.

20 Rochlin, G. (1973) *Man's Aggression: The Defense of the Self*, Boston: Gambit.

21 Uttley, Allison (1937) *Ambush of Young Days*, London: Faber.

22 Grollman, E. (1987) 'Explaining Death and Divorce', in E. Shiff (ed.) *Experts Advise Parents*, New York: Delacourte Press.

23 Riley, J. W. (1968) 'Death and Bereavement', *International Encyclopedia of the Social Sciences* (Vol. 4), New York: Macmillan and Free Press.

24 Krementz, Jill (1983) 'When a Parent Dies', *Parents*, April.

25 Eliot, T. D. (1943) 'Of the Shadow of Death', *Annals of the American Academy of Political and Social Science*, 229: 87–99.

26 Diskin and Guggenheim (1967) cited in Grollman, op. cit.

27 Ibid.

28 Quoted in Hollander, A. (1980) *How to Help Your Child have a Spiritual Life*, New York: A. & W. Publishers.

29 *Mothering*, Winter 1984.

30 Quoted in Seabrook, Jeremy (1982) *Working-Class Childhood*, London: Victor Gollancz.

31 Bordewich, F. M. (1988) 'Mortal Fears', *The Atlantic*, 30–34.

32 Quoted in the *Independent*, 28 July 1987.

33 *Guardian*, 25 October 1988.

34 Quoted in Maugham, G. (1988) *Observer*, 23 October.

35 Ibid.

36 St Exupéry (1982) *The Little Prince*, London: Piccolo/Pan.

37 White, E. B. (1952) *Charlotte's Web*, Harmondsworth: Penguin.

38 Burton, L. (1974) 'Tolerating the Intolerable', in L. Burton (ed.) *Care of the Child Facing Death*, London: Routledge & Kegan Paul.

39 Turk, J. (1964) 'Impact of Cystic Fibrosis on Family Functioning', *Pediatrics*, 34: 67–71.

40 Quoted in Burton, L. (1975) *The Family Life of Sick Children*, London: Routledge & Kegan Paul.

41 Ibid.

42 Quoted in Lindsay, M. and MacCarthy, D. (1974) 'Caring for the Brothers and Sisters of a Dying Child', in L. Burton (ed.) (1974) op. cit.

43 Atkin, M. (1974), 'The "Doomed Family" – Observations on the Lives of Parents and Children Facing Repeated Child Mortality', in L. Burton (ed.) (1974) op. cit.

44 Burton, L. (1974) 'Tolerating the Intolerable', in L. Burton (ed.) (1974) op. cit.

45 Vernick, J. and M. Karon (1965) 'Who's Afraid of Death on a Leukemia Ward?', *American Journal of Diseases of Children* 109: 393–7.

46 Edmund Pellegrino (1988) personal communication.

47 Quoted in Burton (1975) op. cit.

CHAPTER 10   RELIGION

1 Coles, Robert (1986) *The Moral Life of Children*, New York: Atlantic Monthly Press.

2 Ibid.

3 Pinchbeck, Ivy and Margaret Hewitt (1969) *Children in English Society I: From Tudor Times to the 18th Century*, London: Routledge & Kegan Paul.

4 Becon, Thomas (1564) *Worckes*, part 1, quoted in Pinchbeck and Hewitt, op. cit.

5 Pinchbeck and Hewitt, op. cit.

6 Ibid.

7 Townsend, John Rowe (1974) *Written for Children: An Outline of English-Language Children's Literature*, Harmondsworth: Penguin.

8 Barbauld, Anne Laetitia (1786) Preface to *Hymns in Prose for Children*, IV–V, 4th edn, Norwich, Connecticut: John Trumbull.

9 Hughes, Thomas (1983) *Tom Brown's Schooldays*, Harmondsworth: Puffin.

10 'About Ugly Idols', in Leonard de Vries (ed.) (1967) *Little Wide-Awake: An Anthology from Victorian Children's Books and Periodicals*, London: Arthur Barker.

11 Raverat, Gwen (1952) *Period Piece*, London: Faber & Faber.

12 Ibid.

13 de Vries, op. cit.

14 'Home Sweet Home', de Vries, op. cit.

15 'The Case of Goldilocks and Bare-faced Ungodlies', (1986) *Times Educational Supplement*, 22 August.

16 Strommen, Merton (ed.) (1971) *Research on Religious Development*, New York: Hawthorn Books.

17 Goldman, Ronald (1980) quoted in Hollander, Annette, *How to Help Your Child Have a Spiritual Life: A Parents' Guide to Inner Development*, New York: A. & W. Publishers.

18 Donin, Rabbi Hayim Halevy (1977) *To Raise a Jewish Child*, New York: Basic Books.

19 Quoted in Pollock, Linda A. (1983) *Forgotten Children: Parent–Child Relations from 1500–1900*, Cambridge: Cambridge University Press.
20 Ibid.
21 Ibid.
22 Reported in the *Guardian*, 4 November 1985.
23 Reported in the *Sunday Times*, 4 December 1988.
24 Hollander, op. cit.
25 Pennington, Ellen (1988) 'Being Hooked on Jesus', *Sunday Times*, 7 February.
26 Troeltsch, Ernst (1960) *The Social Teaching of the Christian Churches*, 2 vols, New York: Harper.
27 The phrases here are those used by Mormon women in Salt Lake City in conversation with Sheila.
28 Hart, K. R. A. (1955) *A Spastic Wins Through*, London: Bennisdale Press.
29 Maugham, Somerset W. (1963) *Of Human Bondage*, Harmondsworth: Penguin (originally published in 1915 by Heinemann).
30 Raverat, op. cit.
31 Tillich, Paul (1961) quoted in Hook, Sidney (ed.) *Religious Experience and Truth*, New York: New York University Press.
32 Wood, Frances (1926) *A Great Niece's Journals*, in Margaret Rolt (ed.) London: Constable, quoted in Pollock, Linda (1987) *A Lasting Relationship*, London: Fourth Estate.
33 Steiner, Rudolf (1964) *The Kingdom of Childhood*, London: Rudolf Steiner.
34 Traherne, Thomas (1908) in Bertram Dobell (ed.) *Centuries of Meditations*, London: P. J. & A. E. Dobell.
35 Hollander, op. cit.
36 Ibid.
37 Ibid.
38 Ibid.
39 Ibid.

CHAPTER 11   POLITICS & PREJUDICE

1 Sweeny, Elizabeth (1988) Children's Research Unit, reported in the *Independent*, 24 December.
2 Pogrebin, Letty Cottin (1980) *Growing Up Free*, New York: McGraw Hill.
3 King, Martin Luther (1968) *Chaos or Community*, London: Hodder & Stoughton.
4 Kinzer, Stephen (1988) 'Nicaragua', *Asahi Evening News*, 15 February.

5   Hamilton, Masha (1988) 'Middle East', *Asahi Evening News*, 15 February.
6   Smith, Colin (1988) *Observer*, 23 October.
7   Finnish Peace Union, 'Child Martyrs in Iran', in *What Shall We Tell the Children?*, PEP Talk No. 16, Journal of the Peace Education Project: 14–17.
8   *Two Dogs and Freedom* is available from the International Defence and Aid Fund for South Africa, 64 Essex Road, London N1 8LR.
9   Davies Ruth (1988) *Hopes and Fears: Children's Attitudes to Nuclear War*, Occasional Paper No. 11, Lancaster: St Martin's College.
10 Donaghy, Bronwyn (1988) 'War and Peace: How our Children see it', *Parents and Children*, Aug/Sept: 98.
11 Williams, Rick (1978) 'Teaching Underdevelopment', in M. Wolf-Wasserman and L. Hutchinson (eds) *Teaching Human Dignity*, Minneapolis, Minnesota: Education Exploration Center.
12 Rhys-Thomas, Deirdre (1987) *Letters for My Children*, London: Pandora.
13 Stacey, Barrie (1978) *Political Socialization in Western Society: An Analysis from a Life-Span Perspective*, London: Edward Arnold.
14 Greenstein, Fred I. (1969) *Children and Politics*, New Haven: Yale University Press.
15 Stacey, op. cit.
16 Greenstein, op. cit.
17 Nye, Joseph S. (1986) *Nuclear Ethics*, New York: Free Press.
18 For example, Cornell, Joseph Bharat (1979) *Sharing Nature with Children*, Watford, Herts UK: Exley Publications Ltd and Calif.: Ananda Publications.
19 'Fun for Little Green Folk' (1985) *Observer*, 29 December.
20 'Children Take the Lead in Clean-Up' (1988) *Sunday Times*, 23 October.
21 Jenkins, Simon (1989) 'The New Morality', *Sunday Times Review*, 15 January.
22 Drabble, Margaret (1987) *The Radiant Way*, Harmondsworth: Penguin.
23 Frazer, Elizabeth (1988) 'Teenage Girls Talking about Class', *Sociology*, 22(3): 343–58, and quoted in the *Independent*, 21 August 1988.
24 Dickinson, Julie (1984) 'Social Representations of Socioeconomic Status', paper presented at British Psychological Society Conference.
25 Leahy, R. L. (1983) 'Development of the Conception of Economic Equality', *Developmental Psychology*, 19(1): 111–25.
26 Pinchbeck, I. and M. Hewitt (1969) *Children in English Society* (Vol. I), London: Routledge & Kegan Paul.
27 'Home Sweet Home' (n. d.) reprinted in L. De Vries (1967) *Little Wide-Awake: An Anthology from Victorian Children's Books and Periodicals*, London: Arthur Baker Ltd.

28 From 'Tit Bits for Tiny Wits' (1880) reprinted in De Vries, op. cit.
29 Vincent, David (1981) *Bread, Knowledge and Freedom: A Study of Nineteenth Century Working Class Autobiography*, London: Methuen.
30 Ibid.
31 Balsan, Consuelo Vanderbilt (1952) *The Glitter and the Gold*, London: Harper & Bros.
32 Keniston, Kenneth (1970) *Young Radicals*, New York: Harcourt.
33 Stacey, op. cit.
34 Quoted in the *Guardian*, 12 May 1986.
35 Quoted in the *Independent*, 16 June 1988.
36 Quoted in the *Guardian*, 8 February 1989.
37 Bryan, Beverly, Stella Dadzie and Suzanne Scafe (eds) (1985) *The Heart of the Race*, London: Virago.
38 Bryan *et. al.*, op. cit.
39 Anon. (1984) 'Eenie, Meenie, Miney, Mo', in Hannah Kanter, Sarah Lefanu, Shaila Shah and Carole Spedding (eds) *Sweeping Statements: Writings from the Women's Liberation Movement 1981–83*, London: The Women's Press.
40 *Guardian*, 21 November 1988.
41 Quoted in Zehra (1987) 'Different Roots, Different Routes – Ethnic Minority Lesbians', *Trouble and Strife*, 10 (Spring): 11–15.
42 Paul, Rajkumari (1986) 'Schooldays . . .', *Mukti*, 6 (Spring): 9.
43 Salaria, F. (1986) 'Racism in Schools', *Mukti*, 5 (Spring): 12–14.
44 *Independent*, 16 June 1988.
45 Seneviratne, Seni (1988) 'Just Jealous', in *Charting the Journey*, London: Sheba.
46 *Mukti*, 6 (Spring): 11, 1987.
47 Lorde, Audre (1984) 'Man Child: A Black Lesbian Feminist's Response', in A. Lorde, *Sister Outsider: Essays and Speeches*, New York: The Crossing Press.
48 Angelou, Maya (1982) *The Heart of a Woman*, New York: Bantam.
49 Quoted in George, Anthony (1987) 'Doing it For Themselves', *Libertarian Education*, 2 (4): 3
50 *Mukti* 6, (1987).
51 Lal, Solaika (1987) 'Prejudice and Stereotyping', *Mukti*, 6: 11.
52 Fish, Laura (1987) 'A Black Fish in a White Sea', *Libertarian Education*, 2(6): 6.
53 Quoted in Pogrebin, op. cit.
54 Ibid.
55 Gettys, L. and A. Cann (1981) 'Children's Perceptions of Occupational Stereotypes', *Sex Roles*, 7: 301–8.
56 Flerx, V., D. Fidler and R. Rogers (1976), 'Sex Role Stereotypes', *Child Development*, 47: 998–1007.
57 Oakley, Ann (1972) *Sex, Gender and Society*, London: Maurice Temple Smith Ltd.

58 Toynbee, Polly (1988) 'Nature versus Nurture', *Guardian*, 7 April.
59 Quoted in Arcana, Judith (1983) *Every Mother's Son: The Role of Mothers in the Making of Men*, London: The Women's Press.
60 Glastonbury, Marion (1980) *New Society*: 17, 14 November.
61 *Mother Magazine*, February 1989.
62 Ehrlich, Jane (1988) 'Toy Advertising: The Hidden Persuaders', *Good Housekeeping*, December.
63 *Observer*, 16 August 1987.
64 Grabrucker, Marianne (1988) translated by Wendy Philipson, *There's a Good Girl: Gender Stereotyping in the First Three Years of Life – A Diary*, London: The Women's Press.
65 Reported in the *Independent*, 20 October 1987.
66 Arcana, op. cit.
67 Lowry, Suzanne (1986) *Observer*
68 Stein, Sara (1984) *Girls and Boys: The Limits of Non-Sexist Child-rearing*, London: Chatto & Windus.
69 Arcana, op. cit.
70 Jennifer (1988) 'My Mum's a Lesbian – and I'm Proud of Her', *Guardian*, 24 August.
71 Arcana, op. cit.
72 Stratham, June (1986) *Daughters and Sons: Experiences of Non-Sexist Child Raising*, Oxford: Basil Blackwell.

APPENDIX

Books to help talk with children about sexual abuse

For parents:

1 Elliot, M. (1986) *Keeping Safe: A Practical Guide to Talking with Children*, London: Bedford Square Press.
2 Corcoran, C. (1987) *Take Care! Preventing Child Sexual Abuse. A Handbook for Parents*, Dublin: Poolbeg Press.

Books to read with children:

3 Pithers, David and Greene, Sarah, *We Can Say No!* London: Hutchinson.
4 Elliot, Michele, *The Willow Street Kids* (for older children), London: MMB/Andre Deutsch.
5 Irwin, Hadley, *A Girl Like Abby*, London: Viking Kestrel.
6 Chick, Sandra, *Push Me, Pull Me* (for young victims), London: Livewire, The Women's Press.
7 Hessell, Jenny, *What's Wrong With Bottoms?* London: Hutchinson.

INDEX

THE PARENTS' GREEN GUIDE
by Brigid McConville
Printed on recycled paper

Is the food you give your children safe to eat? Is their water
contaminated or their air fit to breathe?

With environmental crises looming, parents urgently
need to know how to protect their children – and their
planet.

In every aspect of daily life, there are things *you* can do to
make the world a safer place for children.

This practical and resourceful guide offers a host of
initiatives, information and advice for parents who want a
safer present – and a greener future. Packed with creative
ideas and exciting projects, it will help parents entertain
and educate as well as protect their children. Covering
every aspect of a child's daily life, it includes chapters on:

- home & garden
- school
- education
- food & water
- pollution
- toys
- transport
- town & countryside

ACT NOW FOR A GREENER TOMORROW

0 04 440564 2
£4.99 pbk

Also Available from Pandora Press

The Hite Report *Shere Hite*	£5.99☐
The Midwife Challenge *Sheila Kitzinger* (ed)	£6.95☐
Drugs in Pregnancy and Childbirth *Judy Priest*	£5.99☐
Miscarriage *Christine Moulder*	£5.99☐
Safer Sex *Diane Richardson*	£5.99☐
Your Menopause *Myra Hunter*	£5.99☐
Parents' Green Guide *Brigid McConville*	£4.99☐
Being Fat is Not A Sin *Shelley Bovey*	£4.99☐
Living with a Drinker *Mary Wilson*	£4.99☐
Infertility *Renate D Klein* (ed)	£4.95☐
Natural Healing in Gynaecology *Rina Nissim*	£4.95☐
Birth and Our Bodies *Paddy O'Brien*	£4.50☐
Your Life After Birth *Paddy O'Brien*	£4.95☐
Women's Health: A *Spare Rib* Reader *Sue O'Sullivan* (ed)	£5.95☐
The Politics of Breastfeeding *Gabrielle Palmer*	£6.95☐
Motherhood; What It Does To Your Mind *Jane Price*	£4.95☐
Until They Are Five *Angela Phillips*	£4.99☐
Women and the AIDS Crisis *Diane Richardson*	£3.95☐
On Your Own: A Guide to Independent Living *Jean Shapiro*	£6.95☐
The Heroin Users *Tom Stewart*	£5.95☐

All these books are available at your local bookshop or newsagent or can be ordered direct by post. Just tick the titles you want and fill in the form below.

Name _____

Address _____

_____

_____

Write to Unwin Hyman Cash Sales, PO Box 11, Falmouth, Cornwall TR10 9ED.
Please enclose remittance to the value of the cover price plus:
UK: 80p for the first book plus 20p for each additional book ordered to a maximum charge of £2.00.

BFPO: 80p for the first book plus 20p for each additional book.

OVERSEAS INCLUDING EIRE: £1.50 for the first book plus £1 for each additional book.

Unwin Hyman Paperbacks reserve the right to show new retail prices on covers, which may differ from those previously advertised in the text or elsewhere. Postage rates are subject to revision.